# THE UNBOUNDARIED SELF

---

*Putting the Person Back into
the View from Nowhere*

LOUIS S. BERGER

Designed, edited and laid out by Amy Langston.

Note for Librarians: A cataloguing record for this book is available from Library and Archives Canada at www.collectionscanada.ca/amicus/index-e.html
ISBN 1-4120-6072-9

*Printed in Victoria, BC, Canada. Printed on paper with minimum 30% recycled fibre. Trafford's print shop runs on "green energy" from solar, wind and other environmentally-friendly power sources.*

# TRAFFORD
**PUBLISHING**™

*Offices in Canada, USA, Ireland and UK*
This book was published *on-demand* in cooperation with Trafford Publishing. On-demand publishing is a unique process and service of making a book available for retail sale to the public taking advantage of on-demand manufacturing and Internet marketing. On-demand publishing includes promotions, retail sales, manufacturing, order fulfilment, accounting and collecting royalties on behalf of the author.

**Book sales for North America and international:**
Trafford Publishing, 6E–2333 Government St.,
Victoria, BC v8t 4p4  CANADA
phone 250 383 6864 (toll-free 1 888 232 4444)
fax 250 383 6804; email to orders@trafford.com
**Book sales in Europe:**
Trafford Publishing (uk) Ltd., Enterprise House, Wistaston Road Business Centre,
Wistaston Road, Crewe, Cheshire cw2 7rp  UNITED KINGDOM
phone 01270 251 396 (local rate 0845 230 9601)
facsimile 01270 254 983; orders.uk@trafford.com
**Order online at:**
trafford.com/05-0973

10 9 8 7 6 5 4 3

*A little error in the beginning becomes a great error at the end.*

    ~  Chinese proverb


*Incompetence consists of wanting to reach conclusions.*

    ~  Gustave Flaubert


*All philosophy can do is to destroy idols. And that means not creating a new one–for instance as in the 'absence of an idol.'*

    ~  Ludwig Wittgenstein

# CONTENTS

## PART I

### PROLEGOMENA: SEVEN HOLISTIC CRITIQUES

## PART II

### AUGMENTATIONS AND ELABORATIONS

## PART III

### EXPLORING APPLICATIONS:
### CHESHIRE CAT RESIDUES

# PART I

## PROLEGOMENA: SEVEN HOLISTIC CRITIQUES

*First, every metaphysical question always encompasses the whole range of metaphysical problems. Each question is itself always the whole. Therefore, second, every metaphysical question can be asked only in such a way that the questioner as such is present together with the question, that is, is placed in question. From this we conclude that metaphysical inquiry must be posed as a whole and from the essential position of the existence that questions. We are questioning, here and now, for ourselves.*

> ~ Martin Heidegger, *What is Metaphysics?*

*To learn, one accumulates day by day. To study the Tao, one reduces day by day.*

> ~ Lao Tzu, *Tao Te Ching*

*There is nothing more difficult than to become critically aware of the presuppositions of one's thought.*

> ~ E. F. Schumacher, *A Guide for the Perplexed*

# 1

# INTRODUCTION

## HISTORY OF WORLD VIEWS

Throughout the history of Western thought, from presocratic to present times, speculations and explorations about the cosmos and our place in it have been ubiquitous. There has been a continuing curiosity about these matters and the host of related questions they raise. Any one period displays a diversity of often conflicting, even warring conjectures, belief systems, theories, ideologies, and approaches. Still, in spite of this heterogeneous, often confusing panorama, each of the four great historical periods—Greek, Christian, Renaissance, and Modern—was dominated by a particular overarching world view.[1]

The Greek era was "based on the principle that the world of nature is saturated or permeated by mind," that it is alive, intelligent, purposive, explainable in terms of ultimate goals and principles, and that furthermore, living creatures are a microcosmic reflection of this all-encompassing cosmic mind, that they are "a specialized local organization."[2]

The Christian world view introduced and emphasized a particular "idea of Creation"[3] that pictured the world as "a harmonious and coherent whole, created by an infinite and good God as an appropriate home for human beings, for whose sake it was made."[4]

The Renaissance saw the rise of the mathematized science of Kepler, Newton, and Descartes which initiated

---

[1]  Marías, 1967; Tarnas, 1991; Kearney, 1994; Bernstein, 1983; Barrett, 1978, 1986; Moravia, 1995; Collingwood, 1945; Melchert, 1995; Cahoone, 1988.
[2]  Collingwood, 1945, pp. 3-4.
[3]  Marías, 1987, 105.
[4]  Melchert, 1995, p. 270.

the tradition the philosopher Richard Rorty characterizes as "Cartesian-Lockean-Kantian (CLK)."[5] That framework famously (although some would say infamously) included the premise of a mind-body dualism, Rene Descartes' well known assumption of "substance dualism," that nature is bifurcated, that everything there is belongs either to the domain of lifeless extended matter—*res extensa*—or else to the realm of nonspatial, insubstantial mind or psyche—*res cogitans*.[6] We should recognize, however, that CLK frameworks entail much more than just the belief in the thinking-subject/extended-object or experience/world dichotomy. Cartesianism is a series of

> interrelated motifs... [namely] the ontological duality of mind and body; the subjective individualism implicit in the ultimate appeal to direct personal verification; the method of universal doubt which was supposed to lead us to indubitable truths; the doctrine that language and signs are an external disguise for thought; the doctrine that vagueness is unreal and that the philosophic endeavor is one of knowing clearly and distinctly a completely determinate reality; and most fundamentally, the doctrine that we can break out of the miasma of our language or system of signs and have direct intuitive knowledge of objects.[7]

We see that Cartesianism is a complex, far-reaching belief system, a network of interlocking concepts and assumptions. Nevertheless, the characteristic that soon emerged to dominate this elaborate vision of the world was its resolute emphasis on mathematization (formalization, measurement), reductive analysis, and mechanization.[8] Consequently, the universe came to be seen as a machine, devoid of life and intelligence.[9] Furthermore, since

---

[5]   Bernstein, 1992, p. 19.
[6]   The distinction dates back to the presocratic era—see Harvey, 1989, p. 38n9; Tarnas, 1991, pp. 21-25.
[7]   Bernstein, 1971, pp 5-6.
[8]   Schumacher calls Descartes' mind "both powerful and frighteningly narrow." (1977, p. 9)
[9]   For a discussion of important precursors of this view, from Plato to Ficino (1433-99) and Copernicus (1473-1543), see Smith, 1984, chapter 2.

machines need to be made, it was logical to retain the idea of a divine creator but one now reconceptualized as the originary universal clock maker who not only created a mathematized cosmos but also wound it up to set it in motion.[10]

The realm of extended matter became the privileged domain in Western thought. By fiat, it was to be science's realm, the domain whose constituents could be objectively measured, the region characterized by "primary qualities" such as mass, time, location, shape. On the other hand, the so-called "secondary qualities" of objects, such as their warmth, color, sound, or smell, were deemed to be unsuitable for scientific treatment since they seemed so difficult if not impossible to quantify or mathematize.[11] In the age of Kepler,

> with astonishing zeal men began to look upon mathematics as the prototype and prerequisite of true knowledge, and quite possibly, as the only source of certitude. It appears that Kepler (1571-1630) was speaking for the entire age when he declared that "just as the eye was made to see colors, and the ear to hear sounds, so the human mind was made to understand, not whatever you please, but quantity."[12]

To remove the difficulties posed by these recalcitrant and supposedly secondary, somehow inferior, not really real (i.e., only projected or imposed by mind), entities, it simply was decreed that since they lacked the tangible material reality of *res extensa*'s ingredients, since they somehow reside "in" mind stuff and not in the real, extended material world, they were unfit subjects for scientific treatment. They should be expelled from the privileged realm of science and exiled to the nether world, the domain of *res cogitans*—and they were. This was highly convenient and

---

[10] Harvey, 1989, chapters 2, 3.
[11] This is another distinction with ancient roots—see Heisenberg, 1958, p. 69; Tarnas, 1991, p. 21.
[12] Smith, 1984, p. 26).

useful for natural science. The move facilitated scientific advances, as it guaranteed that only those entities and phenomena that were properly quantifiable remained in science's realm.

The modern period carried this value system and its practices a step further. Scientists hubristically decided that since science is equipped to explain everything, the previously banished (or at least deprecated, scientifically suspect) "mental phenomena" could and now should be reinstated as proper objects for scientific study. This move is a prime expression of *scientism*, "the doctrine that only the methods of the natural sciences give rise to knowledge...[which] is today widely espoused in epistemology, metaphysics, philosophy of language, and philosophy of mind.... [Science is] a true description of reality.... a true account of the world."[13]

In order to accomplish that assimilation of secondary qualities, however, these heretofore scientifically intractable phenomena would first have to be transmuted so as to make them amenable to natural science's methodologies and theories. In effect, the secondary qualities would have to be transformed into mathematizable, quantifiable and presumably equivalent primary qualities, *which at the same time also transformed "mental" phenomena or subjective experiences into thing-like "objects" that had thing-like properties.*[14] This move completed the mathematicians' and physicists' wordless revolt against Cartesian dualism. *Res cogitans* finally disappeared entirely from science's view, ostensibly leaving only the objective, quantifiable world of *res extensa* and its independently existing objects in its wake.

---

[13] Stroll, 2000, p. 1. The psychiatrist Viktor Frankl notes that "What we have to deplore... is not so much the fact that *scientists are specialising*, but rather the fact that *specialists are generalising.*" (quoted in Schumacher, 1977, p. 5).

[14] See Harvey, 1989; Bergman, 1959, p. 4; Dancy and Sosa, 1992, pp. 362-365.

I note for future reference that this maneuver cannot fail to create paradoxes. For example, it mystifies the presence and role of the observer and mathematizer—where does the scientist belong in this reduced scheme of things? Also, it leads inexorably to a different kind of bifurcation of the world (into an inner, subjective, and an outer, objective, domain); that is, whereas the previous distinctions between primary/secondary qualities and *res extensa/res cognitans* were made on the basis of *qualitative* differences, the inner world/outer world distinction is *spatial* and thus quasi-quantitative.

What enabled this move were the closely related, intertwined positions of scientific naturalism, monistic and physical-material-biological reductionism, and scientism. The resulting frameworks acknowledge only a subset of the total human experience, employ only a subset of the available explanatory resources, and presume to understand, explain and control everything in exactly the same ways that are used to understand, explain and control natural science's physical, insensate world. In other words, by this global, scientistic naturalizing action physical science annexed the domain of the psyche to the world of insensate "extended matter," asserting that as far as natural science is concerned, *in principle* human beings are indistinguishable in all essentials from, say, rocks, or electrons. In the present technological era the paradoxical nature of this claim is reflected in the endless fascination with questions and arguments about the "nature" of robots and computers, such as, Can machines "think"? Do they have "minds"? Can the so-called Turing test settle the matter?[15]

At the same time this naturalizing move ushered in the era of psychology as the separate discipline whose object of study is the psyche, but a field conceptualized from the

---

[15] For early discussions see Anderson, 1964; for more recent ones, see Blakemore and Greenfield, 1987; Sheehan and Sosna,1991; Tallis, 1999a, b.

start primarily as "psychophysics", a mathematizing, quantifying branch of knowledge modeled after the exact sciences.[16]

## REVOLVING DOORS

Opposition to this naturalistic reduction of the mental realm arose almost immediately from humanistically inclined philosophers in "what has been called the Counter-Enlightenment."[17] Prominent figures included Hamann, Herder, Hegel, Goethe, Nietzsche, Marx, Kierkegaard, Dilthey, and more recently Husserl, Heidegger, Merleau-Ponty, and Derrida.[18] Their main objection was that naturalizing the mind was dehumanizing, impoverishing, alienating, degrading, and inappropriate: It "is an error of inestimable magnitude.... to treat human beings as structurally analogous to the objects of study of the natural sciences;"[19] "the maps produced by modern materialistic Scientism leave all the questions that really matter unanswered; more than that, they deny the validity of the questions;"[20] reductionism is "the true nihilism of today;"[21] it is "a very great impoverishment: entire regions of human interest, which had engaged the most intense efforts of earlier generations, simply ceased to appear on the [philosophical] maps.... So the *vertical dimension* [human depth] had disappeared from the philosophical maps."[22]

Furthermore, as many philosophers as well as others have pointed out, this reductive mathematization of the

---

[16] Wundt, Fechner, and Helmholtz are the major early figures (Harvey, 1989, pp. 27-28, 41-42; Audi, 1999, p. 694).
[17] Gardner, 1999, p. 7.
[18] The literature is extensive. See, for example, Harrington, 1996; Berlin, 1994; Barrett, 1978, 1983; Critchley, 2001; Moore, 1992; Harvey, 1989; Bernstein, 1992; Abel, 1976; Solomon, 1972; Berman, 1981; Gardner, 1999; Smith, 1984; Lawson, 1985; Schumacher, 1977; Prado, 1992.
[19] Newman, 1991, p. 6.
[20] Schumacher,1977, p.4.
[21] The psychiatrist Viktor Frankl, quoted in Schumacher, 1977, p. 5.
[22] Schumacher, 1977, pp. 10, 11.

"mental," human, animate, conscious aspect of being-in-the-world raises a host of internal inconsistencies;[23] the idea of identifying the mental with the inert/material is incoherent—a claim that will be made and argued from a variety of positions in this book.

However, opponents of this reductionism have had great difficulty in finding an acceptable, viable alternative to this reductive naturalization of *res cogitans*. It seems that when we attempt to understand ourselves (reflexively, self-referentially) as persons who have a world, we apparently are left only with a small set of explanatory frameworks to choose from. Currently the principal options are (1) some variant of a cognitively-grounded Cartesian dualism, (2) a version of the so-called "dual-aspect" theories, or (3) physical-material reductionism. The last is by far the most popular option, the one deemed to be scientifically respectable. Unfortunately, however, none of these alternatives is viable: "No strictly Cartesian form of dualism is a serious player in the field today.... [but] the main traditional competitor... the so-called identity theory... [which presumes that] mental states are physical states of the brain, has profound liabilities;"[24] "modernity's two options, [substance] dualism and materialism, refute each other;"[25] "to talk about a dual aspect theory is largely hand waving;"[26] "it [dual aspect theory] would be a very odd hybrid indeed."[27]

Incidentally, it is curious that another alternative, panexperientialism or panpsychism—the theory that all of nature has a psychic aspect—is almost never taken seriously or even considered. It is rarely mentioned in the

---

[23] For a particularly lucid and compelling critique, see Harvey, 1989, especially chapter 3.
[24] Stroll, 2000, p. 257.
[25] Griffin, 1988, p. 147.
[26] Nagel, 1986, p. 30.
[27] Tallis, 1999b, p. 132. See also Tallis, 1999a, pp. 59-64; Olafson, 1995, pp. 217-218, 227n.

relevant philosophical literature. For example, one prominent work does not even include it in its list of "Ten types of explanation of behavior and mentation."[28] In the rare instance when panpsychism is mentioned, typically it first is simplistically misrepresented and caricatured, and then on that basis condescendingly dismissed out of hand as preposterous: "If panpsychism is true.... [then] everything has a mental life. But I think that we can safely set this possibility to one side."[29] It supposedly entails "the threat... [of] positing tiny minds everywhere in nature."[30] Yet, even though superficially panpsychism may seem to be an extreme if not bizarre position, well-reasoned arguments grounded in contemporary physics have been advanced in its support.[31] I consider panexperientialism briefly in chapter 14.

At any rate, these are the mainstream alternatives for dealing with the two major branches of the philosophy of mind: *ontology*, the science or study of being, of "existents"—"an account of the nature of the ultimate subjects of predication in the world,"[32]—and *epistemology*, the study of the method and ground of knowledge.[33]

This frustrating status of ontology and epistemology is reflected in the multitude of competing philosophical and scientific proposals that have come and gone over the past 300 or so years, "a series of interminable and inconclusive squabbles."[34] We already have had indications that probably the most prominent bone of contention has been

---

[28] Blakemore and Greenfield, 1987, chapter 22.
[29] Jackson, 1998, p. 7.
[30] Levine, 2001, p. 25.
[31] See Griffin, 1998; de Quincey, 2002; Seager, 2001; Nagel, 1986, pp. 49-51.
[32] Walsh, 1963, p. 55.
[33] The viability of this distinction has been questioned by some philosophers: "In terms going back to Plato, the 'What is X?' question cannot be totally severed from the 'Who am I?' question." (Rosen, 1980, p. 6).
[34] Katz, 1998, p. xiii. Many philosophy texts describe and analyze this state of affairs. See, for example, Stroll, 2000; Armour and Bartlett, 1980; Bernstein, 1983; Moravia, 1995; Griffin, 1998.

reductive, materialistic rationalism. Its apparent scientific credibility and respectability has great appeal for many thinkers, but it also has always been "beset with contradictions" which its advocates have tried to suppress.[35]

There has been, and continues to be, a revolving door parade of proposals. A thinker—a Descartes, a Hume, a Kant, a Hegel—develops a putatively new philosophical system that claims to solve or at least alleviate the extant philosophical difficulties. Often such a system first wins the day only to be rejected sooner or later on the basis of strong, compelling, and apparently new criticisms and counterproposals. In turn, these come under fire and are rejected; then, old solutions tend to reemerge in new clothing, and the cycle repeats. The philosopher Colin McGinn has conceptualized this contentious history of attempts to resolve basic epistemological and ontological dilemmas as an unending, impotent dance around four basic types of approaches, one that gives what he calls a DIME shape to the philosophical landscape: *D* stands for domestication, defanging, demoting, taming (basically evading) the problem to make it manageable; *I* assumes that the problem is irreducible, indefinable, inexplicable, and is reconciled to that state; *M* proposes magical, miraculous, mystical, even mad solutions; and, *E* stands for elimination, for dismissing the problem as bogus.[36]

## THE BOOK AND ITS ORGANIZATION

### Holisms

This history of an unending dance raises two pressing questions for my enterprise: First, is there anything more (let alone new) left to be said here? Second, does it really

---

[35] Lawson, 1985, p. 15. He focuses on the deeply paradoxical *reflexive* nature of experience that reductive materialism cannot encompass. Reflexivity is a topic that will lurk in the background of much of the discussion in the chapters that follow.
[36] McGinn, 1993, pp. 15-18.

matter to anyone other than philosophers whether this constellation of paradoxical ontological and epistemological issues exists? Are the paradoxes, internal logical inconsistencies, ontological impoverishments, and so on, significantly *consequential* for other fields? Outside of philosophy, does it really matter that a field's philosophical ground is paradoxical and problematic, or whether these conundrums are resolved? We know for example that physics and mathematics seemingly have made significant progress in the past several centuries despite their problematic, philosophically untenable foundations. It seems as though "sciences that are misconceived at a philosophical or metaphysical level can make substantive progress towards what seems like the truth."[37] In sum, are there any supportable reasons for offering yet another work about these matters?

Perhaps the situation isn't totally hopeless. Once in a while I encounter works of thinkers who in my view do have something relevant and important to say about our topics. Typically such thinkers identify previously ignored or marginalized issues and demonstrate their import, and/or recognize that some ubiquitously taken for granted assumption is in fact on shaky ground and merits careful reexamination. (Einstein's questioning the nature of the apparently self-evident, heretofore seen as unproblematic, concept of simultaneity is a famous and paradigmatic example of the latter case.) I will use the critiques of seven unusual and creative scholars as my point of departure. The group comes from several disciplines—philosophy, anthropology, English literature, and neurobiology. Part I devotes one chapter to the work of each, the chapters being arranged roughly in order of increasing complexity and unconventionality.

---

[37] Tallis, 1999a, p. 241; his work is the subject of chapter 3.

These scholars are greatly troubled by and intensely opposed to approaches that set out to understand the person in the world naturalistically, reductively. Furthermore, they reject not only mechanistic approaches but also their principal standard alternatives, dualism and idealism. Instead, their thinking rather remarkably converges on the same kinds of unorthodox visions, namely, radical holisms. That is, each in his own way sees the person-in-the-world as an innately unitary, interconnected situation. That is a highly problematic stance, because as it turns out, such holistic approaches are "strictly outside of the reach of any theoretical attitude."[38] As we shall see, any attempt to formally define holisms scientifically automatically turns them back into the standard scientific fragmented and fragmenting reductionist frameworks. We shall also see that the only alternative method of description that anyone has been able to think of is by way of a *negative* approach, a *via negativa*, an indirect route that relies on a careful *positive* specification of what the ineffable unitary position is *not*.[39] Then, what that holism is, is said to be just whatever remains, whatever has not been formally excluded. (As a psychotherapist I see striking, remarkable parallels between this approach to specification of a philosophical or metaphysical position or concept via *removals* and corresponding clinical processes that characterize what I consider to be "good enough psychotherapy.")[40]

Conceptualizing the person-in-the-world as a unitary constellation can have interesting and valuable implications and consequences. For one thing, it calls attention to phenomena we usually take for granted and overlook. In particular, holistic views encourage one to

[38]  Pylkkö, 1998, p. 209; for a representative selection of consonant views by notable thinkers see Capra, 1988.
[39]  See Berger, 2002a, p. 50n39.
[40]  See Berger, 1991, chapters 8 and 9; 2002a, especially chapter 5.

reconsider and reconceptualize the phenomena of boundaries and their concomitants, the apparently independently existing entities. These are two sides of a coin; they mutually create and sustain one another. Boundaries partition, creating separate entities; separate entities—"things"—come complete with boundaries.

Formal disciplines are predicated on the existence of such partitioned-off entities. These are their mainstays, the free-standing "objects" of their study. For example, those who study language (linguists, philologists, philosophers, logicians) and/or use it as a tool (e.g., natural scientists, psychologists—and also linguists and philosophers of language themselves!) take for granted that it is a separate and independent "object" in the sense that it can be excised from the external world and from persons and treated as a kind of quasi-material entity (see chapter 11). Perhaps the most extreme example of a field predicated on the independent existence of its objects of study is mathematics. Numbers, sets, functions, axioms, rules, logic, and the like, are all seen as objects that are just "there," that have their own properties, regardless of whether or not a human being is in the picture (see chapter 12). In fact, history tells us that any attempt to link the ingredients and processes of mathematics to mathematicians as persons has been strongly condemned and scornfully dismissed in the field as unacceptable *psychologizing*, an attempt to ground their independent field of study in psychology's "laws of the mind."[41]

Having thus objectified a given field of study, its practitioners go about their work as though their presence and roles were irrelevant: "Galileo forgets his own being-in-the-world, and so do Newton, Kant, Hegel, et al..... The concept of being-in-the-world goes especially counter to

---

[41]  See, for example, Audi, 1999, p. 404; Harvey, 1989, chapter 2, 3. I consider psychologizing and its critics in chapter 12.

Cartesian modes of thought."[42] In previous publications I have called the effects of this ubiquitous objectifying, reifying position and attendant practices *Cheshire Cat Phenomena*, for obvious reasons.[43] On that view, the entities that are the objects of study in fields such as those just mentioned actually are considered to be impoverished residues of holisms, the feline's grin. Under an holistic approach this fragmenting compartmentalization into world, its objects, and persons is seen not as inevitable or primary but as derivative, undesirable, and to a degree reversible. Holisms recover, and pay attention to, the previously forgotten being-in-the-world constellation.

Another important consequence of a holistic view is that it impels us to acknowledge that our experience of being-in-the-world ultimately is grounded in an ineffable mystery; it does not insist that a discipline's goal is to explain everything. For now I postpone discussing this aspect and its implication. While it will occasionally be mentioned in Part I it becomes a major focus in the last two parts (especially in chapter 9).

## Ontogenetic and Pragmatic Extensions

However valuable the holistic critiques of the seven scholars may be, in my view they necessarily are limited because they all but ignore two additional significant conceptual dimensions. First, with only a few and minor exceptions (see especially chapter 8) the critics' orientation remains *adultocentric*. That is, when the scholars address and explore topics such as perception, or language, or mathematics, they do so almost exclusively from the common-sense standpoint of the adult's world. As one philosopher put it during his discussion of developmental psychology, disciplines fail to address key problems

---

[42] Collins and Selina, 1999, p. 59.
[43] Berger 1985, pp. 55-56, 59, 83, 89.

adequately because they "unhesitatingly approach the issue from the point of view of the mature, conceptually organized subject."[44] That adult's point of view ignores the important dimension that I will call *ontogenetic*. The term refers to a psychodynamically informed way of looking at phenomena that takes into account aspects of human development (especially the earliest phases).[45] As we shall see, adultocentrism stands in the way of certain useful insights that an ontogenetic way of looking/thinking allows to emerge.

Second, the seven critics deal with issues in line with the orientation that I call *the Pure Knowledge Paradigm* (PKP),[46] the position that knowledge is to be sought for its own sake. The disdain for any departures from a purist position has a long history: "We are told the Greeks despised applications."[47] That is, adherents to the PKP position typically examine, analyze, and theorize about issues without taking into account the implications of their domain of application. For example, both linguists and philosophers of language structure, conceptualize, and analyze their subject matter without regard to where and how, by whom, in what kinds of context, for what purposes, language is going to be used.[48] Those working within the PKP assume that such (apparently) pure study uncontaminated or cheapened by crass practical concerns will provide a neutral, acontextual knowledge base from which informed applications can and will follow. (Theoretical physics is paradigmatic of this premise.) One

---

[44] Pylkkö, 1998, p. 193.

[45] For an introduction to this ontogenetic perspective, see Berger, 1996a.

[46] Berger, 1985, pp. 5, 100-110, 144, 166, 171.

[47] Hersh, 1997, p. 185.

[48] See Harris, 1998; I draw on his work heavily in chapter 11. Incidentally, the famous Wittgensteinian approach to the study of language via language games or the emphasis on use is only an apparent exception; it, too, remains "intralogical" (see the discussion in Olafson, 1995, pp. 4-7) and what Harris calls "segregationist."

difficulty with this PKP stance is that it itself is not at all free of all sorts of unstated, unexamined, implicit metaphysical preconceptions; by no means is it pure, presuppositionless. That is generally acknowledged by most mainstream workers in all disciplines; it is widely recognized that observations and investigations are "theory-laden," skewed by their conceptual-theoretical presuppositions, but actually that is only the tip of a very large iceberg.

The alternative to the PKP that I propose is an approach I call *anomalous pragmatism*, adumbrated in previous works.[49] This variant of pragmatism is foreshadowed in the works of the philosophers Martin Heidegger and his teacher Edmund Husserl. Dubbing this pragmatism "anomalous" is intended to mark the difference between it and the familiar pragmatisms associated with philosophers such as Peirce, James, Dewey, and more recently, Richard Rorty: "We must be careful not to confound Heidegger's pragmatism with, say, the American versions of pragmatism which move much more closer to common sense knowledge than Heidegger, and which are also overly optimistic as regards the comprehensiveness of scientific rationality."[50]

These two added dimensions or perspectives (the ontogenetic, and the anomalously pragmatic) will be introduced in Part II; Part III then will explore some of their implications by means of examples showing how they might be applied in four disciplines: linguistics and philosophy of language, mathematics, psychology/psychiatry, and physics. Let us begin, then, with the study of the works that prepare the way for these two expansions.

---

[49] Berger, 1985, pp. 97, 111, 115-118, 125, 129-136, 159-170, 178-179; 1991, pp. 158-169, 175-183, 192, 224n10, 225n16; 1996a, pp. 62-63; 1996b; 2002a, pp. 14, 16n26, 39-40, 54, 71, 77n69.
[50] Pylkkö, 1998, p. 41.

# 2

# MENTAL CONTENTS

## ARTHUR COLLINS

Arthur Collins is Professor of Philosophy Emeritus at the Graduate Center of the City University of New York. In this chapter we will consider his *The Nature of Mental Things*.[1] This monograph is written for his peers, for those working in the philosophy of mind, a sprawling, multifaceted field "that includes the philosophy of psychology, philosophical psychology, and the area of metaphysics concerned with the nature of mental phenomena and how they fit into the causal structure of reality."[2]

Most of these philosophers presume that the subject matter of their studies is "composed of inner entities, states, and relationships to which we [i.e., the philosophers] refer propositions about beliefs, memories, intentions, desires, and perceptual experiences.... [of] states and processes of some kind—if not outer, then inner—if not physical, then nonphysical."[3] This notion of *inner realities* or *mental phenomena,* the assumption that there is something that "is before the mind in thought" goes back at least to Aristotle, who called such "objects", or concepts, *noema.*[4]

## ELIMINATIVIST POSITIONS

Collins' main point is that in philosophy the notion of mental contents is ill-conceived, introduces numerous difficulties, and therefore ought to be abandoned. He wants to "rethink the old paradigms and relax the grip of the idea

---

[1]   Collins, 1987. Unless noted otherwise, in this chapter all citations giving page numbers only will refer to this work.
[2]   Audi, 1999, p. 684.
[3]   pp. ix, 21.
[4]   Crane, 2001, p. 9.

of inner constituents of mental life,"[5] and wants philosophy to stop trying to construct theories that purport to explain "inner mental things."[6]

This is not a new position: "Many philosophers and psychologists have developed critical views about the inner-reality interpretation of mental phenomena"[7] but as we shall see, Collins is no standard eliminativist.

Historically, philosophers (and others, such as some neurobiologists, psychologists, psychiatrists) who would eliminate the idea of mental contents have fallen into two groups: behaviorists, and identity theorists.[8] Philosophical or analytical behaviorism is the orientation that simply rejects by fiat the use of inner mental states and processes in the sciences and in philosophy because such "contents of the mind" are not scientifically observable or quantifiable; they should be replaced by scientifically respectable and presumably equivalent entities, namely, quantifiable or otherwise mathematizable, objectively observable, behavioral data.[9] There is a strong implication that they do not even exist. Collins argues, as have many others,[10] that such radical behaviorist reductionism and eliminativism violates our basic knowledge and intuitions about what a human being is and excludes an entire range of important human phenomena—particularly those that it cannot explain—from disciplines. Collins will not consider behaviorist eliminativism further in his monograph.

The second and currently dominant eliminativist stance comprises two subclasses: mind-brain identity theories ("eliminative materialism"), and functionalist identity theories. The common core concept and mechanism is

---

[5]    p. xviii.
[6]    p. xvi.
[7]    p. 19.
[8]    For a comprehensive overview of eliminativist approaches in general see Levine, 2001, chapter 5.
[9]    pp.16-18.
[10]    See, for example, Tallis, 1999a, b.

*identity theory*, an explanatory logical structure that makes "theoretical identifications"[11] and whose format is, "something equals something else." Specifically, to identify something in that fashion is to say *what that something "really" is*. An identity theory claims to "explain" something already familiar but something that also is only superficially or incompletely understood, some pretheoretical "X," the *explanandum*, by replacing it with something else, some "Y," the *explanans*, a scientific, more rarefied and abstract, legitimate, deeper, and supposedly more illuminating term or concept. The rationale for identity theorizing, then, is that until the philosopher or the scientist furnishes such an explicating equation, our understanding of "X" is and remains inadequate, naive, incomplete, erroneous, and that explaining X as being really Y will correct that heretofore fuzzy, unacceptable, foolishly ingenuous (mis)understanding. In other words, by recasting our inadequate conception of Xs, identifications transform these into scientifically respectable, conceptually purified equivalent Ys. Collins gives several examples: "Warts are ("really") virus colonies," "sponges are animals," "lightening is an electrical discharge," "stars are massive hot bodies like the sun."[12]

This, then, is the formal explanatory template common to both mind-brain and functionalist identity theories. They differ only in their view of what the *explananda* are. Roughly, as the terminology suggests, the mind-brain or eliminative materialism identity theorists' *explananda* are neurobiological entities and phenomena. Mind equals, or is at best a curious illusory side effect of, brain and its neurobiochemical support systems.

Eliminativist functionalists see mind as a formal component—specifically, the transformation-providing

---

[11]    pp. 88-89.
[12]    p. 89

unit—within a mathematics-like input-output system.[13] That is, for functionalists mind is that system component that mediates between inputs to persons (e.g., "variables" arising in the external world, or from proprioception) and outputs emanating from those persons (e.g., overt behaviors, cognitive activities). All that one needs to know about the mind is given when one specifies the particulars of this transformational function. Functionalists do not care whether one conceptualizes mind as biological stuff, or as consisting of some transcendental, immaterial, mysterious substance such as Descartes' *res cogitans*, or simply as an abstract, mathematical cognitive engine. They maintain that all that should matter to workers in the philosophy of mind is the mind's formal function, the specification of how it executes input-output transformations. (The obvious analogy to computer science is frequently drawn.)

What makes Collins' eliminativism unusual is that although he does want to eliminate mental contents from the philosophy of mind, at the same time he does not want to replace or even marginalize pretheoretical and prephilosophical knowledge, the Xs that identity theorists remove from view by replacing them with Ys. He militantly defends the legitimacy of retaining the ordinary naive knowledge about and understanding of our inner life: "The ultimate rejection of inner-state theories about particular mental phenomena is founded on incoherences they are shown to contain and not on the fact that we have no commitment to inner states among our pretheoretical conceptions of mentality."[14] He repeatedly makes the point that people do know with assurance *that* they have thoughts, beliefs, perceptions, desires, memories and that also with equal assurance they can *tell* others *what* these are—what they think, remember, see, etc.: "most people do

---

[13]  See Tallis, 1999a, chapter 5.
[14]  p.13.

know about their own mental states much of the time."[15] When I say, for example, that I have such-and-such a belief, "there is nothing wrong with this way of speaking."[16] When it comes to our own beliefs (or memories, perceptual experiences, and so on), "we do know about them and we can state them."[17] Prephilosophically we believe that all such reports refer to experiences that are private, inaccessible to others, and non-spatial, *"not part of the physical order of things,"[18]* and Collins does not challenge those beliefs. He does not propose to develop a philosophy of mind that would exclude them entirely.

There seems to be an inconsistency here. On the one hand Collins rejects the use of inner mental contents in the philosophy of mind, while on the other hand he wants to retain them in some fashion; prescientific, ordinary discourse seems to be about those very entities. Be that as it may, here I want to focus on the arguments Collins presents in support of his contention that in philosophy the premise of mental contents is untenable, because he illustrates how Cheshire Cat residues come to exist as a discipline's objects of study, and some of the kinds of problems that attend their use.

## ARGUMENTS AGAINST ASSUMING THE EXISTENCE OF INNER CONTENTS

### Sensuous Perception

A central and obvious characteristic of the objects we routinely perceive in the external world is that they have sensual properties—they can be seen, heard, have colors and shapes, and so on. It is easy to automatically take for granted that the putative objects of the mind can be

---

[15]  p. 4; see also pp. 5, 12, 16, 62.
[16]  p. xi.
[17]  p. 16.
[18]  p. 2; see also pp. 1-16.

perceived in the same way, but as Collins points out, that is a subtle mistake: "No philosopher asserts that the phenomena of consciousness are objects of sense perception."[19] While we may say in casual discourse that we *have* a belief, or a memory, or a perception of an (externally existing) object, we cannot really say of these inner objects that we supposedly have also that we also can see, feel, hear, or smell *them*. We cannot legitimately claim that we can *sensuously perceive* them. For example, while we ordinarily would say that we see a yellow lemon, or more formally and artificially, that we "have the visual experience of a yellow lemon," still, we cannot maintain that *that visual experience itself* is yellow, or that we can *see* it. We can only see the lemon: "The act of inner awareness does not have the phenomenology characteristic of a sense modality."[20] In fact, "years ago the pioneer mind-brain theorist U. T. Place labeled [the] failure to respect the nonsensuous character of [inner] experiences 'the phenomenological fallacy'."[21] Thus, even if we want to maintain that there are inner objects, still we must acknowledge that we cannot experience them sensuously.

### Familiarity with the "X" in Identity Statement

As already noted, Collins cites familiar examples (concerning the *explananda* warts, sponges, lighting, stars) emblematic of identity theorizing and says that both mind-brain and functional eliminativists rely heavily on this model to construct what presumably are scientifically respectable equivalents of mental contents. Collins argues that to transfer the use of identity theorizing from scientific or philosophical explanations of entities such as, say, lightening to the corresponding use as explanation of inner objects is flawed and illegitimate. In the case of prescientific

---

[19]  p. 64.
[20]  McGinn, 1997, p. 64.
[21]  p. 91.

*explananda* such as warts, etc., in an important sense we know very well, by direct acquaintance, what these are. In these cases we are quite familiar with the X element of the "X is really Y" structure. We know prescientifically in an ordinary way what a wart is (e.g., a small growth having a certain texture, color, shape, size, hardness, etc.); it is not a mysterious, elusive, ineffable entity. Thus in these instances we comfortably know X even though that knowledge may be naive and limited, and even though in some cases we may want or need to understand the nature of that X more deeply. In those instances we would look for a theoretical identification and thus for a Y, a scientifically-grounded *explanans*.

That is not the case when it comes to putative inner mental contents. Collins shows that our knowledge of these is not at all like our knowledge of, say, bright twinkling points of light in the sky. While we can say, for example, that we know that we have beliefs and can say what we know about them, Collins says

> that we do not have any naive convictions about how it is that we know about our own beliefs and are able to state them upon demand.... We have no conviction that we ought to describe this ability in terms of an inner thing which we consult and report on.... we are not secure about what to say.[22]

We are stymied when asked what a belief *qua* a belief is, for example. Of course, this insecurity reflects the problem I just outlined—that we cannot sensuously perceive the putative inner mental entities. If we have no sensual perception of these, it naturally is difficult to have any solid, defensible "ordinary" opinions about what they are. Furthermore, lacking "a natural conviction" about the nature of these putative mental states, people in general are easily swayed by the expert answers provided by

---

[22]   pp. 15-16, also chapter V.

scientists, psychologists, neuropsychiatrists, even philosophers.

At any rate, whereas our pretheoretical knowledge of things like warts has been more or less stable over time (because humans' direct experiences of them have remained more or less the same), the same cannot be said about our knowledge of inner objects. Because direct acquaintance with the latter is so elusive, because people are insecure about the knowledge they think they have about them, the pretheoretical and prephilosophical knowledge about these presumed has been unstable, fluidly shifting. At any point in history, what that ordinary knowledge is, is biased by the then dominant intellectual belief system.[23] One of Collins's arguments against mental contents, then, is that identity theory explanations of inner objects are untenable because in order for it to be viable, an identification equation must use a pretheoretically familiar, temporally stable X. If we do not reliably and directly know X in a pretheoretical fashion, then using identity theorizing to explain that X is illegitimate.

Therefore in order to make identity theories about inner objects work, philosophers first have to stabilize or tie down the unstable *explananda,* typically by defining them in some fashion. That preliminary move changes them into entities that now no longer are ordinary, pretheoretical, prephilosophical; a kind of pre-identity theorizing has already been implemented. Collins comments ironically about this "little step": "philosophers thinking about mental concepts [via identity theories] take the starting point of their investigations to be somewhat beyond anything definitely suggested by prephilosophical thought about mental things.... I want to secure agreement that this is a little step beyond natural intuitions."[24] The philosophers'

---

[23]   pp. 93-96.
[24]   p. 13.

concerns with mental contents begins too far downstream, at points where pretheoretical knowledge has to some degree already become formalized or structured by theory. Xs have become pre-Ys. Here Collins broaches a special case of the general idea that in order to understand something deeply, one must go back to its origins.

## Descriptions

A closely related other weakness of the notion that mental contents exist is that they elude verbal description; we cannot *say* what they are. That follows directly from the facts that inner contents are not sensuously perceivable, and that our general linguistic resources are limited to descriptions of just those things that we *can* perceive sensuously, that are sensuously describable: "the search for an adequate phenomenological language has yielded nothing so far."[25] Therefore while we may be able to say *what* it is that we believe, still we cannot *describe* that belief itself, at least not in discourse that is any different from our usual ways of describing our real-world experiences. "We have to use derivative descriptions,"[26] metaphors that borrow from the usual descriptive arsenal. We can only say such things as, "my belief in... is as solid as a rock." Descriptions of inner objects degenerate into "the metaphorical language of perception and observation and things we can report on."[27]

## Location and Boundary Problems

Yet another set of problems arises when we ask how and where mental "contents" like beliefs, memories, or names are stored. This is a very old and problematic issue, dating back at least to ancient Greece.[28] These days most

---

[25]  p. 117.
[26]  p. 117.
[27]  p. 65.
[28]  For an overview of ideas about the location of visual images, see Sheldrake,

philosophers, scientists, physicians, and psychologists are likely to say that they are stored in the brain.[29] So would much of the general public, because, as noted above, it is swayed by the experts' opinions.[30] At any rate, most would maintain that such items must be stored somewhere, that to believe otherwise would be to believe in miracles; for philosophers the need to account for a storage mechanism and concomitant location is insistent. Collins notes that it is "characteristic of the pressure to which philosophers succumb without much resistance."[31] Philosophers are not the only ones who so succumb.

Collins takes great care to show that these usual assumptions concerning storage and location are untenable. Take beliefs, for example. For the sake of argument let us assume they are "inscribed" somewhere in the body, say, stored neurophysiologically. If we take someone's belief and write it down, is such a record that person's belief? Few would maintain seriously that it was; whatever else they may be, beliefs are not such "sentential inscriptions."[32] Persons have beliefs, slips of paper do not. The same critical reasoning can be applied to the claim that beliefs (or memories, perceptual experiences, affects, thoughts, etc.) are stored in the brain, or for that matter anywhere else in the material body: "a neural inscription cannot be a belief any more than a notation on a piece of paper can be a belief."[33] Thus, the received views about physiological/ biological location and storage of internal experiences notwithstanding, the premise that entities such as beliefs or memories are neurophysiologically stored is untenable and incoherent—a counterintuitive claim, to be sure. (This

---

2003, chapter 13, (Are images in the brain, or are they where they seem to be?).

[29]  See, for example, Laughlin et al, 1990; Gardener, 1985; LeDoux et al., 1986.

[30]  There also are deeper compulsions at work here—see Berger, 1991.

[31]  p. xii.

[32]  p. xi.

[33]  p. xvi.

theme resurfaces in numerous guises and contexts throughout the chapters that follow.)

In this connection Collins makes a very important though brief observation. In the course of discussing the locus of beliefs he reminds us in passing that material stores of information such as books or computer media are inscriptions that "really deserve the title 'information' only as a consequence of relations to believers such as ourselves."[34] Thus, in addition to criticizing notions concerning physical location and storage, he adumbrates the issue of *neglected, lost or obscured relations to persons*. He suggests that stored "information" becomes actual information only if and when the latent but ontologically central originary ties to *persons* are brought back into the picture. This is the only reference to such ties that I have found in Collins' text, but still, at least he intimates a key issue in holistic positions: the restoration of heretofore obscured or lost relational ties between inanimate, apparently independently existing Cheshire Cat residues that the discipline studies, and their human progenitors. Here is yet another reason why Collins' text is relevant to holisms.

Collins makes still another point in connection with the problem of location. Unless one is a dualist of some stripe, one considers the "inner" (i.e., the interior of the body) to be just as spatial (i.e., just as much in the domain of *res extensa*) as the "outer." That is, while for dualists, "inner" legitimately refers to the nonmaterial domain of *res cogitans* and thus does not refer to the body's interior, to neurobiological matter, for the monistic physical reductionists that option is unavailable, by definition; "inner" can only be a slippery metaphor. The body's interior must be an "outer" for the reductionists. It is observable matter, although to see it may require the services of a

---

[34] p. xvi.

brain surgeon or the use of instruments such as microscopes or spectrographs. Ultimately for mind-body identity theorists, the "inner" of the body must be an "outer;" since they are, or claim to be, monists, that is their only option.

Collins notes that this situation creates still another inconsistency for physical reductionists. Physicalists do not want to say that warts, stars, and so on do not really exist just because they are pretheoretical, insufficiently and only naively understood objects, but they do maintain that inner *mental* objects do not exist. Yet, in their identity theorizings, from a formal perspective they treat both kinds of "objects" equally; both are treated as *explananda*.

The paradox is this. In the first case the mind-body eliminativists' use of identity theories purports to explain what inadequately understood but real entities really are, while in the second the theorizers profess to explain (away) things that they insist do not even exist. Clearly there is an incongruity here, and a problem: *what* do they think they are explaining when they claim to explain, say, what ideas, or memories, really are? (Similarly: What do reductive neuroscientists or psychiatrists think they are explaining when they explain what, say, a suicidal thought really is?) On that basis, Collins argues that monistic physical reductionists must actually be crypto dualists; when they claim to be clarifying the nature of mental contents via identifications they implicitly but surreptitiously must "accept the Cartesian idea of an inner mental realm;"[35] otherwise they have no real Xs for their Ys.

### Comments

I have noted the principal ways in which Collins's critiques are relevant and helpful to the holistic enterprise I am developing and advocating. His work provides an important

---

[35]   p. 61.

example of how disciplines create Cheshire Cat residues, how these then become the supposedly independently, objectively existing subject matter that they can excise and study, and how those practices in combination then create irresolvable paradoxical difficulties and pseudoproblems.

He introduces the idea that at least in some situations, one needs to go back to origins in order to understand phenomena. I note, though, that his idea of a return to origins is ahistorical, not ontogenetic, a conceptually constrained retrograde move that takes place in an atemporal *logical* space.

He also recognizes that demonstrating that the idea of mental contents is incoherent in philosophy will also have implications for neuroscience: "if I [Collins] am right and we come to recognize the intrinsic defects of the theories about inner mental things, this will considerably alter our expectations about the course that neural science may be expected to follow. We will not be so confident that there *must be* inner representations like those whose discovery we have just posited."[36] I expect to demonstrate that the implications would be even wider (see Part III).

He refers to still other matters that will become increasingly important. First, he says that certain questionable linguistic practices are at least partly responsible for the philosophical muddles he unearths. In this he follows in the footsteps of Wittgenstein, the philosopher he says influenced him the most.[37] Wittgenstein's focus was on identifying, logically analyzing, and thereby dissolving, unsolvable pseudoproblems in philosophy introduced by careless, misleading use of language. Collins refers to Wittgenstein's famous (but also obscure, problematic, enigmatic) linguistic analyses of inner

---

[36]  p. xvi.
[37]  p. xviii.

mental concepts such as pains,[38] analyses that usually are subsumed under the enigmatic, elusive umbrella term "private language argument." Collins singles out nominalization, the "grammatical engine that makes a new subject term out of a whole sentence,"[39] as the prime flawed linguistic practice that helps create and maintain the illusion that thing-like mental contents exist. Under nominalization, saying things like "I am thinking of..." becomes changed into "I just had a thought about...." Nominalization has turned a report about a process into a report about some elusive *thing*, in this case, a "thought." It reifies. He, like Wittgenstein, wants to do philosophical-logical linguistic therapy; as one philosopher wrote, "the Wittgensteinian philosophical purpose... [is to make] a piece of disguised nonsense into patent nonsense."[40] Collins wants to remove the inappropriately hypostatized or reified spurious mental objects created by linguistic follies, and instead wants to use more productive, less problematically obscurantist concepts and language in the philosophy of mind.[41, 42]

Second, Collins very briefly and obliquely refers to pragmatic considerations. Although by and large his critiques remain within the Pure Knowledge Paradigm tradition, twice he alludes briefly to pragmatic issues. The

---

[38]   pp. 20-21; see also Johnston, 1993, especially pp. 23, 127; Schulte, 1993.

[39]   p. 86.

[40]   Tallis, 1999b, p.10.

[41]   His most extended discussions about linguistic rehabilitation are in chapter 5, "Visual experiences and theoretical identification."

[42]   Incidentally, in my own field of psychoanalytic psychotherapy there has been a similar attempt at linguistic reform by a notable psychoanalytic practitioner and theorist, Roy Schafer. He saw the "objects" used in mainstream psychoanalytic thinking, research and practice (e.g., resistances, libidos, affects, egos, superegos, ids, barriers between various "mental subsystems") (For a dictionary of these purported objects, see Laplanche and Pontalis, 1973.) Also as inappropriately reified "objects" that create unnecessary and insuperable difficulties for the field that therefore should be discarded. He proposed to replace psychoanalysis' standard reifying discourse with a process-focused language he called "action language." (See Schafer, 1976; also Sass, 1992, pp. 26-32; Berger, 1985, especially pp. 144-146.)

first time is during a discussion of naive, pretheoretical, prephilosophical ways of speaking about one's inner life. As I reported earlier, he observes of such prephilosophical discourse that "there is nothing whatever wrong with this way of speaking,"[43] but since the point of his monograph is that there is something seriously wrong about using such language in philosophy, his comment suggests that there are some circumstances under which it is acceptable to speak as though there were inner contents, and others where it is not. The second hint is that he faults the use of theories about inner realities in the philosophy of mind on the basis that they "cannot possibly do the job that is envisioned for them."[44]

Both comments indirectly raise the further question of what kinds of tools, practices, conceptual frameworks are adequate *for philosophy's purposes,* a specific form of the general question an anomalous pragmatism raise across disciplines. (Collins does not take his comments any further.) In the present context pragmatism suggests that we ought to know more about just what the "envisioned job" of philosophy is. Otherwise, if philosophers don't know that, how can they come to understand issues such as, under what circumstances pretheoretical, ordinary talk may be adequate and acceptable in philosophy, or when the use of flawed identity theorizing might be innocuous or even productive in their field, or whether and what kinds of new conceptual tools might be needed as replacements for formal discourse and identity statements about mental contents? Under the Pure Knowledge paradigm such considerations do not even arise; it is taken for granted that philosophy's job is love of wisdom, and that that is all one needs to know and say about its task.[45] Of course, over the years it has become apparent that the Pure Knowledge

---

[43]   p. xi.
[44]   p. 13.
[45]   See comments on "vulgar pragmatism" in Berger, 2002a, pp. 14 and 71.

Paradigm itself actually is not so pure after all.[46] It is just that the paradigm's underlying pragmatic presuppositions are not readily discernible, because they have been covered over by a sort of Platonic purity.[47]

I stated in the Introduction that in my view the accomplishments of most thinkers whose work is presented in Part I are limited by their adultocentrism and their tacit adherence to the Pure Knowledge Paradigm. Collins is no exception, but still, his critical analyses do help introduce the critiques of theories, practices, and belief systems that create Cheshire Cat residues, pseudo-objects that stand in the way of developing holistic alternatives.

---

[46]   A superficial example of this awareness is the generally recognized so-called "theory-laden" aspect of supposedly and apparently objective, presuppositionless facts.

[47]   See Parts II and III for further discussion.

# 3

# EXPLICITNESS AND NEUROPHILOSOPHY

## RAYMOND TALLIS

Raymond Tallis is an Oxford trained physician, academician, researcher in neurosciences, and author of two major textbooks on geriatric neurology. That, as he says, is his "weekday self". On weekends, he is a highly knowledgeable but radical philosopher, as well as a published writer of short stories and poetry. The Times Education Supplement has described him as "one of the most intriguing figures in the current intellectual scene".[1] Among his philosophical publications are works on Martin Heidegger, on linguistics (Saussure), and the two volumes whose contents I will be discussing here: *The Explicit Animal: A Defense of Human Consciousness*, and *On the Edge of Certainty: Philosophical Explorations*.[2]

While the "weekday" Tallis is heavily enmeshed in the field of medical neurobiology, as his "weekend self" Tallis is a severe and expert critic of the application of neurobiological thinking to philosophy of mind. He develops a neuroscience-grounded critique that fits into the tradition of the humanist critics of physical reductionism. It is most unusual to find a critic who is an expert in medical-neurological fields yet sees and cogently articulates its shortcomings for conceptions of the person-in-the-world.

His central purpose "is to refute physicalism and any other materialist account of what it is to be a human being."[3] He is passionate about this position but also

---

[1]  Grant, 2000, quoted on the back flap of the book jacket.
[2]  Tallis, 1999a and b, hereafter: Animal, and Edge, respectively.
[3]  Animal, p. 3.

recognizes and laments that he seems to be fighting a losing battle. He notes ruefully that

> it is somewhat depressing to reflect that, in the eight years since *The Explicit Animal* was published, the approaches to the philosophy of mind which it criticized, far from being discredited, have become better established in both professional and public consciousness. Computational and biological (evolutionary and neurological) accounts of the human mind have received more widespread attention and appear to be attracting increasing support.[4]

> Much recent philosophy and psychology has been characterised by attempts to deny the peculiar and distinctive nature of consciousness or of its role in human behaviour or, more commonly, both.[5]

Tallis sees various kinds of twentieth-century thinkers as contributing to a climate that supports the mechanistic thinking that rejects or marginalizes consciousness: "Political theorists, in particular Marxists.... Social theorists, as exemplified by Durkheim.... Freud, for whom a large part of the mind was unconscious.... Post-Saussurean thinkers for whom even verbal expression... is determined by structures of the [linguistic, semiotic] system... Helmholtz and his descendants."[6] He sees the common underlying motive to be a need to tidy up the messy phenomena that characterize being human by way of a grand, totalizing scientific theory. I believe that he greatly underestimates the complexity and irrationality of the motives behind this ubiquitous mechanization of human beings in our time. I see it as a defensive expression of a severe, pervasive, dehumanizing and alienating cultural psychopathology that I have described and analyzed elsewhere.[7]

---

4   Animal, p. xi; see also Edge, Preface
5   Edge, 10
6   Animal, pp. 14-15.
7   See Berger 1991 and 2002a; also comments about societal motivation in Parts II and III, below.

Be that as it may, Tallis says that the rationales that support "the scientism that has taken such a hold on much philosophical thought"[8] and traduce the nature of human consciousness, use materialistic theories, principally the constellation he calls neurophilosophy: "In such theories, the mind is animalised and/or mechanised and effectively eliminated, if not in fact, at least as a problem or entity utterly different from those that are currently being fruitfully addressed by science."[9] Neurophilosophy purports to explain mind completely (1) as a neurobiological phenomenon, (2) as computational, the "mind" being the *software* for the "hardware", the biological brain, and/or (3) as a complex material process that arose gradually in the course of *evolution* as a byproduct that has survival or adaptive value.

The alternate "vision of the human creature" Tallis offers is the human being as "an *essentially* explicit animal whose explicit consciousness cannot be explained in terms of biological science or, indeed, captured by any science working within a third-person, materialist framework."[10] It is by no means clear from this comment just what Tallis means by "explicitness" but as indicated by the title of the first of his two books that I am discussing, it is a key term. Tallis's usage needs to be clarified.

## EXPLAINING EXPLICITNESS

As Tallis uses the term, explicitness is an elusive notion, varying along a hierarchically-ordered spectrum representing something like the degrees to which experience is distinctly or clearly expressed, verbalized, not mute or even absent. Tallis represents its lower end point by "?", "standing for my unwillingness to commit myself as

---

8    Edge, p. xi.
9    Edge, p. xii.
10   Animal, p. xiv.

to what the world contains in the absence of consciousness."[11] "?" is whatever there is in the absence of explicitness. It stands for something that is neither object, nor "part of, or the central character in, a state of affairs. At this level, the difference between objects and states of affairs—or between objects and 'That objects are/exist' etc.—has not been established."[12]

With increasing levels of explicitness come increasing levels of description. (Unfortunately, Tallis does not explore the relationship between explicitness and language in any depth. Compared to the depth and complexity with which most of the thinkers in the coming chapters treat language, his work barely touches on what later I will label "the ontology of language problem.") At any rate, increasing levels of explicitness go hand in hand with increasing complexity of language use. The high end of the spectrum is open-ended, representing increasingly nested meta-language (i.e., discourse about discourse about...).

Tallis gives a number of schematic examples of such spectra, for instance:

?—an ineffable state

X—there are existents, but no consciousness: "... a pebble;"

That X exists—objects are beginning to emerge in awareness: "a pebble is;"

"That is an X"—discourse about objects is beginning to emerge: "that object is a pebble;"

"Someone has said 'There is an X'"—beginning of meta-language: "John has said 'there is a pebble there.'"

Explicitness, the opposite of implicitness, I suppose, thus is whatever it is that is absent in the most elementary part

---

[11]   Animal, p. 221.
[12]   Edge, p. 62n7.

of the spectrum and increasingly becomes present and expressible as we move toward the "higher" levels of consciousness and linguistic reflexivity. But, Tallis explicitly says of this spectrum, it "is not meant to depict an evolving process, a chronological sequence of emergence, but rather to mark out a distance, or a series of distances, between what we are and the scientific and metaphysical *notions* of (unconscious) matter.... [It is not] meant to depict ontogenetic relations between different kinds of entities."[13] Tallis's spectrum is an ahistorical, atemporal continuum situated in logical rather than historical space. Movement along the spectrum mirrors neither phylogenetic nor ontogenetic, evolutionary, developmental phenomena; it represents synchronic rather than diachronic dimensions. (We already have met one such example of ahistorical differences, namely, the distinction Collins made between prephilosophical, prescientific and scientific knowledge and understanding. That difference, too, was conceptualized as being situated in logical rather than temporal-historical space.)

Tallis' principal goal is to counter physical reductionism in philosophy and neurobiology, and explicitness is the key conceptual tool for his critiques. I have already said a good deal about this issue of reductionism elsewhere,[14] and it is not the major focus of the present work. I intend to use Tallis's critiques in the same way I use the work of other thinkers whose critiques are examined in Part I: mostly to emphasize those aspects that are particularly relevant to the holistic project I am outlining. What seems to be most relevant in Tallis' work is first, his awareness of what I call the Cheshire Cat residue nature of objects in philosophy of mind (especially in the version Tallis calls "neurophilosophy"), in neuroscience, and in computational

---

[13] Animal, pp. 2-3.
[14] See Berger 1974, 1985, 1991, 2002a, b. For a complete bibliography see Berger 2002b, pp. iv-viii.

models of the mind; and second, his ideas about the nature of origins.

He also points to pragmatic issues, indirectly, when he contrasts the "weekday" position on neuroscience he holds as a physician and researcher with his "weekend" stance when he is working as the philosopher who is a severe critic of neurophilosophy. From the perspective of an anomalous pragmatism, that discrepancy does raise interesting questions, primarily: How does he reconcile or integrate these conflicting positions as he is wearing one or another of his hats? That is, what implications do his critiques of neurophilosophy have for him when he is working as a physician, and what implications do the outcomes of his neurological researches have while he is working as a philosopher? Why, really, are entirely different positions needed in different circumstances and contexts?[15] To my knowledge he does not consider this dimension of his work, and that is unfortunate. Exploring such pragmatic issues might lead to interesting contributions.

## CHESHIRE CAT RESIDUES

Tallis shows in numerous contexts that in philosophy and science the practice of taking entities or concepts as existing on their own, independently of persons, is indefensible and destructive. In our by now familiar terminology: he shows the ubiquitous presence in these disciplines of Cheshire Cat residues, how these are generated, and that and how they are misconceived. Tallis shows that the meaning of such presumably independent entities is parasitic on the conscious experience of the observer or analyzer; the assumption of an observer-independent status is unacceptable. I will outline of what he has to say about several kinds of these "objects" to illustrate the rationale of his critique.

---

[15] There are facile but superficial answers to this question, of course.

## Information

What is information? A representative statement of the mainstream view is in a book that purports to explain consciousness neurobiologically. Speaking about the brain and information, the author asserts:

> Broadly speaking, the function of its cells, or neurons, is to pick up information (in the form of electrical impulses) from other neurons, synthesize the information observed, and pass the (modified) information on to many other neurons. With few exceptions most physiologists believe that the "genius" of the human brain derives from the sheer size and complexity of the information-processing system.[16]

The claims expressed here are (1) that information can be and is encoded electrically in the nervous system, (2) that it traverses a network of neurons that synthesizes and modifies it as the electrical signal wends its way, and (3) that the brain (an organ that can have, does have "genius") is the information-accepting terminus of this process. The statement also implies (4) that this information already exists in the outside world, (5) that it is picked up by the energy-transforming sensory receptors (eye, ear, etc.) that do the initial electrical encoding, and (6) that ultimately someone (!) somehow ends up with inner "representations" that can be perceived—but of course we do not say or even know who that "someone" is, or how the signals become (real) information.[17] Asking who does the perceiving, or who is watching this interior television screen's display, raises the age-old frustrating, unanswerable homunculus problem.[18]

Tallis calls this complex of assumptions and ingredients, the chain that begins with the emission or reflection of energies by objects in the external world and ends with the

---

[16] Cohen, 1996, p. 26.
[17] For a critique of the notion of representation, see Edge, p. 121; Olafson, 1995, especially chapter 1.
[18] Edge, p. 119.

perception of "inner" representations in persons, "The Causal theory of Perception,"[19] a belief system that on the basis of his extended, detailed, and neurophysiologically impeccable critiques he rejects entirely as incoherent and untenable—at least for and in philosophy.

He shows in great detail that when we hold to the Causal Theory of Perception we are inappropriately conflating *energy-to-energy* transductions with energy-to-("true")-*information* transformation. We assume that it is legitimate to begin with "information" in the form of physical energy, trace that through various transformations (e.g., from the mechanical energy of a vibrating ear drum to an encoded electrical signal) and finally take the last, now correctly formatted, version of that information as it arrives at the brain and turn it into something—something that we also call "information"—that subjectively is experienced as informative, as knowledge: "As the impulse propagates centrally, it leaves the world of 'energy transformations' and enters the world of 'signals until, two or three feet and two or three synapses later, it has [truly] become 'information.'"[20] Science has no means of conceptualizing, representing, or accounting for such transformations.

Tallis's major premise is that there are fundamental, drastic differences between physical energies and conscious experiences, including the experience of providing or getting information.[21] Of course, for the mind-body or for the functionalist eliminativists, this is precisely what they refuse to believe, and therefore humanistic critiques like Tallis's cannot influence their position. His premise is self-evident to some, and obvious nonsense to others. One cannot really argue for or against it on logical grounds; ultimately it is a matter of one's credo. As I intimated

---

[19]  Animal, pp. 45-88.
[20]  Animal, p. 83; see also Harding, 2002.
[21]  Edge, pp. 93-95.

earlier, in my view this difference in beliefs reflects characterological differences.[22]

The causal theory of perception often embraces another maneuver and assumption. It reverses the direction of information flow in the sense that the concept of information is extended to include external phenomena. We take the idea that information is encoded as electrical signals in the nervous system, and, reversing the reasoning, in retrograde fashion we now impute information also to the objects and phenomena that exist in the external world outside the physical body—we extrapolate from inner to outer. Now objects in the world, and also the energies they reflect or emit, are said to already "contain information," to become "sources of information," even before the physical energies have reached the human sensory receptors, or for that matter, even when there are no humans present: "According to some, information is actually present in the energy that impinges on the nervous system!"[23]

Overall, in terms of Tallis's conceptual framework we can say that explicitness is totally absent from this entire picture until it somehow magically and suddenly appears in the neighborhood of the neurological terminus, the brain. The concepts of coding and information-bearing signals are Cheshire Cat residues, inanimate, meaningless in and of themselves. What, then, leads to and sustains the ubiquitous beliefs that in and of themselves these pseudo-independent material phenomena can bear information?

As Tallis sees it, the main mechanism and culprit in this prestidigitation is what he calls *thinking by transferred epithet*, a devious, two-way sliding back and forth between mentalist terms (e.g., information, memory, knowing, understanding, searching, comparing, reasoning) and

---

[22] See Scharfstein, 1980; Cahoone, 1988.
[23] Edge, p. 94.

physicalist terms (e.g., computation, coding, storage, transmission, energy transduction, information processing):

> Machines are described anthropomorphically and, at the same time, the anthropic terms in which they are described undergo a machine-ward shift. These same terms, modified by their life amongst machines, can then be reapplied to minds and the impression is then created that minds and machines are one....[24] We are so used to hearing talk about the nervous system 'encoding' the outside world that it is easy to forget that this is a metaphor.[25]

Such unsavory juggling of descriptive terms is employed widely within neurophilosophy, medicine, technology, and in the exact as well as in the human sciences, to create and sustain the naturalization of mind. Tallis devotes an entire chapter specifically to this subject,[26] and extends this discussion further elsewhere.[27] As Tallis observes, "once information is uprooted from consciousness—and from an informant or from the experience of being informed and of wanting to be informed—then any kind of nonsense is possible.... Once the concept of information is liberated from the idea of *someone being informed* and from that of *someone doing the informing*, anything is possible."[28] Esoteric but otiose theorizing can flourish. Here, then, is a prime example of how the notion of explicitness can be used to articulate and reveal the spurious nature of a discipline's Cheshire Cat residue objects of study.

Parenthetically: I see at least one conceptual difficulty here. On the one hand, Tallis conceptualizes explicitness as a phenomenon that manifests along a spectrum, spanning an infinity of levels stretching from the ineffable to infinitely nested discourse. According to this conception, whatever else explicitness may be, in general it presents as

---

24 Edge, p. 73
25 Animal, p. 72.
26 Edge, chapter 2
27 E.g., Animal, pp. 72-73, 82-101.
28 Animal, pp. 100-101.

a hierarchy of gradations, of degrees. However, in the present case, the transmission of information, we seem to have an all or none situation: as Tallis sees it, when it comes to information, explicitness is totally absent in material entities and processes such as electrical signals in the nervous system, and then suddenly appears when these signals have become what he considers to be true information. Explicitness appears when information appears, and vice versa. For instance, Tallis says about language that "in the absence of consciousness, [spoken] language is merely variegated sound rather than the rich varieties of meaning that are embodied in, for example, Shakespeare's texts."[29] Tallis does not consider or even mention this inconsistency between the two models of explicitness. It does raise questions about his premise that explicitness is a dimension along a spectrum.

In any case, Tallis offers a similar critique of a second technical-scientific version of what information is, namely, of the engineering concept as defined in the mathematical theory of communication (information theory), namely, a statistically quantifiable measure of uncertainty and entropy of material or logical states.[30] Tallis shows how this artifice, developed for its usefulness in certain engineering applications, becomes untenable when wrongly extended beyond its legitimate domain of application, i.e., when in non-technical contexts such as ordinary discourse it is conflated with and equated to what is ordinarily understood by the term "information." The engineer's conception of information as specified in statistical theories of communication "has little to do with information in the ordinary sense."[31] Nevertheless, it has gained general use and acceptance even in some disciplines that lie outside of the natural sciences and engineering (e.g., in linguistics,

---

[29] Animal, p. 73; see also Edge, pp. 105-106
[30] Animal, pp. 91-101.
[31] Edge, p. 91.

and in literary theory). Information theory has bred another version of Cheshire Cat residues. Furthermore, its extension into nonengineering areas resonates with Collins' observation about the ways in which experts' views about the nature of inner contents influence the nonexperts' understandings. Uncertainty about the meaning of a term, about the nature of the entity to which it presumably refers—in this case, "information"—breeds insecurity, and that in turn breeds gullibility, vulnerability to being brainwashed by the experts.

**Truth and Falsehood**

Truth and falsehood, and the closely related notion of fact, receive treatments that parallel closely the critique of information as an independent entity. He begins by noting that explicitness is a necessary condition for

> the emergence of truth (and falsehood) out of existence. Existence by itself is insufficient to create the categories of truth and falsehood: a pebble is in itself neither true nor false.... Truth is neither an inherent property of the material world, nor is it a creation of consciousness. It is the result of the material world being made explicit in consciousness; and of that explicitness being made explicit; and of *that* explicitness being made explicit; and so on.[32] Truth and falsehood share *existence conditions*: the explicitness that creates the possibilities that are actualised.... explicitness creates the conditions for the emergence of truth [and falsehood].[33]

Tallis presents long, intricate explorations of the intertwined notions of explicitness, consciousness, truth and falsehood, assertions, reference, fact, and correspondence which I will not attempt to summarize.[34] I only note that what emerges out of these intricate critiques is, once again, that one cannot legitimately consider any of the concepts and the entities to which they presumably

---

[32] Animal, p. 226.
[33] Edge, p. xii.
[34] Animal, 226-230; Edge, pp. xii, xv, 1-70.

refer just by themselves, i.e., without taking explicitness (human ties) into account. Truth, for example, can arise only in the presence of explicitness. By now it should be evident that this is Tallis's way of saying that in order for these terms to be meaningful, they must be (re)connected to an aware human being who has a world. The proximity of Collins' critiques to Cheshire Cat residue critiques is obvious.

## ORIGINS AND MYSTERIES

Tallis not only grants but insists that explicitness is beyond description, ineffable, astonishing:

> Man is, above all, an explicit animal and that it is the capacity for making things explicit which lies at the heart of all that human beings are and do. This capacity is, moreover, utterly mysterious, being underivable from anything else. It has no place, for example, in the world as described by the physicist or the biologist....[35] Explicitness is "*underivable*, least of all from matter, however the latter is conceived....[36] We cannot assimilate human beings to the materialist, physicalist, biologist, computationalist world pictures because those world pictures are confined to descriptions of automatic mechanisms, perhaps rooted ultimately in the laws of physics, while human beings are not, ultimately, mechanisms.[37] Consciousness cannot be fitted into the scheme of the things that it is conscious of, for "that scheme of things is posterior to consciousness.[38]

At times Tallis's discourse about this ineffability seems almost incoherent, perhaps deliberately so in an effort to mirror the baffling nature of its subject: "To try to describe consciousness is to attempt to make explicitness explicit—in language that is itself the explicitness of things made explicit."[39]

---

[35] Edge, p. xi
[36] Animal, p. 3.
[37] Edge, p.3.
[38] Animal, p. 223.
[39] Animal, p. 223; to me, this is a Heidegger-like, gnomic pronouncement. We

This view of explicitness as an ineffable mystery resonates with the statements about holisms in the preceding chapters. The recurring themes are that discourse is ill suited for the description of this facet of human experience, and that all that remains is recourse to hints, allegories, metaphors, poetic and evocative language. However, we also see that Tallis explicitly and emphatically rejects the idea that the spectrum of explicitness has any temporal, onto- or phylogenetic features. In my view this leaves Tallis's mystery floating. I emphasize the position articulated in previous remarks: my aim is not to *explain* (or explain away) the kinds of mysteries that both Collins and Tallis identify and explore, nor those that will be posited and explored by the others whose work I discuss in Part I. Rather, I seek to anchor such root mysteries in a conceptual frame (ontogenesis) that is no less mysterious but, as I hope to show in Part II, more intuitively accessible and grounded, instinctively more satisfying.

---

might remember that Tallis did write a book (Tallis, 2002) about Heidegger.

# 4

# A CHINESE HIGH-MEDICAL PRESCRIPTION

## BRUCE HOLBROOK

With Bruce Holbrook we begin to consider the work of unorthodox thinkers who stand well outside established, familiar, easily comprehended frameworks. Holbrook is a Yale-educated cultural anthropologist who as a graduate student, after studying Chinese language and culture for six years, went to China to study with a traditional physician-scholar for several years before returning to complete his graduate studies. Here is how he introduces his book *The Stone Monkey: An Alternative, Chinese-Scientific, Reality*:

> As I see it, the Western sciences, from physics to political science, are based on a dead and deadening view of reality and consequently—despite the brilliance, creativity, and good intentions of our best scientists—they transform the world more negatively than positively. These effects, interacting exponentially, are creating a catastrophe at all levels of survival: physical, biological, psychological, social, political, and spiritual.... Our problem requires an *unanticipated solution*, and that in turn requires an unconditionally heretical procedure of discovery.... This book... shows the basic defect in Western science and explains how it generates negative effects; gives my reasons for believing that Chinese science is superior to it; and introduces an alternative, originally Chinese, worldview, science, and, potentially, reality.... There is one basic, universal Chinese scientific theory of which each discipline is a further specification, and Chinese medicine is at the center of and overlaps with all of them.... [It is] lively and enlivening; it makes connections among all things, recognizing their interdependence and harmony; thus it

fosters unity, health, and life, whereas the Western paradigm fosters conflict, illness and death.[1]

This unified, integrated Chinese science has evolved within an unbroken, self-correcting tradition for at least 3000 years. In contrast, Western science has been discontinuous, chronically disrupted by major social, political, religious, ideological upheavals, and evolving to its current form in only about 350 years—"an unnaturally rapid and probably short-lived aberration."[2] Yet, it takes a patronizing, hubristic, defensive stance toward non-Western alternatives, unable to imagine that such "primitive" relatives could be superior to any significant degree. Holbrook calls these two drastically contrasting world views *Absolute-Fragmental* (The Western view), and *Polar-Complete* (the Chinese view).

The book's introductory chapters characterize and discuss the general defects of mainstream Western world views. The later sections offer often obscure and difficult to follow expositions of Chinese thinking about specific issues, especially in physics and medicine but also in politics, social engineering, technology, psychology, and philosophy, along with critical comparisons between the Chinese and Western approaches.

## CHARACTERISTICS OF WESTERN THOUGHT

### Binary Categorizing

The Western world view, at least since Aristotle's time, is rooted in binary logic, exemplified by the syllogism. When one strips away the particulars it becomes apparent that the structural-logical foundation of virtually all formal thinking in virtually all disciplines, from physics and

---

[1]  Holbrook, 1981, pp. 8-10, 114-115. Unless otherwise noted, citations in this chapter refer to that work.

[2]  p. 28

mathematics to psychology and anthropology, is the assumption that there is some entity, *A,* which in turn implies the existence of a complementary entity, that which is *not-A*. These two categories are seen as mutually exclusive and jointly exhaustive. That is, everything (i.e., all constituents of the domain under consideration) falls into one or the other, and only into one or the other. Thus, inevitably and immediately two contrasting classes are created that are rigidly separated from each other. Then, usually these two basic categories are subdivided, creating any number of equally disconnected subcategories, which in turn typically leads to atomism. The basic categories-cum-subcategories provide the primitive, irreducible, independent building blocks from which more complex entities can be assembled in the domain under investigation. Holbrook gives many examples, e.g.: water-Matter/spirit-and-light; that world/this world; science/common sense; sacred/secular; Being/non-Being; positive charge/negative charge; animate/inanimate; only-male/only-female; ruling class/ruled class; Monarchists/Democrats; Capitalists/Communists; Progressives/Reactionaries.[3] The list can be extended indefinitely; we have, for instance, the wave/particle duality in physics, or good/evil in ethics.

One might object to this picture of the Western worldview as being made up of discrete and disconnected atomic elements, claiming that there also is integration or merging of disparate ingredients. On closer examination, however, such would-be integrations or continuities are only apparent; they do not leave the binary process behind. Holbrook gives the example of male and female. Under the Western binary paradigm one can apparently "integrate" and undo the rigid boundary between the two concepts in one of two ways. One can subsume both within a single higher-level category, for example, "human," but this step

---

[3]    pp. 91, 113.

actually retains binary thinking because "human" itself is conceptualized as a part of yet another polarizing and polarized dichotomy: human/not-human. Alternatively, one can conceptualize male and female as end points of spectrum, but spectra in Western thought really are made up of subcategories. (Examples are the color spectrum, and the presumably integrating approaches developed in so-called "fuzzy logic."[4])

Contrarily, true integration of elements is an essential feature of the Chinese world view—a baffling feature that is almost impossible to understand from the perspectives of Western world views. Apparently opposing categories in a sense actually contain one another. (The yin/yang "duality" is a famous example.) Holbrook's monograph contains many attempts to illustrate and explain this puzzling aspect of Chinese thought, but it will not be considered further here. What is relevant is the fragmenting and fragmented picture that Western thought inevitably generates.

## Sensuousness

Holbrook emphasizes that in his view (and, presumably, also in the Chines world view), "the Western sciences, from physics to political science, are based on a dead and deadening view of reality..."[5] (I already have introduced this important theme in earlier discussions pertaining to the distinction between primary/secondary qualities and the latter's Cartesian expulsion from the domain of the natural sciences. It will recur frequently throughout this work.) He traces this position back to the Greeks. He quotes Plato:

> Of the world of sense it is true that opposites intermingle. The same object may appear simultaneously as hot and cold, the same experience as pleasant and painful, the same amount as double and half. But this signifies only that sense-experience is not a

---

4    See Priest, 2000, chapter 10.
5    p. 8.

valid medium of truth. For truth... must be rational, i.e., characterized by perfect self-consistency.[6]

Holbrook says that he "will devote much attention to the extent to which Western science, in contrast with the Chinese, *is deliberately misaligned with human perception;* to the fact that Western science and our general culture, which it configures, drastically decreases human perception."[7]

He extensively discusses the differences in Western and Chinese views about the nature of color, using it as a vehicle for his critiques concerning the role of sensuousness in science. The Western conception of color is based on a one-dimensional, linear, quantified spectrum of radiation frequencies, while the Chinese view is grounded in sensuous experience. The latter view leads to a most peculiar and elusive conception regarding the nature of color, but, strangely enough, to one that has affinities with another anomalous view, namely the one promulgated by Goethe more than 200 years ago: "The idea of a purely physical determination of color... was anathema to Goethe when he started his own explorations of it."[8] Goethe's ideas were ridiculed and dismissed even in his own time, but "then, in 1957, something singular happened. Edwin Land (already famous for his invention of the Polaroid instant camera...) staged a demonstration that stunned everybody who saw it and was wholly inexplicable according to classical color theory."[9]

Another example of the benefits of retaining sensuousness in one's scientific framework is acupuncture, a subject to which I return briefly below:

When people have said they can feel pain in a certain area, Chinese medical scientists "concluded" that they feel pain there.

---

[6]    p. 112.
[7]    p. 28.
[8]    Sacks, 1995, p. 155; see also Berman, 1981, pp. 185-187.
[9]    Sacks, 1995, p. 156.

When dissection of cadavers failed to reveal nerves in that area, they concluded that there are fine, invisible ones there. A therapeutic technique was then based on the theory consistent with this conclusion, and found to work. In contrast, Western physicians tend to discount their patient's reports of pain fro which gross evidence of anatomical-physiological causes is lacking. Either they deny that there is pain or they call it "psychosomatic..."[10]

It seems that Western science's dismissal of sensuousness may carry penalties, while granting sensuousness a prominent place in the natural sciences (and elsewhere) may pay off.

## CONSEQUENCES

### Limits on Knowledge and Understanding

The first kind of limitation on what Western philosophy and sciences can know arises from the *fragmenting of the whole*. What one can know and do while working within this tradition is drastically circumscribed because it "is based on a view of the universe that takes into account only one part of it at a time, in isolation,"[11] because it is based on "an always defective and fragmental view of the whole,"[12] and because it is grounded in "a scientific paradigm which fragments reality into disoriented little so-called parts and deals with each so as to side-effect [more about this term and its meaning below] every other [part]."[13] In support of his claim Holbrook offers many examples taken from medicine (especially the fragmented and fragmenting practice of treating individual diseases in isolation), from social and political planning and policy execution, from technology, and from the natural sciences.

---

[10]  p. 82.
[11]  p. 52.
[12]  p. 107.
[13]  p. 76.

The Western world view even isolates its disciplines from one another. Academia is divided into hermetically sealed compartments and although in principle, cross-disciplinary studies may be said to be admirable and avant-garde, in actual practice these are frowned on. For example, Gerald Bruns, whose work I will outline in chapter 6, speaks of himself as an English professor commenting on "the most obscure of a notorious philosopher's writings"[14] and adds: "I guess no one will misunderstand me when I say that departments of philosophy and of language and literature work hard to discourage this sort of thing—call it trafficking outside the normal curriculum and its official canon."[15] Compare this with the Chinese practice:

> What I [Holbrook] have called "Chinese physics, chemistry, biology, and social science," on the one hand, and "Chinese medicine," on the other, are not separate disciplines. There is one basic, universal Chinese scientific theory of which each discipline is a further specification, and Chinese medicine is at the center of and overlaps with all of them. That is, Chinese physics is partly Chinese medicine, Chinese social science is partly Chinese medicine, and so on.[16]

Furthermore, the individual disciplines themselves have a tendency to fragment into esoteric specialized subdisciplines that do not communicate with or even understand each other. Mathematics and physics contain prime examples.

The above-mentioned banishment of the human being and sensual experience from the sciences is yet another major factor that limits the understandings that the Western worldview can achieved. In Holbrook's opinion that is because the ejection removes "that sector [which] is *most* of reality."[17] Of course, in a sense that removal is a sham;

---

[14] Bruns, 1998, p.1; the philosopher is Heidegger.
[15] Ibid.
[16] p. 10.
[17] p. 25.

sensuousness must be covertly retained even in the most formal of the natural sciences—how else could one observe, measure and refer to phenomena, construct theories, propose axioms, or evaluate and report empirical results? The starting points of scientific reductionism, like those of any other of the mainstream monist alternatives, "presuppose the very dualism they try to eliminate."[18] It is just that in the Western scientific world view the *"connections* between sensed data and between people"[19] are camouflaged. (We shall see in Part III that this concealment is at work even in contemporary physics' quantum and relativity theories, unorthodox frameworks that apparently acknowledge the central theoretical importance of the observer and observation. Actually, as far as these theories are concerned, a human observer's functions could just as well be carried out by instruments—although paradoxes do arise.[20]) Holbrook, citing once again examples from a variety of disciplines, shows that, and how, this partial, person-less view (Thomas Nagel's "View from Nowhere") limits one's understanding, and leads to a deficient kind of theorizing and to constricted scientific and technological practices. One example to which he frequently refers is acupuncture, a procedure whose success is inexplicable from within Western theoretical frameworks (although that claim should be qualified—see below) but understandable within the Chinese "whole, balanced, stable, life-promoting system,"[21] as I indicated above. We saw that not only is acupuncture understandable within the Chinese system, but that this system with its retention of sensuality actually led to the discovery of acupuncture in the first place. Another example is the field of biology. Excluding sensuous elements from its framework leads to a "biology

---

[18]  Loy, 1988, p. 94.
[19]  p. 194.
[20]  See, for example, Lindley, 1996; Albert, 1992.
[21]  p. 107.

[that] is without a definition of life.... our biologists' central doubts are about what their very science concerns—*bios*: life (or, better, living)."[22] That is the kind of paradox to which a lifeless framework leads.

Yet another way in which the fragmenting, partial, sensuousness-removing Western approach, this "destructive, lethal little paradigm,"[23] limits understanding is that it induces a blind spot. The lifeless, depersonalized framework does not have the conceptual resources needed for a critical self-examination. It is a "paradigm [that] directs our science in ways of which they [the scientists] are quite unaware and of which, under normal conditions, they could not be aware even if they wished."[24] When one has removed the person from the framework, how can that framework be aware of itself, refer to itself, recognize its limitations, and so on?[25] Perhaps this inability to step outside the fragmenting framework accounts for the "2500-year-long dispute [in philosophy] about which of its variants is true."[26] Perhaps that lack of capacity for self-knowledge helps to account for the situation identified by Lewis Thomas in his *The Medusa and the Snail:*

> The only solid piece of scientific truth about which I feel totally confident is that we are profoundly ignorant about nature. Indeed, I regard this as the major discovery of the last one hundred years of biology.... It is this sudden confrontation with the depth and scope of ignorance that represents the most significant contribution of twentieth-century science of the human intellect.[27]

Thomas's awareness suggests that although the sciences' self-understandings remain greatly deficient there may be a

---

[22]   p. 43.

[23]   p. 113.

[24]   p. 25.

[25]   See Bologh, 1979, for an intriguing study of Marxism as a framework that *does* have this reflexive potential for including its own theory within that theory.

[26]   p. 110; see also similar remarks in chapter 1 concerning the "revolving door" phenomenon," and Colin McGinn's idea of the "dance" in philosophy.

[27]   quoted by Holbrook, p. 44.

small ray of hope. Scientists may be able to recognize their profound ignorance even though they are unable to reflexively identify and examine its roots and take appropriate and effective corrective measures.

## Side Effects

A central point in Holbrook's work is that the sciences have been and are fundamentally destructive:

> As I see it, the Western sciences, from physics to political science... transform the world more negatively than positively. These effects, interacting exponentially, are creating a catastrophe at all levels of survival: physical, biological, social, political, and spiritual.... [The Western world view] has given us pogroms, genocide, and "holy" wars, and their secular transform, wars "for freedom," that were actually waged for wealth and power, and the wealth and power of a few. It has given us "divine" instead of *human* justice.[28]

He gives a large number of other examples from across the spectrum of formal disciplines and their material offshoots (e.g., technology).[29]

As Holbrook says, "Of course, many share this perception of emergency,"[30] but his analyses differ from the usual ones. Typically, the noxious results of natural science/technology, medicine, political science, psychology/psychiatry, and so on, are ascribed to avoidable "side effects"—that is, they are seen as unfortunate outcomes, products of *misapplied* sciences and technologies. Holbrook sees it differently. For him, the apparent side effects actually are the inevitable concomitants of the core features of a Western world view: its "dead and deadening view of reality,"[31] and its innately fragmenting framework. Western science

---

28   pp. 8, 105.
29   See, for example, his chapters 1 and 2.
30   p. 8.
31   p. 8; see also pp. 43, 82, 93, 105, 107, 113, 115-116.

is not unified science based on universal theory. That it has measured many physical, biological, and social phenomena and expresses the results numerically does not constitute *theoretical* unity, as is claimed, but mere *notational* unity. Our scientific paradigm cannot be a unity not only because its theoretical foundations preclude that, but also because it lacks *Humane purpose.* In fact, according to our scientists, it has no purpose at all, because its standard justification, "knowledge is sought for knowledge's sake," is circular, totally meaningless. Research that leads to truth, to universal, unexcepted, logically consistent, empirically grounded theory, must be conditioned by a goal, and that goal, inexorable, is *to serve human beings, as aspects of the whole of Nature....* Actually... our science does have a purpose; our scientists do not wish to admit what it is. It is to discover a phenomenon or technique that will permit merchants to make more money, or, governments to coercively or manipulatively maintain power, and will commute material weal, fame, or both, to the researcher.[32]

(Let us remember that this was written more than 25 years ago; surely, subsequent political, military, technological, ecological, and societal events and developments lend further credibility to this position.) Holbrook's constantly reiterated theme is that the Western world view is fragmented, wrongly motivated, coldly detached and lifeless (actually, worse than that: disdainful and dismissive of humans, denigrating life, "anti-life"), and that it must produce noxious results.

## Manifestations of Defensiveness

Western science is arrogant, hubristic, and ethnocentric. One sign is that when it encounters some practice or accomplishment in another culture that is inexplicable within its own schemas, Western science has great difficulty in accepting "the idea that a superior alternative,"[33] a totally different way of understanding, exists. If, for example, Western medical science is unable to

---

[32]   p. 48.
[33]   p. 26.

explain the efficacy of some non-Western therapy in terms of its own theoretical belief system, then it either rejects that therapy as bogus, as some conjuring trick, or else explains the results in terms of some mechanism that already is available n its arsenal (e.g., acupuncture "really" is suggestion, hypnosis) even though that explanation cannot adequately and honestly account for the clinical data.

Another symptom of hubris is Western science's unwillingness to face the possibility that its negative "'side'-effects are its principal ones,"[34] that, as discussed above, these actually are *necessary,* and not accidental, concomitants of the scientific enterprise. The received view is not only that the many catastrophes brought about by supposed technological advances were in principle preventable, unfortunate mishaps, but also that these problems can of course be fixed by applying still more science—for example, by developing anti-missile technology to counter the threat of cataclysmic nuclear exchanges, by developing "clean energy" to fix the constellation of pervasive ecological disasters spawned by an irresponsible technology; the examples are endless.

Finally, science's arrogance is also evidenced in its rigid resistance to basic change, a position famously documented and superficially explained by Thomas Kuhn. Holbrook believes that basic change must in one way or another be imposed, and identifies three situations that can exert such pressures: (1) since reality cannot be denied forever, sooner or later science when it can no longer support its illusions will be forced to abandon unrealistic, counterproductive theories (a variant of the Kuhnian view of the roots of paradigm change); (2) Western culture may be confronted by a culture whose world view is more mature, may be able

---

[34]   p. 50.

to recognize that, and change accordingly (unlikely, in my opinion); and (3) by forceful foreign intervention.[35]

In my view, Holbrook's analysis of scientific hubris and defensiveness has merit but does not go nearly far enough. His structural and motivational analyses (i.e., of binary structures, and of anti-sensuousness) neglect more basic and salient underlying primitive societal forces that drive that defensiveness: psychodynamic cultural forces that drive Western beliefs and practices and in turn are sustained by these.[36] I return to the issue of the resistance to change at the conclusion of chapter 14.

## COMMENTS

Three aspects of Holbrook's work seem particularly relevant to and useful for the holistic perspectives I wish to develop. First and foremost, much of what he says analyzes and demonstrates the limiting if not noxious consequences of compartmentalizing, boundarying, creating Cheshire Cat objects in formal disciplines; that, and his advocacy of the Chinese Polar-Complete world view, lends support to my holistic proposals.

Second, he challenges a science that claims to be seeking knowledge for knowledge's sake, in two ways: (1) he shows that this position leaves out the humane motivations that have productively guided Chinese science and medicine, and that therefore the Pure Knowledge Paradigm is destructive of life, and (2) he unmasks the Western science's facade of neutral objectivity by showing that actually there are covert noxious motives (such as greed, lust for power, desire for fame) at work.[37] The apparently objective neutrality is just that, only an appearance.

---

[35]   pp. 87-88.
[36]   See Berger, 1991; 2002a, chapter 6.
[37]   pp. 48, 75-76.

There is still another line of thought in Holbrook's work, one that I have not previously mentioned, that is relevant to my project. He briefly but evocatively refers to the ultimately mysterious ground of one's being in the world, and mentions two contrasting ways, *"composting"* and *"non-composting"*, in which societies can deal with that mystery. Non-composting cultures simply eject and dismiss anything that does not fit into their world view; the Cartesian banishment of the secondary qualities from the realm of the sciences is a prime example. The contrasting "composting variety... confronts the mystery... and uses it as fertilizer for the growth of the relatively definite worldview it doesn't fit."[38] In composting, the mystery is neither explained away nor disdainfully dismissed as unscientific nonsense, as mystagogy; instead, it is used to engender significant growth, a movement past extant conceptual limitations. I have mentioned that certain kinds of holisms are mysterious in that they necessarily evade linguistic specification or formal conceptualization—a theme that will continue to be present in most of the remaining chapters—and also mentioned that I do not propose to explain or remove that mystery but rather to "reposition" it productively via an ontogenetic perspective.[39]

---

[38]  p. 123; he borrows the terms and concept from *Purity and Danger* by the anthropologist Mary Douglas; for similar concerns, see Berman, 2000a, pp. 19, 166, 168-169.

[39]  See chapter 9, and Part III, this book.

# 5

# NONDUALITY

## DAVID LOY

David Loy is Professor in the Faculty of International Studies at Bunyko University, Japan. He is a philosopher, a critic of scientism in the tradition of Nietzsche, Wittgenstein, and Heidegger who has studied Eastern nondual thought in a number of contexts, including those pertaining to the "therapy" of those ills that plague Western culture as a consequence of its near-total immersion in the dualist modality.[1]

This chapter will examine his first book, *Nonduality: A Study in Comparative Philosophy,*[2] an expanded version of his doctoral dissertation in philosophy. The book is in two parts. The first explores nonduality as a general phenomenon, although primarily from the perspective of Asian (Chinese and Indian) thought. The attention is on nonduality *as an experience*, and Loy's goal in part 1 is to "extract and elucidate a 'core doctrine' of nonduality from these various claims."[3] These "various claims" differ in *ontology*. Some [Asian] doctrines are monistic, others dualistic, while yet others deny "both that things exist and that they do not exist."[4] Furthermore, the book retains traces of its academic origins and has a thesis: through applying the core theory about nondual experience developed in part 1 in a number of analyses, Loy wants to demonstrate in part 2 that the apparently different claims

---

[1] Loy, 2002
[2] Loy, 1988. In this chapter, citations giving only page numbers will refer to this work.
[3] p. 6.
[4] p. 185.

about the nature of duality made in a variety of Asian traditions—primarily but not exclusively Mahāyāna Buddhism, Advaita Vedānta, and Taoism—and also by some thinkers in the Western tradition (Loy singles out Blake, Nietzsche, Wittgenstein, and Heidegger)[5] "arise not from different experiences but from emphasizing different aspects of the same nondual experience."[6]

We have seen that Holbrook also espouses holism, but there are differences between his and Loy's expositions of non-Western thought. Holbrook emphasizes integration rather than nonduality, and focuses on its everyday roles and applications—in medicine, physics, politics, and so on. His emphasis is on integration as it is manifested or violated in the familiar, ordinary, everyday. Loy's interest, on the other hand, is in the mystical, ineffable, direct experience of nonduality, on the liberating force of the experience, on the ways in which that experience enables a seeker to shed the illusions and delusions that dual ways of being in the world bring to both East and West.

Loy's emphasis also differs from mine in several ways. First, his take on nondualities is primarily adultcentric (although as we shall see, there are minor exceptions). He is looking almost exclusively at what the *adult's* experiences are pertaining to duality and nonduality. Second, he is looking at the salvational or soteriological, mystical, liberating potential that nonduality harbors for the *individual* adult who seeks enlightenment. By contrast, my emphasis will be first, on the ontogenetic aspects of nonduality; second, on its role as an underlying ground in adult life rather than a quasi-mystical, quasi-religious, directly experienced alternative view, and third, on the implications that an ontogenetically-based view of nonduality has for the theories and practices in various

---

[5]  p. 184.
[6]  Ibid.

academic and professional disciplines. Nevertheless, we can profit from Loy's informative general observations about the nature of an holistic, nondual alternative to the usual bifurcating, isolating, alienating, Cheshire Cat-residue producing dualistic world views.

## CHARACTERISTICS OF NONDUALITY

### Ineffability

Nonduality is an extraordinary notion that "naturally tends toward self-negation and paradox, due to its apparent violation of logic, especially the law of identity." As such, it stands in almost diametric opposition to the Western sciences' dualist worldview. Loy does point out, however, that when examined carefully and nondogmatically, that latter view is really no less paradoxical, that it is generally regarded as unproblematic only because it "seems to accord better with common sense, despite whatever puzzles arise when one tries to develop this belief philosophically."[7]

The ineffable nature of pervasive holisms, of nondualities, is a constant theme in the works of virtually all who write about the subject. We have already met that claim in the earlier chapters, and will continue to do so. From Loy's salvational perspective, there are two kinds of reasons. First, "that nonduality is difficult to understand is necessarily true.... If we did understand it fully we would be enlightened.... The intellectual attempt to grasp nonduality conceptually must give way to various meditative techniques..."[8] Second, "something about... [nondual manifestations] is always indeterminable by intellectual analysis.... [T]he problem with any attempt to describe the nondual Absolute is that it amounts to dualistically separating oneself from it."[9]

---

[7]   p. 19.
[8]   p. 5.
[9]   pp. 88, 115.

Loy says there are various manifestations of nonduality, and that "as the negative construction of the word in all languages suggests, the meaning of each [appearance of] nonduality can be understood only by reference to the particular duality that is being denied."[10] This is a point made in earlier chapters; one of the few ways of elucidating an ineffable experience is by way of a *via negativa*.

Trying to explain nonduality in terms of its origins is also problematic. While discussing "the difference between reasoning/conceptualizing/dualistic thinking and the type of [presumably nondualistic] thinking that occurs after deep enlightenment," Loy notes that "Insofar as this involves looking for a 'first cause'—in this case, the origin of delusion [of a separate self]—no definitive answer is given in the nondualist traditions, presumably because none can be given."[11] Loy dismisses explanations that attempt to make the origins rationally understandable, "for example, as an 'oceanic' feeling due to womb memory, Freud's formulation."[12] Instead, Loy mentions a cryptic saying of the Japanese Zen master Dōgen: "Originally, there is no distinction between 'internal (mental) and 'external' (physical),"[13] which leaves the meaning of "originally" obscure. Perhaps the quotation does adumbrate ontogenesis, however, and I find two additional brief comments by Loy that can be seen in the same light. One is a suggestion that a particular kind of fragmentation of a unitary experience (in this instance, one brought about by the superposition of thought-constructions on "raw" percepts) may be due "to language acquisition and other socialization."[14] The other is a remark that language-acquisition may be "the process that gives birth to our

---

[10] p. 17.
[11] p. 146.
[12] p. 8—but see the ontogenetic point of view developed in chapter 9, this book.
[13] p. 140.
[14] p. 40.

phenomenal world of multiplicity, breaking up the primordial whole into objects—one of which is the subject, since the sense of self is also reified in the process."[15] This issue becomes central in chapter 9.

## Classes of Nonduality

Nonduality is elusive not only because it thwarts attempts to define it or to place its origin, but also because it is a term used in multiple ways and in various kinds of contexts:

> No concept is more important in Asian philosophical and religious thought than *nonduality*... and none is more ambiguous. The term has been used in many different although related ways, and to my knowledge the distinctions between these meanings have never been fully clarified. These meanings are distinct, although they often overlap in particular instances.[16]

Loy identifies five kinds of meaning: "the negation of dualistic thinking, the nonplurality of the world... the nondifference of subject and object.... the nonduality of duality and nonduality... [and] a mystical unity between God and man", adding that "no doubt other nondualities can be distinguished, but most of them can be subsumed under one or more of the above categories."[17]

Following Loy, I will outline the sense of the first three of these five meanings. I should note that his work elaborates greatly on these, showing how the concepts become meaningful and useful within the various apparently disparate Asian traditions.

*The negation of dualistic thinking* means a rejection of the kind of thinking that "differentiates that-which-is-thought-about into two opposed categories",[18] echoing Holbrook's criticism of what he designated "Absolute-

---

[15]  p. 117.
[16]  p. 17.
[17]  Ibid.
[18]  p. 18.

Fragmental" Western dichotomization or, more generally, categorization into discrete, mutually exclusive and jointly exhaustive contrasting classes. Supposedly, the (mostly Western?) mind's tendency is to dichotomize and polarize values, experiences, situations by setting up mutually exclusive linguistic dualities such as good/bad, love/hate, being/non-being, life/death, success/failure, pure/impure imposes frameworks that prevent us from seeing reality "as it really is." In an obviously paradoxical manner, nondual approaches call this dichotomizing "wrong thinking" and nondual thinking "right thinking", thus using the very type of dichotomy it faults. (Loy attempts to explain this inconsistency, but it, itself, probably is one of the ineffable aspects of nonduality and resists cognitive elucidation.) Furthermore, "the critique of dualistic thinking... often expands to include all conceptual thinking or conceptualization."[19]

*Nonplurality of the world* rejects as illusion/delusion the belief that the external world is "a collection of discrete objects (one of them being *me*) causally interacting in space and time."[20] Instead, nonduality in this second sense means "that the world itself is nonplural, because all the things 'in' the world are not really distinct but together constitute some integral whole."[21]

The third and for us probably most basic and important sense of nonduality is *the nondifference of subject and object*. Loy points out that

> this third sense, like the other two, must be understood as a negation. The dualism denied is our usual distinction between subject and object, and experiencing self that is distinct from what is experienced, be it sense-object, physical action, or mental event.[22]

---

[19]   p. 20.
[20]   p. 21.
[21]   Ibid.
[22]   p. 25.

He notes that this is an extraordinary and counterintuitive idea, yet "an essential element of many Asian systems (and some Western ones, of course)."[23]

The first part of Loy's monograph consists mostly of explorations illustrating and analyzing how these three aspects of nonduality come into play. One important area is perception. As previous chapters have already suggested (see, for example, Tallis's critique of the causal theory of perception, or Collins's of mental representations) and as the following chapters will further demonstrate, this is an extraordinarily messy topic in mainstream Western thought in general and in Western science in particular. There are perennial, baffling paradoxical problems raised by basic assumptions such as those concerning "pure" sense data or percepts, internal representation of those external data (of "reality"), the bifurcation into an experiencing person or observer and an independently objectively existing external world (which leads, among other difficulties, to the so-called homunculus problem), the nature of referential language, the problem of the two kinds of qualities (primary and secondary). The Western world view seems to have no candidates for a viable holistic alternative. Loy shows that the three kinds of dualities he discussed and criticized—percepts, actions, and thoughts— "somehow interfere with each other, thus obscuring the nondual nature of each."[24] These various manifestations of nondualistic thinking are interrelated, and "work together to sustain the dualistic sense of a self."[25] This pernicious synergism makes it even more difficult to seriously question and challenge the normal, deeply entrenched dualistic thinking.

---

[23]  p. 26.
[24]  p. 11.
[25]  p. 121.

## Asymmetry

Another issue that deserves mention is *cognitive asymmetry*. Let us take for granted that at least at present, science is unable to illuminate nonduality. The reverse, however, is not true: "apparently, dualistic phenomena can be understood from the perspective of nonduality, but not vice versa.... [Science] accepts duality as valid and dismisses nonduality as delusive; the latter accepts nonduality as revelatory and criticized duality as a more common but deluded interpretation of what we experience."[26] In other words, while the nondual perspective recognizes and to a degree legitimizes dualistic phenomena, the reverse is not true. With few exceptions, Western formal-scientific thought is disdainfully dismissive of nondual worldviews and phenomena.[27, 28]

## Validation

One obvious problem raised by nondual claims or frameworks is the matter of *proof* or *justification*. If proponents of a nondual approach admit that it is not only paradoxical but escapes attempts to define it, then how could one justify its validity or importance? While there are exceptions, historically the vast majority of proponents of science have divided views, beliefs, perspectives into two distinct, mutually exclusive and exhaustive categories: those that are scientifically legitimate and respectable, and those that are not—that are indefensibly mystical, magical, deluded, poetic, emotive, or downright fraudulent. (An

---

[26] pp. 7, 8.

[27] In spite of appearances to the contrary, this remains true in contemporary science, including quantum and relativity theories—see, for example, Smith, 1984.

[28] It reminds me of a similar point I made some time ago about various clinical perspectives; these, too, are asymmetrical. I claimed that psychodynamic thought and practice can illuminate behavioral or clinical cognitive thought and practice, but not vice versa, Berger, 1991.

extreme formal expression of this scientistic position was the Vienna Circle's Logical Positivism and its verifiability criterion: meaningful statements were those that could lead to experimental verification or disconfirmation; those that could not be "operationalized" and tested were deemed meaningless for science, and could simply be dismissed. One difficulty with this position was that the criterion itself failed to meet its requirement.)

Now, as I have pointed out in a number of publications (most recently, in *Psychotherapy as Praxis*)[29] there is at least one other way, basically one that does take the *source* and *context* of such apparently nonscientific and therefore not credible claims into consideration. Science makes a firm distinction between the so-called *context of discovery* and *context of verification*. The point is, science says, it does not matter who discovered something, or how that occurred; all that matters is whether the discovered theory or phenomenon can be publicly and objectively verified, the findings replicated, and so on.

Loy discusses this issue at length.[30] In Asian thought at least, the history and source of some kinds of "discoveries" and claims do matter. If there are some phenomena that cannot be validated through the theories and methodologies of "normal science" (Kuhn)—and whether or not there are such phenomena is itself contentious—then tradition, report, the subjective experiences of those willing to investigate the claims, just might be relevant and meaningful. Loy identifies only three kinds of decisive arguments against the standard scientistic demands for validation or justification: a person's own intuition; reports of credible persons who have attained enlightenment; and, a person's own direct meditative experiences and their consequences. Sometimes the context of discovery does

---

[29]  Berger, 2002a.
[30]  See especially pp. 6-8, 17.

matter; in certain situations it ought to influence how one judges a claim that is being made.

I mention the matter of proof and credibility here not because the issue of the veracity of Asian views about nonduality is particularly relevant to my thesis, but because I want to begin questioning the scientistic premise that any and all proposals or claims ought to be empirically verifiable (or, if you like, disconfirmable) at least *in principle* in order to be taken seriously. We shall encounter variations on this critique at several junctures in the remainder of the book since most of its proposals and claims are nondual and thus cannot be "scientifically" validated or disconfirmed.

## Applications

It is to Loy's great credit that he does not stop with a philosopher's analysis of abstract generalities about "world views" and nondual experiences but at least demonstrates with examples of how nonduality might be relevant to our way of life. He briefly considers how it might pertain to *ethics, aesthetics,* and *society.*[31] The last of these three is a subject that has been particularly significant for me,[32] and I want to call attention to a very important point Loy makes:

> From a nondualist perspective, what is most striking about the present world situation is the curious parallel between it and our perennial personal situation. The personal situation is of course the subject-object dualism.... Once the correspondence between this and the collective social problem has been noticed, the natural question is whether the latter problem too may be subject of a parallel solution. In this century it has become clear that the fundamental social problem is now the relationship between humankind as a whole and our global environment. It is because of our alienation form the earth that we are destroying it.... But this is nothing other than the individual situation writ large.... In

---

[31] pp. 292-304.
[32] See Berger, unpublished (October 2002); 1991, chapters 4 and 5; 1985, p. 191; 2002a, chapter 6.

both cases the problem is a delusive sense of duality between oneself and the world one is "in."[33] This issue, here set in a soteriological context by Loy, is exactly the one I raised in a clinical, psychodynamic context: can what is known about individual, dyadic psychotherapy be transmuted and applied at a societal level?[34]

## Martin Heidegger

I have mentioned the philosopher Martin Heidegger several times in previous chapters, but so far his influence has not been obvious. Neither Collins nor Holbrook mention him, and Tallis says little about him in the two books we examined in chapter 3 although he studied Heidegger's work closely and has written a book about him.[35] Loy devotes several pages to arguing that Heidegger's later work can best be seen as nondual thought.[36] That is hardly surprising; after all, Heidegger is considered by some as "the undisputed master of dichotomy destruction."[37]

Loy identifies and briefly considers some parallels between Heidegger's later thought and nonduality, especially the rejection of the subject-object duality;[38] On the whole, though, Heidegger's work seems to be peripheral in Loy's text. Incidentally, since *Nonduality* was written, the ties and close affinities between Heidegger's and Asian thought have come to be more widely recognized, explored, and appreciated.[39]

---

[33]  p. 302.
[34]  Berger, unpublished, October 2002; see also Berger, 2002a, chapter 6, and 1991, chapters 4 and 5. For valuable parallel analyses, see Berman, 1981, 1989, 2000a.
[35]  Tallis, 2002, chapters 4 and 5.
[36]  See especially pp. 163-177.
[37]  Pylkkö, 1998, p. xxi.
[38]  see, for example, Mansbach 2002, Introduction.
[39]  Parks, 1990; Zimmerman, 1993; Pattison, 2000; Caputo, 1978. Loy and Heidegger also share an interest in what might be called a mystical kind of psychotherapy. Heidegger did collaborate with the psychiatrists Medart Boss, Ludwig Binswanger, and Rollo May in an attempt to develop an existential psychotherapy—an attempt which I believe is clinically ill-conceived (see Berger 2002b, chapter 14)—and Loy has addressed similar Heideggerian

Heidegger's thought does become central in the following three chapters. Accordingly, I want to offer a preliminary overview of the man and his work. Here is how an encyclopedia entry introduces Heidegger:

> Martin Heidegger is acknowledged to be one of the most original and important philosophers of the 20th century, but also the most controversial. His thinking has contributed to such diverse fields as phenomenology (Merleau-Ponty), existentialism (Sartre, Ortega y Gasset), hermeneutics (Gadamer, Ricoueur), political theory (Arendt, Marcuse), psychology (Boss, Binswanger, Rolo May), theology (Bultmann, Rahner, Tillich), and postmodernism (Derrida). His main concern was ontology or the study of being. In his fundamental treatise, *Being and Time*, he attempted to access being (Sein) by means of phenomenological analysis of human existence (*Dasein*) in respect to its temporal and historical character. In his later works Heidegger had stressed the nihilism of modern technological society, and attempted to win western philosophical tradition back to the question of being. He placed an emphasis on language as the vehicle through which the question of being could be unfolded, and on the special role of poetry. His writings are notoriously difficult. *Being and Time* remains still his most influential work. [40]

That emphasis on language becomes pivotal not only in the next three chapters but continues to resonate throughout the remainder of this work.

---

therapeutic issues in his *Lack and Transcendence*.

[40] Korab-Karpowicz, 2001, p. 1.

# 6

# HEIDEGGER AND POETRY

## GERALD BRUNS

Gerald Bruns is William P. and Hazel B. White Professor of English at the University of Notre Dame. Here is how he introduces *Heidegger's Estrangements: Language, Truth, and Poetry in the Later Writings*, the principal work to be discussed here:

> This is a book about the relation of language and poetry in Martin Heidegger's later writings. Or, more exactly, it is about the way in which the space between poetry and language is mediated, or more accurately held open, or breached, by Heidegger's strange notion of truth as *a-lētheia*, where *a-lētheia* is no longer simply the old Greek word for unconcealment or disclosure (*alētheia*) but is also a complex pun that preserves the darkness or otherness of truth, its strangeness or reserve, its self-refusal, its "untruth." In this book I try to follow the later Heidegger's attempt to speak about this unspeakable subject.... This book is about the way poetry and language belong to this unspeakability, that is, it is about their archaic darkness or strangeness, their *dichten*, their resistance to discourse, their refusal of clarification and assimilation into frameworks of meaning or structural description. Of course, my subject thus puts me in the awkward position of not being able to say, exactly, what this book is about, or what its point is.[1]

In general, "Heidegger's criticism of the traditional view of... language is regarded as shattering the very foundations of modern philosophy:"

> Heidegger "rejects the traditional view of language presupposed by the [Cartesian] philosophy of the subject, which relegates language to a tool for representation, for mediation between subject and objects, the human being and the world... [the view of language] as a system of signs that contain meaning and relay

---

[1]  Bruns, 1989, p. xv; in this chapter citations having page numbers only refer to this work.

those meanings to entities, situations, or events.... [Heidegger] refers to language as 'primordial poetry,' or 'primordial language'... [or] 'poetic 'saying.'"[2]

Bruns notes that Heidegger's

writings on language and poetry do not represent the unfolding of a theory. They are rather a lingering with a subject matter, where lingering means holding back, not seeking advancement or mastery, refusing to determine the subject conceptually, acknowledging Plato's judgment 'that everything that lies before us is ambiguous'... the questions of language, truth, and poetry that he [Heidegger] raises (as does no one else)... evade the grasp of our concepts.... [He] leave[s] everything open....[The] refusal to conceptualize is where the later Heidegger is to be found.[3]

*Estrangements* necessarily covers a very large territory because for Heidegger, language (or, for that matter, just about anything else) cannot be properly treated in isolation. So, Heidegger's (and Bruns's) excursions into language involve a large and complex constellation of obviously as well as not so obviously related topics such as philology, truth, being, identity, logic, understanding, knowing, thinking, perceiving, questioning, metaphysics, technology, the work of art, letting go—to mention just some of the more prominent constituents elements in this open field.

We see again that Bruns, too, refers to the ineffability of a holistic position and point of view, and predictably, therefore relies primarily (but, as we shall see later, not exclusively) on explicating the Heideggerian views about language by emphasizing what they are *not*—resorting once again to the by now familiar pseudo-specifications by means of the *via negativa*. What is it, then, that language is *not*? If we are going to understand Heidegger/Bruns' thoughts about language better, and if these are specified as the logical complement of what I am calling "the received views," if the Heideggerian notions are the "other" of those

---

[2]   Mansbach, 2002, pp. 2, 4, 5.
[3]   pp. 125, 150, xxviii, 55.

mainstream views, then we first need to be clear about just what it is that Heidegger is rejecting.

Bruns addresses that question primarily in the context of the ancient Greek polarizing distinction (and quarrel) between philosophy and poetry; elsewhere he sets it within the clashing views of the logicians and their humanist or hermeneutic critics (the important logician Gottlob Frege and Martin Heidegger, respectively, are representative figures).[4] Irrespective of such specific contexts, however, we can identify salient features of what the Heideggerian view of language opposes—what its *other* is. In that way, we can indirectly catch a better glimpse of the Heideggerian view.

Let us begin by specifying the received view's principal characteristics. (The received view will be considered in more detail later, especially in chapter 11.) As we shall see, the received view of language will continue to play a key role as a foil in many if not in most of the explorations and discussions in the later chapters; therefore, we need to become well aware of its salient features.

## THE RECEIVED VIEW OF LANGUAGE

### Enframing

The received view is a special case, a restricted instance, of the broader general position Heidegger calls enframing (*Gestell*): "As the mind-set that underlies the rise of technology and that permeates our daily habits of speech and thought, enframing is Heidegger's term for a way of objectifying our world and our experience;"[5] it is a mind set that is "a way of revealing."[6] It is a way of thinking and conceptualizing the world, persons included, that Heidegger variously calls technological thinking, or rational-representational-calculative thought, but that does *not*

---

4   Bruns, 1987, p. 239.
5   Pattison, 2000, p. 2.
6   Polt, 1999, p. 171.

mean enframing is roughly equivalent to a technological way of life. Technological thinking is not technology; the latter is but one side effect of the underlying world view, one of its surface manifestations, albeit an obvious and important one. Heidegger is talking about a way of life.[7]

Enframing is, roughly, formalized thinking—roughly, mathematized and mathematizing thinking, a way of perceiving, structuring, and conceptualizing both "inner" and "outer" entities, events, processes, phenomena, in a manner that is objectifying, reductionistic, quantifying—the enshrining of that aspect of Cartesian thought that privileges the domain of primary qualities and discards the remainder.

According to Heidegger, enframing is just what has been happening with increasing intensity in the Western world for the last several millennia. The travel along this trajectory was launched by the ancient Greeks and received a major impetus with the rise of modern science. The enframing mind set and its attendant practices have come to spread into everything. That is, while initially enframing's proper domain of application had been natural science, it soon reversed direction and infiltrated common sense. In other words, what originally had been a derivative, reduced version of experience posited for the convenience of scientific work, a limited world comprising only the phenomena pertaining to primary qualities, soon came to be taken in retrograde fashion. The world constructed by rational-calculative thinking became the totalizing common sense view of the world. Thus, the initial reductive move underwent what Husserl, Heidegger's teacher, called "the ontological reversal."[8] The reduced vision reversed direction and now was imposed as a template cast over the world through which all reality came to be seen: "our present-day everydayness is... already

---

[7]  For a highly useful introductory overview, see Bernstein, 1992, chapter 4.
[8]  Harvey, 1989, pp. 62-74.

ineradicably contaminated by the scientific culture."[9] Increasingly, reality became a reality of primary qualities until virtually *everything* comes to be seen by *everybody* (i.e., not only just by scientists) in technological, rational-calculative, reduced terms; the derivative world becomes the originating reality for just about everybody. (A paradigmatic example is the mental health field's wholesale reductive neurobiologizing of "mental disorders" and other psychological phenomena.)[10] Technological thought is applied in all areas.

## Language as a Semiotic System

This "everything" that comes to be seen in terms of the rational-technological enframing architecture includes language, and so we come to the *received view of language*: it is language perceived *technologically*. Language "really" is (or ought to be) a *syntactic, logical, semiotic system* composed of basic building-block ingredients (e.g., letters, words) and of syntax, rules that specify which assemblages of these elements are legal and meaningful, and how such "strings" of language are to be correctly transformed to others (e.g., "the boy hit the ball" may be transformed to "the ball was hit by the boy"). This system *refers* to non-linguistic as well as other linguistic entities (to objects, phenomena, "facts," or other language strings).

Ordinary language is viewed as defective, untidy, sloppy, degraded language, in need of being cleaned up, of being replaced by "an ideal or logically perfect language, a language of pure syntax and transparent terms"[11] which will transform it into a scientifically respectable, strictly formalized or axiomized, sanitized language. Mathematics and symbolic logic are the ideal models. The paradigmatic linguistic representational format is the proposition,

---

[9]   Pylkkö, 1998, p. 14.
[10]  See, for example, Tallis's views, outlined in chapter 3; also Berger, 1991; 2002a and b.
[11]  p. 162.

statement, or assertion—a logical structure whose subject-predicate logical structure is said to mirror the object-attribute structure of objects in the nonverbal domain.

Basically, language is considered to be a tool, just like mathematics. (There seems to be some uncertainty about whether it is made or found.) It can be used as an instrument for reasoning (e.g., as in syllogisms, or contemporary logic), for communicating information, meaning, for controlling, exploiting and manipulating. As a communications tool, language is said to represent, mean, refer, name, point to, describe, mirror some external and/or internal phenomena, events, facts. In other words, language is seen instrumentally, as just one useful tool in science's armamentarium where it facilitates theorizing, calculating, manipulating, controlling.

## Language as a Cheshire Cat Residue

As a formal system language is said to exist (somewhere) as a somewhat peculiar kind of an object which is "out there," having its own independent existence and legitimacy. For those who study it formally, it is the objectively and independently existing subject matter of their discipline. In that sense, it is boundaried, strictly segmented off from users. (The user disappears from view, leaving language behind—a Cheshire Cat residue phenomenon.) As noted above, one can then analyze its various "objective" features (its logical structure, laws, ingredients, truth value) just by studying this "object" *qua* object. Its erstwhile human ties become irrelevant, lost. In previous chapters we already have had several examples of this kind of objectifying, decoupling attitude, for example, in discussions concerning the locus and storage of information, or of beliefs. This aspect of the received view of language, its objectifying, Cheshire Cat residue producing effects together with its practice of then analyzing these isolated residues, will be considered more closely in chapter 11.

# HEIDEGGER'S LANGUAGE

## General Rejection of Enframing

Heidegger resolutely rejects enframing in general when it is ensconced *outside its legitimate domain of application, the natural sciences.* (But even in that context he has reservations about its worth, legitimacy, safety.)[12] It reductively impoverishes, dehumanizes, flattens out the world: "This frame of mind leads us to a kind of experiential desert or waste land."[13]

When applied outside its legitimate domain, it becomes dangerous: "Where enframing reigns, there is *danger* in the highest sense."[14] (We have already seen analogous critiques of the dangers of misapplied science made by Tallis, Loy, and especially by Holbrook.) For Heidegger, the danger is that we do not, will not, realize that by closing off certain avenues of perception and thinking, certain "ways of being," and constraining us to others, enframing necessarily brings with it a terrible kind of destiny—devastating alienation, mechanization, damage to the environment, coercive domination and control, exploitation—abstractly: the "forgetting of Being:"

> The danger... is that the essence of man and of truth will be perverted once for all, that the grip of the *Gestell* will be unbreakable, that the world-night will grow darker.... [The danger] is a concealment of the Truth of Being. It [the "essence of technology"] distorts the meaning of nature, of dwelling in the world, of thinking, and of man himself.[15]

History seems to be vindicating his speculations.

---

[12]  Heidegger's critiques of *Gestell* have been discussed extensively—see especially Lovitt and Lovitt, 1995; also Pattison, 2000, chapter 4; Bernstein, 1971; 1983; 1992, chapter 4; Caputo, 1986; Barrett, 1978; Polt, 1999, pp. 43-45, 55-60, and chapter 5, especially pp. 171-174; Berger 2002a, 15n6, 76n50, pp. 90-91.

[13]  Pylkkö, 1998, p. 113; also pp. xxiii, 51-52, 209-211.

[14]  Bernstein, 1992, p. 108; see also Mills,1997.

[15]  Caputo, 1978, pp. xviii, 248.

## Rejection of Boundaries

The rich concept of enframing has numerous aspects, but it always implies the presence and application of boundaries, especially of boundaries that create dichotomies. One way to look at Heidegger's work, then, is as a deframing move, a strategy for undoing boundaries, compartments, sets, polarities, structures, indubitably certain foundations. One of his most central notions, *Dasein,* can be seen in that light. *Dasein* is "the German word for 'existence' or 'being-there' which Heidegger uses to refer to the structures of humans that make possible an understanding of being."[16] He develops this eccentric terminology in order to separate his thought from that of his precursors; he wants a fresh and unique philosophic start. Subject-object boundaries are no longer honored: "What is central to Heidegger's thought... is not the individual subject but Being itself."[17] Heidegger "consistently describes *Dasein* as transcendence, as extending beyond its own borders."[18] The person, no longer separate, is necessarily embedded in a world that *Dasein* "always already" understands, is familiar with, is coping with. Boundaries are softened even if not entirely dissolved.

An extreme example of how he negates boundaries is the later Heidegger's strange, complex notion of the Fourfold:

> Earth and sky, divinities and mortals—being at one with one another of their own accord—belong...together by way of the simpleness of the united fourfold.... Each of the four mirrors in its own way the presence of the others.... Out of the fourfold, the simple onefold of the four is ventured.[19]

Furthermore, the four engage in a unifying "round dance." I will not attempt to say more about what at first glance appears as such a weird, incomprehensible notion. My point

---

[16]  Audi, 1999, p. 371.
[17]  p. 13.
[18]  Mansbach , 2002, p. 4.
[19]  pp. 78-79.

is that even in this puzzling, possibly willfully obscure narrative (the kind of Heideggerian discourse that often is dismissed by his many opponents as simply obfuscating, mystifying nonsense) one can see the thrust toward de-framing boundaries in his emphasis on unitedness, mirroring, singularity, dancing. Standard categories are negated. (The kinship with the various nondual conceptions discussed in several of the previous chapters is apparent.) Cut loose from conceptual structures and classifying categorizations, things become mysterious, unsettling, strange, aporetic, leaving us at sea—we are in the presence of *Estrangements.*

## Rejection of Language as an Object

Heidegger's holistic views about language can be interpreted as a subset of this general de-framing, de-boundarying impulse. Thus, to put it baldly, for Heidegger language simply is the *other* of everything that enframing explicitly and implicitly thinks language is; for him, language is that which remains when one rejects and removes everything that technological-rational-calculative thinking believes about it. Thus he can say, for instance, that "To speak a language... is totally different from employing a language.... Common speech... merely employs language."[20] When enframing is rejected, language is no longer instrumental, a tool. Neither is it a mathematics-like system with a subject-predicate-, substance-attribute-inducing syntax. It becomes poetic.

I am grossly oversimplifying Heidegger's thought here. For him, the very dichotomy of formal-scientific discourse versus poetry, literal versus figurative language, received views and his views, becomes untenable. In the first of these dualisms, language is a "sedimented," perverted, desiccated remnant of the second. "Formal," literal language is "the familiar language of analytical

---

[20]  p. 75.

distinctions, binary oppositions, signifier and system, subject and object, literal and figurative, poetry and philosophy"[21] that Heidegger cannot accept. Elsewhere in an excellent exploration of this issue Bruns refers to "two traditions of giving an account of language: that of the [logician] Gottlob Frege, the other that of Martin Heidegger."[22] Obviously, Frege's is the enframing account; it also is the version that is almost universally accepted explicitly in Western scientific thought, and implicitly by the general public.

Even though Heidegger's notions of language are most faithfully presented by way of a *via negativa*, still, he throws out some positive hints, as Bruns demonstrates. For one thing, language is no longer seen as a separately existing entity. It is indissolubly linked up with and interpenetrated by Being, *Dasein*, truth, poetry, events, stillness. Its boundaries are breached. Obversely (and also paradoxically), it extends its own boundary without limit. Language encompasses everything: one "can never step outside of it and look at it from somewhere else."[23] We have here two complementary and strange ways of conceptualizing the dissolution of boundaries: either as a mutual interpenetration of language and other aspects of *Dasein*, or as language becoming unitary, swallowing up all those other aspects. Specifically, for Heidegger the old and apparently unchallengeable distinction always made between user and language is disestablished; language falls "entirely outside the subject-object relationship,"[24] entirely outside "the Cartesian-Kantian axis of subject and object." [25]

---

[21] p. 128.
[22] Bruns, 1987, p. 239.
[23] p. 172.
[24] p. 49.
[25] Bruns, 1987, p. 246; this is part of Heidegger's so-called antihumanism [an unfortunate, misleading term]—see Mansbach, 2002.

A further example is the repudiation of internal structure. Language is no longer conceptualized as constructed from the traditional building blocks or constituent elements, or analyzable in terms of logical or formal structure, or the rules of grammar.[26] Yet, paradoxically, in his writings Heidegger continually asks about and extensively explores the meaning of certain key terms: Being, truth, thought, a thing, metaphysics, logic. Like Nietzsche's, Heidegger's thought has a strong philological turn. He is particularly interested in the meanings of certain presocratic terms (especially "being," and "truth"). He engages in such questioning primarily to reveal the impossibility of getting to some end point—a foundational definition, a final answer, a final point of rest. For him, a worthwhile question is something generative one "dwells with;" the event of questioning, the following of the path which it opens up, and not reaching some ultimate answer, is what matters to him, is what thinking is for him.

## Origins

We have been considering Heidegger's notions about language from the perspective of boundaries and their dispersals. Heidegger also tries to flesh out his vision of language by saying something about its origins. Predictably, these remarks also are enigmatic and gnomic. His notions about origins are especially unconventional because he consistently and frequently gives listening and silence priority over speaking:

> The unspoken is the true source of what is said.... The priority of hearing over speaking is one of the constants in Heidegger's thinking with respect to language, perhaps the only constant.... Listening leads not to language as such, whatever that is, but to the being of language, which occurs in talk. And there is more to talk than speaking.... Stillness is something you can hear if you

---

[26] See "Do words exist?", pp. 128-136.

> listen for it.... *Language speaks as the peal of stillness....* The peal
> of stillness is not anything human.[27]

Bruns adds, "here uncanniness turns sinister."[28]

In sum, "language for Heidegger isn't a problem; rather... it is a mystery. A mystery isn't anything anyone can solve. One doesn't probe a mystery; one cannot approach such a thing analytically, or at all." [29] Something other than further analysis, something unspecifiable, not capturable conceptually, must be envisioned. We give up "the human will to explain"[30] via cognitive-rational-scientific-scientistic methods.

Once again a holism has led to a mysterious origin. Can one go further in understanding the phenomenon of language-cum-*Dasein*? My by now familiar position is that one cannot do so as long as one maintains an adultocentric stance. In Heidegger's thinking about language, *Dasein* is treated and conceptualized almost exclusively as an *adult Dasein*, a being-in-the-world that already has language, understands, thinks, knows, experiences "internal" moods, is able to use tools that are at hand, and so on.[31] I say "almost" exclusively because Heidegger does characterize *Dasein* as being "thrown into the world," thus pointing abstrusely to a personal origin, an individual history. But, as I want to show in chapter 9, that kind of global, amorphous pointing to personal early history hardly does justice to the kind of importance and relevance that of personal origins have that is revealed by detailed and psychodynamically informed ontogenetic exploration.

---

[27]  pp. 67, 21, 22, 94, 163.
[28]  p. 163.
[29]  pp. 125, 112.
[30]  p. 81.
[31]  Heidegger's adultocentric stance is also reflected and demonstrated in his existential approach to psychiatry, which I see as a profoundly limited—see Berger, 2002b, chapter 14.

# 7

# HEIDEGGER AND THE HUMAN BEING

## FREDERICK OLAFSON

Frederick A. Olafson is Professor Emeritus of Philosophy at the University of California, San Diego. The principal work on which this chapter will draw is his *What is a Human Being: A Heideggerian View* (1995), although I will occasionally refer to material from two of his other books, *Heidegger and the Philosophy of Mind* (1987), and *Naturalism and the Human Condition: Against Scientism* (2001).

While these three works cover much the same important and extended ground, they differ in emphasis. The first book argued primarily that while the rejection of Cartesian dualism is virtually taken for granted by the majority of contemporary thinkers, "Heidegger's way of moving against and away from Descartes constitutes a significant and deeply conceived alternative."[1] Olafson believes that this alternative is insufficiently appreciated and offers his explications as a remedy. In *Human Being*, Olafson elaborates and further develops Heidegger's ideas about being and *presence* ("the term that Heidegger uses to express the fundamental character of being as such"[2]) that he had presented in the earlier work. Olafson says of this middle work that it "is an essay in the philosophy of mind, although, paradoxically, it will turn out that the concept of mind itself has to be abandoned"[3] and that "it forces a reappraisal of commonsense notions of mind as our 'inner'

---

[1] 1987, p. xx; in this chapter, citations without an author's name refer to Olafson's work.
[2] 1995, p. xvii.
[3] 1995, p. 2.

reality."[4] The most recent book focuses on naturalism, vehemently rejecting the currently dominant naturalizing, scientistic, mechanizing views of what the human being is.

Olafson's principal concern in *Human Being* is first and foremost the Heideggerian being-in-the-world: presence. Olafson argues for and explicates his key concept through numerous dense, extended discussions set in several topical contexts: perception, "absence" (involving memory, thought, belief, imagination), individuation, feelings, agency, and the human being's being embodied. A major aspect of these presentations is a wide-ranging, vigorous critique of science's practice of naturalizing the human being (i.e., of subsuming it under the other, inanimate phenomena that populate the domains of the natural sciences), and it is in the course of these latter arguments that Olafson discusses three major and interrelated topics that are particularly relevant for my project: *boundaries, language,* and *formal* (e.g., scientific, or philosophical) *observation.*

## BOUNDARIES

The first and most basic, pervasive boundary issue that Olafson analyzes is the matter of the boundary between ourselves and the rest of the world—the "inside/outside," "me/not-me" dividing line. He argues that for his goal of reconstructing "the central concept of the philosophy of mind... the famous contrast between the inner and outer... [is] egregiously inappropriate to that task."[5] On the one hand the "assimilation of our mode of being in the world to the mode of spatial inclusion that characterizes such entities as chairs and walls is profoundly mistaken."[6] We are not *in* the world in the same way as are chairs; chairs are not *Dasein.* We cannot properly conceptualize the

---

4    Ibid.
5    1995, p.14.
6    1987, p. 33.

person simply as just another object set "in" the dimensionality of space of the world. "Space" is *not* a container that contains us. (This already is a peculiar claim, to say the least. Common sense sees persons and their bodies as entities that obviously *are* located in space.) One the other hand, neither is the world in *us* in any sense. We are not separated-off objects (or subjects) that perceive, represent, or internally contain the world.

Olafson develops an idiosyncratic critique of the familiar received view of what it is to be a human being in the world—that, for example, we experience a variety of "internal" psychological states or events. I see Olafson as idiosyncratically addressing essentially the same basic problem raised by Thomas Nagel: "how to combine the perspective of a particular person inside the world with an objective view of that same person, the person and his viewpoint included.'[7] Olafson begins by examining what happens when "we" observe a human being other than ourselves. We see such a person "as a distinct unit within a larger natural environment."[8] We observe that certain kinds of things happen outside that person, and others (thinking, *as reported by that person*) apparently within her or him. Thus, it is natural to conclude not only that "for this distinction the contours of the body offer a ready line of demarcation."[9] Olafson labels this conception of the person observed by "me," "Picture 1."

Furthermore, because that picture seems to be valid for all other people we observe, we infer that it must be valid for ourselves as well; we can and must understand ourselves from the same kind of externalist standpoint. Since, however, in Picture 1 we also implicitly are the person who does the *observing*, Olafson asks whether it is

---

[7]  Nagel, 1986, p. 3.
[8]  1995, p. 18.
[9]  Ibid.

proper simply to transfer Picture 1, the picture developed when observing another, to all humans, including the observer. He notes that the usual taken for granted answer is, yes; we are essentially just like the observed, with the same demarcations and boundaries. Why should we be different? Picture 1 applies to everyone, observer and observed alike.

Here Olafson raises idiosyncratic objections. He points out that when we are observers observing another, "it may be questioned whether we form any picture of ourselves at all."[10] We are unaware of any boundaries between ourselves (whatever that entity is) and what it is that we observe. We aren't in the picture; we simply observe. This in a sense observerless picture is "Picture 2." In that picture there is no place for the inside/outside distinction we imposed on the observed other in Picture 1; there is no such segmentation. The question is, is it nevertheless legitimate to conceptualize ourselves as boundaried even in that situation? (This consideration echoes the kinds of issues Loy raises about the nature of "thought." And, as previously noted, Heidegger did have an affinity with Asian thought.)

There is yet a third modality: we apparently can observe "ourselves," we can "introspect," essentially suspending observations of anything that is going on "outside." It is tempting to infer that in this situation, "our" thoughts, images, feelings, proprioceptions, memories, and so on, are the same kind of target of observation as other persons are in Picture 1, to believe that what we are observing "inside us" are the same kinds of objects as the external objects observed in Picture 1. Let us call this deliberately self-observational third position, "Picture 1a."

Olafson says that two points follow from these constructions. First, he claims that Pictures 1 and 2 are much more closely linked with one another than with

---

10   1995, p. 19.

Picture 1a. Although he does not spell out a supporting argument, I assume that he thinks the claim is obvious because the first two positions are natural and immediate, while deliberate self-observation or introspection is a second-order, artificial, reflexive modality.

Second, he argues that "there is not only an intuitive difference between the two pictures [i.e., 1 and 2]; there is also a demonstrable lack of fit between them."[11] In Picture 1, boundaries, that is to say, the internal/external distinction, are important components, while in Picture 2 they and the distinction they bring with them are absent (but to a degree self-consciously restored in Picture 1a). The crux of the matter is that therefore, when one forces an integration between Pictures 1 and 2 one automatically introduces logical-ontological incoherences. Olafson presents detailed, intricate arguments demonstrating the genesis and nature of the paradoxes that follow from the attempt at integration.[12] At any rate, the resulting picture obtained from forcing an integration of Pictures 1 and 2, perhaps including traces of Picture 1a—let us call it Picture 3—is a mess, although presumably it is science's picture. The amalgam entails the host of familiar and traditional philosophical difficulties: *Who* is the observer? What is the nature of perception? How can impinging physical energies become perceptions? How should the boundaries be treated and reconciled? How can we span the gulf between a presumably inner and outer world? What are we "observing" when we observe ourselves (and what is it that we are doing when we use language to describe such observations—e.g., of pain)? The several kinds of pictures just cannot be reconciled or synthesized in any acceptable, unproblematic scientific or philosophical construct (hence Colin McGinn's dance).

---

[11]   1995, p. 21.
[12]   1995, pp. 21-45.

Olafson's attempts toward a solution drawing on Heideggerian thought are for me less convincing or lucid than his analyses of these boundary issues and the various difficulties they raise (particularly the difficulties pertaining to the notion of inner representations [one type of "inner contents" whose existence Collins challenged], which occupy him greatly).[13] What is important for us is that he demonstrates the aporetic, paradoxical, perennial unresolvable difficulties that attend attempts to make sense of positing an inside/outside boundary, regardless of whether these attempts are based on monisms or dualisms—on some version of idealism, or reductive materialism, or neutral monism, or Cartesian dualism. The implication seems to be that there is something profoundly wrong with the entire idea of inside/outside boundaries and their concomitants, and it is that implication that matters most for the position I am attempting to develop

## LANGUAGE

An important merit of Olafson's work is that he shows explicitly and in considerable detail that there is an *ontology of language problem*. The simplest statement of that problem is this: If we assume an ontology that posits the two mutually exclusive and collectively exhaustive domains of self and world (i.e., everything that there is belongs to one or the other domain only, without remainder), if we believe that there are two boundaried domains, then where does language belong in this ontology? *What is its nature?* That this problematic question exists remains largely unrecognized; Olafson points out that "there has not been any significant reassessment of the mode of being of language itself,"[14] and worse still, that the

---

[13]  Critical discussions of the concept of inner representations are ubiquitous and too numerous to cite, but see especially1995, pp. 24-47.

[14]  1995, p. 4.

consensus among those concerned with linguistic matters is that there is no such problem. The ontology of language is thought to be no more problematic than "the standard, usually quite uncritically espoused ontology of the subject."[15] We already "know" what language is, at least enough so for the usual purposes:

> It is taken for granted that language use is an overt and observable function of the human organism and thus takes its place unproblematically within the same natural milieu as all the other processes with which the sciences are concerned... it tends to be simply assumed that language, particularly its distinctive semantic and referential functions, presents no special problem for a naturalistic account of human nature....[16] Language and language use are not seen as raising any interesting ontological issues at all....[17] Through an effective separation of language from its users and their distinctive mode of being in the world, all questions about the ontological status of language itself may be elided and even never raised at all....[18] Taken in isolation from the world, they [words] are just sounds and marks, not words...[19][they are] assimilated... to the status of things.[20]

There is also the closely related ontological paradox raised by the capacity language has to refer to itself: "Philosophers and linguists in the Western tradition have always taken for granted that there is nothing paradoxical about using language as a tool for the rational description and investigation of language.... The philosopher is trading on the assumption that lay people and specialists alike all understand what a language is."[21]

A telling example of this assumption appears when in the course of his investigation of the mind-body problem, the philosopher Sergio Moravia asks, "what is 'mental'?

---

[15] 1987, p.125.
[16] Ibid., pp. 4, 5.
[17] Ibid., p. 124.
[18] Ibid., p. 123.
[19] 2001, p. 49.
[20] 1987, p. 125.
[21] Harris, 1996, pp. 111, 4.

Isn't it time we thought this question through? We have agreed that it is not a thing.... What if it were first and foremost a *word*."[22] We might expect that this line of thought will lead him to ontological considerations, but that is not the case. His investigation quickly turns into a conventionally "intralogical," epistemological rather than ontological, analysis of the *term* 'mental,' a standard approach that assumes a rigorously formal analysis of concepts, words, and so on, will clear up the meaning of a term—a premise that is ubiquitous in the philosophical literature. (Perhaps there would be no philosophy as we know it without that assumption.) Moravia says, for example, that the word 'mental' "has to be decoded and interpreted..., [that it is] a word which, properly examined, may turn out to allude to experiences that are not physical but in some sense '*meta*-physical'."[23] He demonstrates that for him, language simply remains a semiotic system— referential ('mental' must allude or refer to... something), consisting of segmented basic units (e.g., words) that carry encoded meanings, and that if these are obscure, they can be made clear by careful logical, exact explorations—an approach perhaps taken to its extreme by Ludwig Wittgenstein's treatment of philosophy as a sort of linguistic-logical therapy that cures by revealing pathological use of language. Moravia's investigations are typical of those philosophical investigations that "must take the form of an analysis from a logicolinguistic point of view of the concepts deployed."[24] Like so many others concerned with linguistic matters, he fails to consider the possibility that the source of problematic muddles may be ontological rather than logical-analytical-epistemological.

The received view of language prevails. Language remains seen as an independently existing symbolic,

---

[22] Moravia, 1995, p. 16.
[23] Ibid.
[24] 1995, p. 3.

semiotic system having "logical properties and functions"[25] that can be objectified, empirically studied and scientifically analyzed in isolation. There *is* no "ontology of language" problem or issue: linguistic philosophers have shown no interest "in the idea that language itself raises ontological issues."[26] There is "an artificially maintained obliviousness."[27] The usual approaches to various linguistic issues retain the "familiar empirical means," remain "intralogical," are "ontologically neutral,"[28] while Heidegger's approach is profoundly and primarily ontological, a position foreshadowed in Bruns' discussions.

Olafson's proposed solution to these issues (by employing the concept of *presence* in his ontological analyses) is not particularly relevant to my project. What is of interest, though, is that in principle he recommends re-embedding language in its original unitary context, in *Dasein.* Somehow, language has to be (re)tied to perception, memory, and other "mental" functions, and to the "external"world.[29] Severed links need to be restored, somehow. That is the strategy to which his ontological analysis of language has led. It is easy to comprehend the goal, but obscure as to how one might translate that position into a strategy.

Lastly, concerning language ontology we ought to consider Olafson's thoughts regarding issues in origins. His discussions are almost entirely adultocentric, but the topic of genesis does arise obliquely in the course of his discussion of the individuation of *Dasein.* He notes the obvious, that "birth and death are the terminal points," and then considers the roles an understanding of these might play in illuminating further the nature of *Dasein.* As to the

---

[25]  1987, p. 124.
[26]  2001, p. 47.
[27]  1987, p. 126.
[28]  1987, pp. 128-129; 1995, p. 6.
[29]  2001, pp. 48-51

beginning of life, he says that this is complex, not simple "like turning on of a light," that instead "a human life emerges gradually out of another kind—that of the fetus or infant—in some way that we have great difficulty conceiving."[30] So far so good, but then he concludes that therefore "it seems more feasible to use death rather than birth as a way of trying to understand the temporal boundedness of presence."[31] As far as I can see, that is the only time in the three books under consideration here that he mentions fetal life and birth, and, sadly, when he does so he deems it to be unsuited to further exploration or philosophical use because that early phase "is difficult to conceive." We will see in Part II that this matter can be treated quite differently.

## OBSERVATION AND OBSERVERS

At several points Olafson discusses the problem of scientific or philosophical observation, and the place of the observer/theorizer. He shows that the mainstream naturalizing views render the observational event incoherent. Let us consider two examples.

Olafson shows that

> in its treatment of human beings, linguistic philosophy uses a concept of language as verbal behavior that is quite different from (and dubiously consistent with) the understanding of language as a semantic and referential function that is implicit in its own enterprise.[32]

In other words, linguistic philosophers' own use of language is not subsumed under their theory of verbal behavior. Olafson observes that "as long as this peculiar duality remains unaddressed, there will be something inherently

---

[30]   1995, p. 142.
[31]   1995, p. 143.
[32]   1995, p. 8.

unstable about this conception of [linguistic study in] philosophy."[33]

A similar problem arises when philosophers and scientists reductively assume as a given fact that mental states of persons (e.g., thinking, perceiving, feeling, remembering) "really" are states of the central nervous system, especially of the brain. (In Collins' terminology, we here have an identity theory.) In principle, the scientists or philosophers observing the subjects or objects of their investigations and theorizing presumably could observe those central nervous system states and thereby could understand and explain their subjects' "subjective" experiences. Once again, the question arises, what are we to make of the observers' or theorizers' *own* experiences? Scientists and philosophers generate and employ

> theories [about human beings] for which there are no data except those derived from observation of other human beings—nothing, in other words, that registers the reflexive character of the subject matter with which it deals. Theory has so completely devoured fact under these circumstances that the people who propose these theories have been altogether eclipsed; and there is no longer any sense in which these theories are about them.[34]

In both cases, to make sense of the theorists' own experiences or behaviors in terms of their own theories requires the presence of a meta-theoretician, a meta-philosopher, a meta-observer who can observe, understand, and explain the experiences of the observing theoreticians, scientists, and philosophers.

Olafson's numerous and thorough discussions of prototypical examples show that in order to avoid the dilemma of this infinite regress, the observer is not considered and thus is made to disappear. The theorists who promulgate a material reductionist view of the person

---

[33]  Ibid.
[34]  1995, p. 240.

become invisible, in the sense that their own consciousness, *Dasein*, use of language, perception, all disappear from the theoretical picture. Their presence and experience is considered a non-issue. All that remains in a given discipline is the now disembodied observation of "the objective fact," of a Cheshire Cat residue. We have the situation the philosopher Thomas Nagel famously calls the "View from Nowhere," sometimes also called the "Gods-eye view."

So far we have been considering the scientific or philosophical observation of and theorizing about persons, but essentially the same considerations apply in the natural sciences. There, too, the ontology of the observer is swept under the rug.

While both of the dominant theories of contemporary physics, quantum theory and relativity, do recognize the theoretical (epistemological) importance of the observational process, physics' understanding of that process is far from ontological. Physics simply takes the ordinary views concerning the nature of human perception for granted. It assumes either that perception already is well enough understood (by someone else, though—say, the neuroscientist, or the neuropsychologist), or else that for physics, the ontological particulars are irrelevant, that all that matters is that observers can and do observe and report. Thus, although physics talks a good deal about the observer's place in its theories (e.g., in quantum theory, the moment of "observation" of the "system" is presumed to have the major effect of producing the so-called "collapse of the wave function"), actually it fails to treat the process of observation in any depth; apparently it does not even appreciate that here is a significant and highly problematic issue.[35] Without being aware of it, the natural sciences are left to deal with Cheshire Cat residues without any

---

[35] See Smith, 1995, 1984.

understanding of the complexities and paradoxes concerning observation. I have not even considered the complications that obtain when languages (i.e., discourse and mathematics) are introduced into the observational picture—e.g., when describing, reporting, theorizing. I return to these matters later, particularly in chapter 14.

I have only sketched several of the key issues and arguments presented by Olafson in his rich, carefully and densely argued *What is a Human Being?* The book is not easy reading, but it certainly merits close study by anyone who is interested in a Heidegger-grounded phenomenological exploration of ontology.

# 8

# HEIDEGGER AND SCIENCE

## PAULI PYLKKÖ

Pylkkö opens his highly unconventional *The Aconceptual Mind: Heideggerian Themes in Holistic Naturalism* with a summary of a portion of the seventeenth song of *Kalevala*, the great Finnish epic which grew out of a rich oral tradition with prehistoric roots. The fragment concerns the seer Väinämöinen's visit to the mythical shaman Antero Vipunen. "Vipunen appears to be deceased, almost decayed already, or at least his body can hardly be separated from the thick vegetation of the forest where he used to live."[1] Väinämöinen has gotten stuck in his sail boat building project because he cannot find the tool needed for that task's completion—the right words of a song—and he wants Vipunen to supply these. The relationship between the two is not an easy one. Although it is grudgingly respectful, it is mostly antagonistic, primitive, and eventually becomes violent. In his attempt to wrest the words from the shaman, Väinämöinen forcefully enters Vipunen's mouth who attempts to rid himself of the intruder by swallowing him. That does not work. Vipunen is tortured in his stomach by the now sword- and fire-wielding Väinämöinen who eventually succeeds; Vipunen provides the needed song.

This strange, magical, tantalizing, suggestive fragment is an allegory for the difficult, complex master-disciple relationship between Pylkkö and Heidegger. Heideggerian themes are central to the book, as the subtitle suggests. They pertain to social, political and cultural (e.g., Nazism, Fascism, nationalism, culturally unique meanings, cross-

---

[1] Pylkkö,1998, p. xiii; in this chapter, references with pages numbers only refer to this work.

cultural communication), as well as to a host of philosophical, scientific, and linguistic issues. Yet, while Pylkkö draws heavily on Heidegger's thought he also is highly critical of certain of its aspects, and of his behavior; he does not treat Heidegger "softly."[2]

Pylkkö develops a nontraditional, elaborate, rich, evocative, but also elusive ontological-epistemological framework designed to address the cluster of Heideggerian issues, and this framework is the common ground that integrates his critical analyses of apparently highly diverse, unrelated themes. His major concern, however, is with "naturalized" science and philosophy: "In what follows, one of the leading ideas will be that now the postphenomeno-logical thinking should take a naturalistic turn, and it should do it without adopting the metaphysical machinery of standard scientific realism."[3] He calls that kind of realism *dogmatic,* and much of his text is devoted to exploring whether an alternative, a nondogmatic naturalism that would include both a nondogmatic *science* and a nondogmatic *philosophy,* is possible, and how it might look.

## HEIDEGGER'S CRITIQUE OF NATURALISMS

Heidegger refers to and describes the naturalizing he criticizes in a variety of idiosyncratic ways and terminologies. One of Heidegger's principal pejorative words is *metaphysics,* a term which in his special sense refers to the attitude he says saturates standard Western natural science and "also regular philosophical work and its language."[4] It includes "the habit of straightforward realism [taking the external world at face value] and objectivism

---

[2]    p. xviii.
[3]    ibid.
[4]    p. xx.

[assuming that the world exists independently of its observers]."[5]

A second and essentially equivalent major term is *onto-theo-logic,* referring to a nefarious mix of wrong ontology, theology, and logic. It is "the attempt to ground all entities in one supreme entity,"[6] "the discipline that classifies and explains beings in general and subordinates them to a supreme being."[7] It posits a dichotomous ontology of subject and object, is steeped in the structure of logic, is able to see only beings (i.e., specific entities of various kinds—in Heidegger's terminology, it is "ontic" rather than "ontological"), is unable to see Being (which for Heidegger is not an entity), and is "unable to think of its own essence."[8] For onto-theo-logic "the human mind becomes a mechanism or device whose main purpose is to reflect [conceptualize, represent] entities and their relations."[9]

Another alternative Heideggerian term is *metaphysics of subjectivity,* which refers to the dogmatic belief in "the modern picture of man,"[10] to an understanding of persons "based only on the subject's consciousness and rationality."[11] It is a subject-centered "humanism" which "separates the subject from the object and dictates that the main role of the subject is to represent the objects of the world... [a position that] reifies the human mind into a system of internal entities (a system of concepts) which will eventually begin to resemble the external objects which the system is supposed to represent."[12] A metaphysics of

---

[5]   p. 12.
[6]   Audi,1999, p. 373
[7]   Polt, 1999,p. 144.
[8]   p. 27.
[9]   ibid.
[10]  p. xxiii
[11]  p. 77.
[12]  p.189.

subjectivity presupposes the "strong objectivization and reification of experience."[13]

The attitude which these terms attempt to capture is also labeled *theory-centered*: "Regular theoretical work attempts to describe the structure of its subject matter, say, the structure of natural language, as accurately as possible and reach as powerful generalizations as possible."[14]

## PYLKKO'S CRITIQUE OF THE HEIDEGGERIAN CRITIQUE

Pylkkö calls Heidegger the arch-enemy of dichotomies, "the undisputed master of dichotomy destruction"[15] who disrupts dichotomies in various complex, ambiguous, amorphous, essentially mysterious ways—most especially through his holistic development of *Dasein*, Being, the unitary situation alluded to by the cryptic, hyphenated term "being-in-the-world" ("authentic *Dasein* experience dissolves the boundary which separates the subject from the object").[16] Heidegger's development of *Dasein* includes: a reconceptualization of truth that transforms it from something concerning assertions and states of affairs into an event, an occasional, reluctant, elusive revealing that again recedes into concealment; the previously-mentioned notion of an unfathomable Fourfold of earth, sky, divinities and mortals; and, a reconceptualization of language, e.g., as "the house of being," as we saw in the last chapter.

Heidegger, the severe critic of naturalism, presents detailed, meticulous recurring critiques of enframing (*Gestell*), of technological-rational-calculative thinking in general, but in doing so he *does* dichotomize: natural science's thought is severely demarcated from non-

---

[13]  p. 213.
[14]  p. 147.
[15]  p. xxi.
[16]  p. xxiv; also p. 3.

metaphysical thought. Science is innately enframing, Heidegger claims. Here Pylkkö disagrees strongly, claiming that Heidegger's critique is mistaken, that the dichotomy on which it is predicated is not inevitable, that a non-metaphysical, non-enframing naturalism is possible.

## PYLKKÖ'S "A-..." WORDS

Pylkkö's approach is *genetic* (but not *onto*genetic), predicated on the premise that "experience"—itself an elusive notion—has roots, that it is "originally" amorphous and unitary, and only "later" becomes structured, dichotomized. (I will have more to say about "original" and "later" below.) The conceptual and linguistic device Pylkkö employs to articulate this vision of unitary, boundary-less states is a collection of "a-..." words. That is, he takes terms and their implied polar opposites and attributes a common root to each dyad. He envisions a precursor of both that is neither one nor the other pole but a unified, "lower," originary "something else." The dominant term in this collection of originations is found in the subtitle of his book: *aconceptual.* It is the state that precedes the coming into being of the conceptual/nonconceptual dyad:

> If the human mind and language are originally aconceptual experience which is not controlled by a rational, representative and autonomous subject, then the study of the human mind and language cannot simply begin with concepts and theories.... Let us take immediate and unstructured experience as our philosophical starting point. This unarticulated and prelogical experience which we call *aconceptual* is what mind and language primarily *is*. It is not yet organized by concepts.... [It is] experience which is so unstructured with respect to conceptuality that even the contrast of the interior and the exterior (subject and object; subject [in the grammatical sense] and predicate) isn't yet discernible. This is experience that cannot be captured by such

conceptual or theoretical tools which cut everything into logical and grammatical structure.[17]

With some obvious modifications, the same holistic, prestructural characteristics also hold for his other a-words, mostly derived from Heideggerian terminology: a-subjective, a-metaphysical, a-mechanical, a-ontotheo-logical, a-historical, a-theoretical, and so on. There are, for example, *asubjective* states where the polarized pairs of subjectivity/objectivity, the me/not me, inside/outside distinctions and associated boundaries have not yet arisen.

A-experiences are associated with a quality Pylkkö calls "intensity," a continuous dimension, an informal "scale" that ranges from originary ("a-") states (high intensity) to those that have become strongly articulated (low intensity): "experiential intensity should be associated with the dissolution of structure."[18] Take, for example, the difference between and contrast of the aconceptual, asubjective, nameless, object-less experience we call dread (*Angst*), and the structured experience we call fear (*Furcht*). Fear is a "subjective attitude,"[19] an articulated, structured fear of *something;* dread is objectless. According to Pylkkö's schema, "*Angst* isn't anything categorically more than something that is ranked high on the intensity scale of *Furcht* feeling."[20] In other words, while for Heidegger fear and dread are distinct contrasting pairs, for Pylkkö they are endpoints of a spectrum. In this and other similar cases Pylkkö faults Heidegger for going against his own policies, for dichotomizing and reverting to dogmatic, dualistic, metaphysical thinking.

In terms of Pylkkö's a-notions, structured entities such as subjects, objects, concepts, perceptions and the like are all products of articulations that arise from aconceptual

---

[17] pp. xxii, 11-13.
[18] p. 10.
[19] p. 6.
[20] p. 7.

experiences; in that sense, they are "special, reified forms of experience."[21] "This reificational aspect of experience floats like a sloop on the high seas of aconceptual experience."[22] The amorphous, holistic primary states are the quicksand substratum of our everyday, apparently grounded, solid, structured, bifurcated, articulated, dichotomized experiential world. What we believe we can be, are sure of, actually rests on uncertain, shifting, insubstantial bases.

A perennial problem with holistic notions that we now have encountered in several contexts (e.g., with regard to Tallis's "explicitness," Loy's "nonduality," Holbrook's "polar-complete" Chinese world view) is that they are said to be impossible to define by formal means that meet the usual scientific standards of precision. That holds specifically for aconceptual experience as well; it cannot be defined "comprehensively in terms of such notions as person, rationality, intentionality or consciousness."[23] In earlier chapters I suggested that the only viable option is the *via negativa*, but Pylkkö believes otherwise. While he acknowledges that the a-states cannot be characterized comprehensively in cognitive-scientific-philosophical-theoretical terms, he also maintains that they are "not necessarily completely ineffable."[24] They *can* be described, up to a point:

> If we decide to describe aconceptual experience verbally, we have (infinitely) many different discourses available, ranging from poetry and religious language to neurobiological and connectionist language. One of the main restrictions that we want to impose upon these languages, as well as upon an adequate description of these languages, is that they should not resort to strong structural notions, especially not to standard logical, grammatical, Newtonian and ethical notions. Any attempt to use such notions

---

[21] p. xxii.
[22] pp. 50-51.
[23] p. xxii.
[24] p.15.

would preclude the possibility of finding an adequate description.[25]

## NONDOGMATIC YET NATURALIZED SCIENCE AND PHILOSOPHY

Pylkkö's belief that aconceptual experience can be described discursively in some way is consonant with his belief that one can have "anomalous, nondogmatic, a-ontotheological, ametaphysical" scientific and philosophical naturalisms, disciplines that somehow are formal, scientifically sound and respectable yet also reject the standard scientific, metaphysical, subjectivist attitude that

> still views the world as a set of external things, language as a set of labels for the things and actions, and the human mind as a mechanisms which handles the labels and related concepts in order to say something about the things.[26]

As I mentioned at the beginning of the chapter, he wants to have sciences and philosophy "take a naturalistic turn... [but] without adopting the metaphysical machinery of standard scientific realism."[27]

In Pylkkö's view, Heidegger's critique of naturalization, with its implied dichotomizing of thinking into naturalizing, rational-calculative, enframing thought on the one hand and meditative, authentic, meditative, "dwelling-with" thought about Being (rather than beings) on the other hand, failed to take into account certain non-metaphysical potentials that soften the supposedly rigid boundaries. He claims that in physics these are latent in quantum theory and the theory of relativity, with precursors in the thinking of Hume, Mach, Ostwald, Pauli and Bohr, and that in philosophical antecedents can be found in what he labels

---

[25] p.13.
[26] p. 37.
[27] p. xviii.

the "Schelling-Schopenhauer-Nietzsche" tradition[28] and also in Wittgenstein's "relentless attacks on any theoretical and explanatory attitude toward language."[29] Pylkkö maintains that "it seems that Heidegger exaggerated the extent to which externalization and reification [necessarily] characterizes modern natural science."[30] Science does not have to be dogmatic.

How does Pylkkö propose to approach the development of such *adogmatic* yet naturalizing fields of study? As far as I can see, he bases his vision of an adogmatic naturalized science on a two-step argument, namely, first, that the findings of physics (and he singles out and emphasizes quantum theory) force us away from the usual metaphysics of subjectivity (see above), and second, that we can change the nature of these disciplines by reinterpreting their extant data and theories. Then, he wants to extend and apply that model of an adogmatic science to transform philosophy into an adogmatic discipline as well.

He claims that contemporary physics takes us away from dogmatic science and philosophy by the introduction of "such notions as chance, indeterminacy and inseparability [Bell's theorem],"[31] and/or by way of the so-called Copenhagen interpretation of quantum theory which "destroyed the last remnants of the thing ontology."[32] This is how in science one moves away from the metaphysics of subjectivity.

As we have seen in numerous contexts, dogmatic (mainstream, normal) science "by its very definition, attempts to obliterate all traces of its humble human origin: it tries to attain knowledge which is purified of its ties to

---

[28]  p. 7; see also pp. 38-39, 59, 73, 81, 171, 182-183.
[29]  p. xxi
[30]  p. 21.
[31]  p. 24.
[32]  p. 59; also p. 29.

human experience."[33] The new, nondogmatic, naturalism will reverse this stance and reintroduce the person; it "will mean man's peculiar willingness to understand his relation with nature.... For example, its concepts, external objects, and so on, will never be able to become fully independent of or separated from the primordial aconceptual origin but will always remain partly entangled with it."[34]

It seems, then, that Pylkkö proposes to move toward his envisioned kinds of nondogmatic yet naturalized disciplines by continuing to *practice* natural science—most especially physics—along the familiar theoretical and empirical lines but radically reinterpreting (the meaning of) its results. As a guiding exemplar he cites Niels Bohr's "heroic attempts to design adequate *atheoretical language* in which microphysical phenomena could be spoken of."[35] The quantum phenomena remain, but their interpretations are transmuted. The language in which one speaks about science, its results, meanings and implications, will be changed, and that will be the beginning of the kind of science Pylkkö is seeking.

In my terminology I would say that clearly, Pylkkö recognizes and appreciates at least some of the problems generated in a field when its practitioners think they are "objectively studying" phenomena while what they really are investigating are impoverished Cheshire Cat residues, when the human ties are concealed and neglected. He, too, wants to somehow restore the hidden, ignored, but nevertheless omnipresent and still consequential linkages between "objectivity" and humans in both disciplines. I applaud this aspect of his vision of naturalized holistic sciences and philosophy, but cannot agree with the ways in

---

[33]  p. 33.
[34]  pp. 31, 34.
[35]  pp. xx-xxi.

which he proposes to move toward it. I will explain my reasons for this opposition to his approaches in chapter 14.

## "EARLIER" AND "LATER"

So far, as I have outlined Pylkkö's ideas about aconceptuality and related notions I have followed his own terminology of describing the holistic states as *earlier, primary, primitive, primordial, predifferentiated.* As I have emphasized, what he often says about such states is that they are unstructured "originally," and/or that it is only "afterward," "later," that they do become structured and articulated—typically by bifurcating into separate, independently existing, bounded contrasting and separated-off entities such as objects, observers, mental contents, etc. The question I want to raise is: do these kinds of descriptors refer to *synchronic* or to *diachronic* aspects of the processes? That is, are the movements from "earlier", primordial, to "later", structured, states conceptualized as occurring over a limited, relatively short time, more or less within the adult's day-in, day-out present (synchronically), or as occurring historically, over appreciable periods of a person's growth (diachronically)? Pylkkö states clearly that these movements can and do occur in both senses. He distinguishes between them by using separate terminologies. When he wants to speak of earlier aspects of experience in the synchronic sense he uses a-words, while when he wants to refer to a diachronic aspect (to what at times he refers to as "empirical or historical" aspects), to a developmentally early period of maturation—he uses the prefix *pre-* . For example, he might use "preconceptual" as referring to developmental or maturational eras in which conceptual thinking had not as yet become possible.[36]

Take the matter of sleep, for instance. As the adult begins to fall asleep there is a qualitative movement in

---

[36]  p.12.

experience from the structured "later" state, a state full of boundaries and dichotomies, toward a hypnagogic state where "what we call 'external' in colloquial language becomes inseparably entangled with 'internal'."[37] Conversely, when persons are dreaming they may suddenly become aware of that *in their dream* and make an effort to return to a waking, organized state (typically, because they become frightened). These are synchronic phenomena, and they would be described as moving rapidly toward or away from the aconceptual condition. In terms of Pylkkö's dimension of intensity, falling asleep would be a movement from lesser to greater "intensity", to an "earlier", "more primitive" state, while the movement in waking up would be in the opposite direction.

What about examples of movement along the diachronic dimension? Most of Pylkkö's book is about synchronic aspects of the movements between less and more structure and about their implications for a variety of issues and themes, as already noted. In contrast, he has relatively little to say about the "pre-" (maturational) dimension. He makes several short statements about its nature. He notes that it deals with the formation of external objects (reification) and internal concepts; that it concerns the mother-child differentiation, the establishment (in the growing child) of an internal/external world, me/not-me distinction; and, that the polarizations or structuralizations that characterize this movement are never entirely stable or perfect, that "even afterwards [I assume he means with further maturation] the internal and the external always remain inseparable to some extent."[38] (He says nothing more about the last aspect, one that is critical in my scheme of things.) Thus, there is a marked difference in his treatment of and emphasis on the two types of movements.

---

[37] p. 8.
[38] p. 9; also p. 48.

Even though I greatly admire and value Pylkkö's work, I submit that this one-sided stressing of the synchronic aspects of (adults') experiences at the expense of the diachronic aspects is an important shortcoming. In spite of his great sensitivity to matters pertaining to emerging structuralizations, his orientation remains basically adultocentric (i.e., he is almost exclusively concerned with those matters to which his a-words refer), and that is a pity. I will conclude this overview of *The Aconceptual Mind* with some preliminary thoughts about this limitation.

## "EXPLAINING" THE DIACHRONIC DIMENSION

Pylkkö attempts only brief explanations of the diachronic movement in humans. Basically, he asserts that these processes "are partly innate, coded into our genetic heritage, partly caused by maturation and learning;"[39] that the development arises from "repetition and habituation;"[40] that it is gradual in that "experience has to be reified by repeated associations which eventually shape the experience"[41] into the inside/outside framework; that parenting plays a role ("first comes the mother, and then, due to the mother-child differentiation, the external world").[42] In short, he offers sketchy, cursory, dogmatic, *and entirely conventional* assertions and supposed explanations about the movement along the ontogenetic dimension, maintaining that maturation arises from a mixture of neurobiological, behavioristic, and interpersonal-relational factors.

It seems to me that Pylkkö has not thought much or deeply about this dimension. At times he even seems to be confused about whether he is talking about the diachronic

---

[39]  p. 49.
[40]  p. 156.
[41]  p. 69.
[42]  p. 35.

or synchronic dimension, indiscriminately mixing "a-" and "pre-" terminology.[43] And, he takes for granted that scientific psychology is "unable to explain how subjects arise."[44] The last is quite true up to a point, but it nevertheless is a telling statement. First, it suggests obliquely and rather offhandedly that such an explanation may exist. Second, if one includes psychodynamic thought within the domain of scientific psychology, then in a broad sense the claim is inaccurate, as we shall soon see.

With regard to the latter point: if his occasional asides about Freud are any indication, Pylkkö has only the most superficial, academic, retricted knowledge and understanding of psychodynamic thought. (He cannot be faulted for this shortcoming, though; after all, he is a philosopher, not a dynamically-informed, experienced psychotherapist, although given his interest in holistic states one would think that he might have made an effort to explore the large and readily available clinical literature about ontogenesis.) He obviously has read some Freud, but knows him only as a mechanistically inclined theoretician of the unconscious—for example as the "explainer" of the phenomena of pleasure, humor, and narcissism in terms of various reductionist models.[45] Pylkkö shows no awareness of the considerable and readily available body of psychoanalytically-informed clinical knowledge about early development that has accumulated over the past century (both from clinical practice and from empirical observations including those of infant-mother interactions), or, for that matter, seems quite unaware of the importance of what I see as Freud's principal *conceptual* as well as clinical contributions: his evolved, sophisticated ideas about free association and the defenses to which it leads when patients in dyadic psychodynamic therapy are invited to

---

[43]  e.g., pp. 9, 13.
[44]  p. 193.
[45]  pp. 96, 128-129, 236.

attempt it.[46] In what follows I hope to show that psychoanalytically-based knowledge about ontogenesis does have considerable bearing on the topics that interest Pylkkö.

---

[46] See Berger, 1991, 2002a.

# PART II

# AUGMENTATIONS AND ELABORATIONS

*All essential philosophical questioning is necessarily
untimely.... Philosophy is essentially untimely because it is
one of those few things that can never find an immediate
echo in the present. When such an echo seems to occur, when
philosophy becomes fashionable, either it is no real
philosophy or it has been misinterpreted and misused for
ephemeral and extraneous purposes.... But—it is in the very
nature of philosophy never to make things easier but only
more difficult.*

> ~ Martin Heidegger, *An Introduction to
> Metaphysics*

*One limit encountered by the pursuit of objectivity appears
when it turns back on the self and tries to encompass
subjectivity in its conception of the self.*

> ~ Thomas Nagel, *The View from Nowhere*

*The slenderest knowledge that may be obtained of the
highest things is more desirable than the most certain
knowledge obtained of lesser things.*

> ~ Saint Thomas Aquinas, *Summa Theologica*

*Once, in the Greek New Testament class on Sundays, taken
by the Head Master, I dared to ask, in spite of my
stammering, what some parable meant. The answer was so
confused that I actually experienced my first moment of
consciousness—that is, I suddenly realised that no one knew
anything....*

~ Maurice Nicoll, *Psychological Commentaries*

*The most important part of any inquiry or exploration is its
beginning.*

~ E. F. Schumacher, *A Guide for the Perplexed*

# 9

# ADULTOCENTRISM AND ONTOGENESIS

*If we meddle with fundamental principles... we reach a remarkably ambiguously lit, not to mention perilous, province.*

> ~ Martin Heidegger, *The Principle of Reason*

*It would be important to consider the child's sense of oneness with the natural world.... this is a topic that has received almost no attention in psychology.*

> ~ William Crain, *Theories of Development*

*If one begins by assuming a separation of subject and object or of mind and body, the boundary between them sooner or later becomes problematical. And such separations are so fundamental to our thinking that it is difficult to conceive of alternatives.*

> ~ Roger S. Jones, *Physics as Metaphor*

*Now the difficulty in determining a valid scope of reality lies precisely in the fact that no individual can successfully separate this subjective reality, which is the aggregate of his personal sense-impressions, from the objective reality which he has acquired from contact with other individuals, present or past.... The nearest we can come to grasping this subjective reality is the psychology of an infant; and, since we cannot successfully reconstruct our own impressions as infants, we must rely on the studies which adults have made on infants, studies which are invariably colored by preconceived notions.*

> ~ Tobias Dantzig, *Number: The Language of Science*

## EXPLANATION AND UNDERSTANDING

If we want to adequately understand the languaged human being's being-in-the-world, do we need to invoke a person's history?[1] The question has surfaced several times, most recently in the discussion concerning Pylkkö's handling of synchronic and diachronic approaches that closed the previous chapter.

Let us start with the general case in the natural sciences: In order to understand or explain a given physical situation, phenomenon, event, entity, do we need to have its history? Do we need diachronic information, or will synchronic knowledge do? The classic expression of the natural sciences' position was clearly articulated long ago by the French mathematician and astronomer Pierre Simon de Laplace (1749-1827):

> We ought to regard the present state of the universe as the effect of its antecedent state and as the cause of the state that is to follow. An intelligence knowing all the forces acting in nature at a given instant, as well as the momentary positions of all things in the universe, would be able to comprehend in one single formula the motions of the largest bodies as well as of the lightest atoms in the world, provided that its intellect were sufficiently powerful to subject all data to analysis; to it nothing would be uncertain, the future as well as the past would be present to its eyes.[2]

Here, in a nutshell, we have a description of what for some time I have been calling "State Process Formalisms."[3] These imply and presuppose that in order to understand something (typically, the behavior of some physical "system") all one needs to have available is a comprehensive description of that something's present *state* (typically, its condition as specified in terms of the value of

---

[1]   I acknowledge that understanding and explanation are large and controversial topics—see for example Mayes, 2000; Potter, 1994; Dancy and Sosa, 1992, pp. 129-132; Audi, 1999, pp. 298-299.

[2]   Quoted in Berger, 1985, pp. 41-42.

[3]   Berger, 1978, 1985.

variables in some descriptive co-ordinate system—"all the forces... [all the] momentary positions"), along with the laws and so-called boundary conditions (circumstances that limit the system's behavior) in order to know how that system will behave, how it will evolve over time, and how it got to its present state. In other words, the state process formalism assures us that we can accurately and comprehensively predict or retrodict future and past behavior from a complete description of the current conditions, and it assumes that this is all that "understanding" something amounts to. For physicists, this understanding *is* historical.[4]

An abstract example is a single particle moving in space. If we know that particle's position and velocity at a given time, the characteristics of the force field in which it is located, and the presence and nature of constraints, if any (e.g., the presence and location of an impermeable wall), then we know all we need to know about that particle. We can tell where the particle is going, and, if we like, where it has been. To make these predictions we do not need to know its history; all that we need is a complete description of the system at this moment.

The classical real-world example in physics is the behavior of the planets in our solar system. If we select one of these, say, the earth, as our system, then its behavior— that is, its past and future paths—is specified when we know its present position and momentum, the (gravitational) force field in which it is moving, and Newton's laws. For the natural sciences, the great power of the state process formalism is that it is generalizable, extendable to very complex systems in mathematically highly sophisticated ways. In the present example we could also treat the entire solar system as one single (but complex, high-dimensional, abstract) system, and state

---

4    Berger, 1995.

formalisms would allow us to specify its entire behavior (which or course subsumes the motion of all the individual bodies), at least in principle.

Thus, physics does not need to know anything about the past behavior of a given system in order to be able to understand, predict, and control its properties and behavior. (We already encountered the natural sciences' disdain of history in chapter 5 in the form of privileging the context of verification over the context of discovery.)

Currently that is also the majority position in most other disciplines that have scientific pretensions. It is essentially true in my own field of psychotherapy (and in contemporary clinical psychology and psychiatry in general). The need to know a patient's history is given lip service, but actually the focus is very much on the present, both in diagnosis as well as in therapy.[5]

Furthermore, even when historical aspects are taken into account in, say, philosophy or psychology, the framework is adultocentric. For instance, even when psychologists investigate developmental aspects of language, or of intellectual function, they do so "unhesitatingly... from the point of view of the mature, conceptually organized subject."[6] That position is considerably modified in psychodynamic-psychoanalytic thought, a framework which "is unthinkable without the theory of [an individual's] evolution and of ontogenesis of mental development,"[7] the subject to which I turn next.

## PSYCHOANALYTIC NEONATE MODELS[8]

Currently there are two chief classes of psychoanalytic neonate models. One is the "revolutionary" model of the

---

5   See Berger, 1991, 2002a.
6   Pylkkö, 1998, p. 193.
7   Loewald, 1980, p. 139.
8   This section is based on revised portions of Berger, 1996.

"competent infant... the new psychoanalytic theory of infancy as represented by Stern's work;"[9] let us label it "CI"(for *competent infant*). The other is an older conception, exemplified in Margaret Mahler's infant researches,[10] in which the neonate is assumed to be undifferentiated, merged, in a unitary state; let us call that model "UN" (for *undifferentiated, unitary neonate*).

## The Competent Infant ("CI")

Models in the first, CI class postulate an infant who from the start is capable of relating "competently" to the external world, who "arrives with an array of innately determined perceptual predilections, motor patterns, cognitive or thinking tendencies, and abilities for emotional expressiveness and perhaps recognition."[11] This is an infant who already has a rudimentary sense of me and not-me, an "integrated sense of a core self and others."[12] In the current scientific climate such models invite being set within a genetic and/or neurobiological framework. That is, such competencies tend to be seen as "pre-wired" into the biological organism. These innate characteristics are inferred primarily from observational studies of infants' behavioral responses to caregivers or experimenters. Such empirical observations find that the infant can initiate, terminate, modulate, or even avoid social interactions; can make rudimentary discriminations between stimuli; does relate interpersonally, and so on. An important example of such built-in competence is Noam Chomsky's premise that as far as language is concerned, the neonate has "an inner design—a genetic program"[13] composed of rules that govern the acquisition and use of language,[14] that "the child brings

---

[9]   Zuriff, 1992, p. 19; the reference is to Stern, 1985.
[10]  Mahler et al., 1975, pp. 4-43
[11]  Stern, 1977, p. 35.
[12]  Zuriff, 1992, p. 21.
[13]  Crain, 2000, p. 344.
[14]  But, a small problem: Chomsky is "silent on semantics" (Katz, 1998, p. xxiv).

to the task [of acquiring language] a significant, genetically determined predisposition to construct grammars according to a well-defined pattern."[15]

However, what is usually ignored is that such empirical findings are virtually guaranteed by the scientific methodologies employed.[16] The researcher imposes or superposes a rational-computational-cognitive template over the phenomena, and then necessarily finds that the thus observed infant indeed does exhibit behaviors that support cognitive hypotheses and models—a prime instance of Heidegger's enframing and its consequences: the imposed conceptual frameworks predetermine and constrain the range or nature of the possible observations. Discussing the parallel situation in animal research (concerning the "linguistic" behavior of the chimpanzee Washoe) one linguist puts the issue succinctly: "The animal makes a movement and the psycholinguist talks about an 'internal state' without further ado."[17] In other words, those are the only kinds of findings that the employed methodologies and underlying conceptual frameworks can and do allow; anything else, any other kinds of observations, any other kinds of hypotheses, inevitably are filtered out at the front end, so to speak.[18] In Heideggerian terms: technological or calculative-cognitive-rational thought sees the essence of technology everywhere.[19]

How, then, is the neonate's *experience* conceptualized under these models? Almost not at all. The CI model is an *external observer's* model. Basically, it is a scientist's model that treats the infant as a "black box." The functionalist model describes the world in terms of external inputs (e.g., the caregiver's behaviors), and the neonate's outputs

---

[15] Audi, 1995, p. 352.
[16] See Zuriff, 1992; Solnit, 1987; Rangell, 1990; Berger, 1996.
[17] Robinson, 1975, p. 158.
[18] See Berger, 1978, 1985.
[19] This is very much like Husserl's "ontological reversal" discussed in chapter 6.

(behavioral responses). In between these two classes of variables is the neonate—functionally, a black box that serves a transformational function. The scientist's goal is to infer or invent a suitable mathematical function for that interior that will account for the observed relationships between input and output. Formally, this is just like the engineers' black box: one puts something (usually, some kind of a signal) into a system, and observes what comes out, how that input is transformed. Then, one designs the black box to functionally, mathematically account for the changes between what is put in and what comes out. (That is, one creates a mathematical *function* that will correctly transform observed input variables into observed output variables.) For the purposes of science it does not matter what the CI "really" is, that is, what one would find were one able to open up this black box and actually examine its interior. All that matters is that the box's function is modeled correctly mathematically.

In these terms, if the CI is modeled "correctly," then the infant's actual experience is not at issue for the scientist. It does not seem to be of much interest to CI researchers. I would guess that for researchers who embrace such functionalist frameworks any concern about what "really" might be going on in the "black box," what a neonate's experience actually might be like, would seem like so much idle, indefensible, pointless, unscientific speculation.

### The Undifferentiated, Unitary Neonate ("UN")

Models of second, UN type postulate a neonate who is profoundly merged with the environment, who lacks spatial and temporal boundaries, who is entirely undifferentiated, for whom self or other does not exist *in any sayable sense,* who lives in a unitary, boundaryless world. Not only is there thought to be no sense of me or not me, no distinction between self or other, no temporal sense of the past, present, and future, but the UN lacks even a rudimentary representational, let alone linguistic, capacity: "It is only the observer who can distinguish between the individual and the environment... the individual [i.e., the neonate] cannot do so."[20] On this view, the infant cannot possibly have anything even remotely resembling an adult's experiences: "The world comes to be for human beings only through and within language. Language, world, and human being are co-ordinate terms."[21]

In psychoanalytic jargon this infant state has been called the state or stage of "normal autism"[22] or "primary narcissism."[23] The terminology tends to be misleading because it suggests that in some sense, this infant is somehow aware of itself (it is "narcissistic," can be "satisfied," is "hungry," etc.) even though it is presumed to be totally unaware of anything external. Thus, we find what I see as misleading statements such as, the neonate "focuses on inner physiological states.... protected from the outside by what Freud called a stimulus barrier, a kind of shell, that keeps out extremes in stimuli."[24]

This unstructured, preverbal, pre- and undifferentiated, pre-boundaried experience is virtually unimaginable, ineffable, inexpressible in adult terms: "Our scientific conceptual language... appears to be particularly inadequate for statements about early mental functioning;"[25] "we could not *say* of a nonlogical [i.e.,

---

20 Winnicott, 1975, p. 266. Before he became an analyst, for many years Donald Winnicott was a pediatrician; his psychoanalytic theorizing is probably the one most empathetic with the infant, and with the infant-mother situation—or, as he calls it, "the environment-individual set-up."(Ibid.) For an excellent non-clinical general overview of this merged condition and its subsequent fate see Berman, 1989, especially chapter 1: The Basic Fault (a reference to an important book by the psychoanalyst Michael Balint).

21 Barrett, 1978, p. 43.

22 Mahler et al., 1975, pp. 41-42. This is "a preconscious unity with the environment... that has been called by many names" (Berman, 1989, p. 25).

23 Loewald, 1980, p. 8; the term is problematic—see, for example, Laplanche and Pontalis, 1973, p. 337; Balint, 1969.

24 Crain, 2000, pp. 299-300.

25 Loewald, 1980, p. 186.

nonlinguistic] world what it would be like, because our saying would be language, and language must be logically articulated to some minimal degree at least."[26] As soon as we try to put it into words, we subvert or misrepresent it. A discussion of a closely related issue in a different context is Thomas Nagel's famous critique of what "it is like" to be a bat.[27] Thus, for example, attempting to treat the experience "scientifically," as an object of formalized, structured, scientific study is simply inappropriate enframing.

Here we once again encounter the problem of how to articulate the properties of a unitary, nondual domain—a problem we had encountered ubiquitously throughout Part I—but this time we do so in a quite different context. By and large, the kinds of holistic, undifferentiated states to which most of the critics in Part I pointed each were aspects of the *adult's synchronic experience.* Tallis's explicitness dimension, Loy's nonduality, Pylkkö's aconceptual pole, all were conceptualized as synchronic and adultocentric phenomena, one pole in a temporally "vertical" (i.e. non-temporal) dimension.

Furthermore, for all these thinkers that unstructured end point of the experiential synchronic spectrum is as far as one can go. What I mean is this. Within their frameworks the unstructured pole is a conceptual dead end. The end point comes out of nowhere, and it is unsupported—it "floats." By comparison, the unstructured infant's experiential era that I am outlining, while no less mysterious, while still afloat, nevertheless provides a broad and integrating basis in the sense that *all* the (developmentally) later aspects and experiences that come to characterize a maturing or mature person's life are seen as special structuralizations that emerge out of this global,

---

[26] Barrett, 1978, p. 43; see also Coulter's discussion of what he calls the prelinguistic infant's "opacity" (1983, pp. 108, 111, 124, 163).

[27] Nagel, 1974.

foundational, unitary domain. That includes *everything*, from the me/not-me distinction to becoming languaged: perception, memory, reasoning, the different sensual-perceptual modalities, the distinction between mind and body, proprioceptions, imagining, dreaming, creating, and so on. It may be a matter of my own proclivity, but an ontogenetically-grounded mystery seems much more conceptually, intellectually and emotionally satisfying and tangible than does an adultocentrically- and synchronically-grounded holistic foundation (e.g., Tallis's explicitness). I will add to these general introductory comments later in several contexts.

The idea of an UN is not accepted widely. It seems that such conceptions of an undifferentiated neonate state often evoke strong defensive reactions. The notion of a structureless, unbounded, non-languaged, ungrounded state tends to stir up unseen archaic dreads in many adults and elicit corresponding defensive surface maneuvers (the intellectualizing, structuring natural sciences can be seen as one kind of defensive response to anxieties that are outside of awareness),[28] including the summary dismissal of the entire idea as absurd. For example, one physicist asks rhetorically "what our world would be like... [without] the hand-eye coordination and integration of sense data that enable us to live an efficient, ordered life" and answers that it would be "a chaos, unintelligible, unnegotiable; a schizophrenic nightmare, the experience of an infant mind, or perhaps even of death."[29] It must be shunned like the plague. Even Freud, the pioneer clinician, was unwilling to plunge into such depths. Throughout his working life he much preferred to focus on the later stages of development, especially and famously on the œdipal era, the time when triangular, competitive (and comparatively mature)

---

[28]  See Keller, 1979.
[29]  Jones, 1982, p. 15.

relations take center stage. He examined this era and the consequences it has for later life in great specificity, both from theoretical and clinical (case study) perspectives. By comparison, his coverage of the earlier, developmentally more primitive periods of development was much more global, sketchy, generalized, abstract. Freud not only avoided deeper and more focused exploration of early dyadic interactions (the core focus of highly productive work by later analysts such as Melanie Klein, Michael Balint, Donald Winnicott, Hans Loewald, Heinz Kohut) but apparently was unwilling to plunge into unstructured depths altogether.[30] Perhaps that accounts at least in part for his insistence on making and keeping psychoanalysis a science cast in the mold of the natural sciences.

I am convinced that whether one accepts the CI or the UN model is matter of a characterological makeup rather than of rational argument. Some persons greatly need the safety of structure and therefore will find rationalizations that support their belief in a structured infant and the concomitant dismissal of the UN model. Others are drawn to and comfortable with less structured, deeper, perhaps more poetic or mystical realms. People are "inexorably subdivided into two kinds: materialists and transcendentalists."[31] This issue has received but little attention; I know of only two philosophers who have explored it in any depth in their own field: Ben-Ami Scharfstein, and Lawrence Cahoone.[32]

---

[30] See Loewald, 1980, especially pp. 9, 142, 168.
[31] Rota, 1997, p. 266.
[32] Scharfstein, 1980; Cahoone, 1988. This psychodynamic ontogenetic orientation is fundamental, however, in the works of Morris Berman, a cultural historian (see Berman 1981, 1989, 2000a).

# THE TWO CLASSES OF MODELS AND PSYCHOLOGICAL DEVELOPMENT

## Development and the Competent Infant

Let us next see how development is conceptualized within each of these two classes of neonate models. According to CI models, development is a straightforward matter: the infant already has available in primitive form the three key standard ingredients of the Cartesian adult: the perceiving subject, the external object, and the capacity for internal representations (e.g., sense data; ideas; concepts) which structure and facilitate the commerce between the adult's inner and outer world.[33] The assumption is that there "is a logic within the womb.... The organizational principle is present in the baby upon entry into the world.... We shall call it 'Logos', or the logic of the womb."[34] Mainstream psychologists and philosophers alike typically assume that "a genetic psychology requires some innate structures at the start."[35] The neonate comes already equipped.

Consequently, for these models human development poses no special conceptual difficulties. No conceptually new elements enter the picture with maturation; there merely is an unfolding and elaboration of characteristics that are already present, albeit in primitive form, in the neonate. One could say that under this model, development is mostly a quantitative rather than a qualitative matter. Development is only a matter of a series of straightforward, unproblematic transformations of what is already there. The "innately determined perceptual predilections, motor patterns, cognitive or thinking tendencies, and abilities for emotional expressiveness and perhaps recognition,"[36] the

---

[33] See, for example, Danto, 1989.
[34] Feher, 1981, p. 31.
[35] Taylor, 1985, p. 144.
[36] Stern, 1977, p. 35.

CI's already present rudimentary sense of me and not-me, its "integrated sense of a core self and others,"[37] gradually just become elaborated, more complex, nuanced, realistic, and effective as maturation proceeds, but for theorizers the presence of these elements and competencies in the older child or in the adult pose no fundamental conceptual modifications or paradoxes. "Learning" and its various behaviorist or cognitivist adjuncts and cognates becomes the magic key to understanding maturational changes.

## Development and the Merged Infant

When we turn from this picture to the individual psychological development of the Mahlerian, merged neonate we encounter a very different and highly problematic scene. How can one conceptualize the move from the UN's holistic, ineffable and unstructured, prelinguistic, pretemporal state—a condition that cannot, indeed must not, be described or conceptualized through any of the conventionally available, mainstream (i.e, linguistic or language-like) means—to the various later structured, differentiated, boundaried, languaged capacities that characterize the toddler, the adolescent, or the adult?

One of the most comprehensive psychoanalytic attempts to articulate this question is by the late Hans Loewald. It is not coincidental that as far as I know, this notable Yale clinician and theoretician was the only psychoanalyst to have studied with Martin Heidegger.[38] Surely that experience opened him to the issue of holism, mystery, and its problems. For example, when he says that psychoanalysis as a discipline requires conceptual frameworks which are fundamentally different from those which ground "sciences such as physics, chemistry or

---

[37]  Zuriff, 1992, p. 21.
[38]  Loewald 1980, p. viii; also Stan Leavy, personal communication, May 8, 2004 ("I have it directly from Hans Loewald that he studied with Heidegger as his graduate student.").

biology,"[39] or that we all "are still more or less captives of an erroneous understanding of objectivity and objective reality,"[40] we can hear echos of Heidegger's thought about *Dasein*, and about rational-calculative thinking. Yet, Loewald's use of Heidegger is "indeed more than an application, but an extension into a sphere of understanding foreign to their creator, the sphere of human development, and of the unconscious life in which the past survives, and the future is in process of becoming."[41]

Loewald describes the process during which the self is differentiated as occurring "through the modifying influence of external reality.... The psychological constitution of the ego [roughly: the self] and outer world go hand in hand.... An organized ego and organized reality have been differentiated from each other.... Ego and reality [arise together from] a unitary whole that differentiates into distinct parts.... Ego and reality cannot be considered separately as they evolve together."[42]

Furthermore, on the way to adulthood "the early levels of psychic development are not simply outgrown and left behind but continue to be active, at least intermittently, during later life including adulthood;"[43] persons carry their past within themselves as their "living history."[44] This important notion was adumbrated by Pylkkö during his discussion of the adult's experience of external "things" when he noted that "this reificational aspect of experience floats like a sloop on the high seas of aconceptual experience."[45] The neonate state is very much present in Loewald's clinical thinking about the later stages of development—their general characteristics, pathologies,

[39]  Loewald, 1980, p. 298; see also pp. 96, 123-124, 296-297.
[40]  Ibid., p. 277.
[41]  Leavy, 1989, p. 235.
[42]  Loewald, 1980, pp. 4, 5, 11, 25.
[43]  Ibid., p. 81.
[44]  Ibid., p. 144.
[45]  Pylkkö, 1998, pp. 50-51.

and therapeutic implications. This is an example drawn from the clinical world illustrating how an ontogenetic perspective can illuminate a discipline.

I have emphasized Loewald's contributions, but it should go without saying that he is but a part of a vigorous, long and valuable psychoanalytic tradition. The contributors are too numerous to mention, but I want to point out one unusual, relatively recent and fascinating addition, namely, Allesandra Piontelli. This Italian psychoanalyst not only has observed and studied fetuses ultrasonically *in utero* but in some cases has seen these children later as patients, noting astonishing continuities and parallels between their pre- and post-birth observed lives.[46]

## Covert Conceptual Difficulties Inherent in the CI Model

Let us reconsider the CI's maturation. I have pointed out that this journey does not seem to pose any significant conceptual problems in the sense that if one starts out from the premise of a CI, then one encounters no radically fundamental qualitative changes in the course of maturation because the basic conceptual ingredients (e.g., a differentiating sense of self/other, a representational capacity) have been there all along, as was discussed above. However, that does not at all mean that the CI model and the maturation picture that develops out of that state truly are without significant difficulties.

The CI model, as well as all the subsequent maturational stages that follow from it, are trapped within a naturalizing framework. In Part I we have seen its limitations identified and discussed from a variety of positions and in a variety of contexts. We have seen that the holistically-oriented critics insist that there is no intelligible way to scientifically

---

[46] Piontelli, 1992; for related clinical and theoretical observations by a psychiatrist made in a quite different context, see Grof, 1985.

understand, for example, consciousness, the nature of perception, the problem of other minds, the mind-body problem, language acquisition, semantics, thought, self-reference or reflexivity, free will, or cognition—the litany of all the familiar issues that have been a principal preoccupation of Western philosophy. What development according to the CI model actually does, then, is to conceal a whole set of paradoxes and enigmas that already are implicit in that infant model (e.g., *that* a neonate can discriminate is taken as unproblematic).

The CI model is circular right from the start. It implies that understanding the CI's competencies poses no fundamental conceptual problems because in all essentials these abilities are rudimentary versions of the adult's competencies which presumably are well understood. In turn, the adult's abilities are seen as unproblematic because they are just the end points, elaborations of the CI's basic equipment which is well understood. Where is understanding in this picture?

One of my main objections to this kind of thinking is that it pretends to provide answers—or at least to be on the way to providing such answers (promising that these will come with further advances in neuroscience, experimental psychology, etc.). It covers over the fundamentally imponderable, mysterious nature of the phenomena which it purports to explain. The fact—or at least what many others, myself included, take as a fact—that this entire spectrum of phenomena and experiences is essentially shrouded in mystery is made invisible.

There is yet another issue here. Why model the infant at all? The question brings up the issue of the utility of the pure knowledge paradigm. When, under what circumstances, in what disciplines, for what kinds of purposes, are evasive, dissembling models such as that of the CI useful and legitimate in a limited sense, and when do they become impediments or worse? The next chapter begins to address these kinds of questions and issues, and Part III extends the discussion.

## THE PROBLEM OF EMERGENCE IN THE MERGED INFANT MODEL

When we turn to consider human developmental from the perspective of the UN model, we encounter a set of baffling transitions—how can one conceptualize the change from what essentially amounts to having no structure, no articulable awareness, no differentiation, no boundaries, to the developmentally later states that are replete with structure? This is basically a problem of *emergence*: how *qualitatively* totally new phenomena, structures, objects, experiences, and the like, can emerge. We are dealing with a conceptual discontinuity, with something like the kind of change engineers call a step function.

Structurally this poses the same problem the naturalizers face when they attempt to "explain" consciousness as a phylogenetically emergent property, as something that somehow emerges from a presumably insentient, inert, inanimate material world, assuming that consciousness, lived experience," unfolds at certain levels of cognitive complexity that require a brain and a higher nervous system. In other words, consciousness is a special kind of cognitive process that emerges when cognition reaches a certain level of complexity."[47] The premise is that even though we now do not "quite" understand how that can happen, sooner or later materialistic science *will* explain it. This hubristic claim is ubiquitous. For example, Steven Weinberg, a Nobel-Prize winning physicist, proclaims that future advances in physics and allied progress in neurobiology will "identify something, some

---

[47]   Capra, 2002, p. 38.

physical system for processing information... [that] may not be an explanation of consciousness, but it will be pretty close;"[48] he devotes two pages to a discussion that includes snide remarks about those who do not agree with that assessment. What does "pretty close" mean here? Isn't it like being a little pregnant? No one has the slightest idea not only about *how* to explain such a jump (it "requires a miracle.... has materialism stumped"),[49] but furthermore, no one has even an inkling of what the very *nature* of such an explanation could be, what it could look like, what its ingredients might be, in terms of "what" consciousness would be explained. Physical science only allows *correlations* between its material phenomena and those belonging to other realms (e.g., correlating behaviors and neurobiological phenomena), and correlations do not explain. They only correlate. Neither does saying that emergence is a gradual process (as does, for example, Pylkkö)[50] explain anything; is only begs the question and obfuscates.

Scientists are not alone in this matter. Philosophers also tend to explain the mystery away. Pylkkö explains the developmental changes from "pre-" to "a-" states (from infant to some adult experience) by asserting that these processes "are partly innate, coded into our genetic heritage, partly caused by maturation and learning," partly arise from "repetition and habituation," that gradually "experience has to be reified by repeated associations which eventually shape the experience" into the inside/outside framework, and that parenting plays a role: "first comes the mother, and then, due to the mother-child differentiation, the external world."[51] Another philosopher says that

---

[48] Weinberg, 1994, p.45.
[49] de Quincey, 2002, pp. 34, 222; see also Tallis 1999b, pp. 32-44; Seager, 2001.
[50] 1998, p. 159.
[51] Pylkkö, 1998, pp. 49, 156, 69, 35.

the newborn does not at first distinguish itself from the environment.... Only when its needs, wants, and desires are frustrated does it begin to recognize that the environment is distinct from and over against it.[52]

"Explaining" the change from, say, having no language to acquiring it in some rudimentary form by terms such as learning, interactions, or frustrations merely substitutes a set of ultimately obscure terms for the paradoxical transition or emergence; the advantage is that these terms seem eminently unproblematic, that they are thought to stand for processes that at least in principle are said to be well understood and stand in no need of further fundamental explanations.

Similarly, mainstream psychoanalysis has attempted to explain (and circumvent, blur) the problematic aspects of maturation by positing all sorts of "mechanisms" that supposedly can account for the qualitative changes: internalization, introjection, projection, externalization, differentiation, identification, mirroring, or laying down of memory traces.[53] Now, such a superficial pseudo-understanding of development may be useful in clinical work (and I believe that it is), but as a purportedly conceptual explanation it is mere hand-waving. It is yet another instance of a mystery apparently being explained by expert science in impressive specialist terminology when actually the puzzle is merely translated into language that tends to hide its presence. Closer examination demonstrates that the explanatory terms and mechanisms themselves are no less problematic than the phenomena they presume to explain. (What is internalization? Identification with? Projection/ introjection? Learning? Habituation? Genetic coding? Mental representations?)

---

[52]  Potter, 1994, p. 22.
[53]  For a comprehensive and up to date overview see Sass, 1992.

Always, the presence of an ultimately unfathomable mystery is being denied, one way or another, but as we have seen, the mystery that is being explained away or at least marginalized in adultocentric, naturalizing ways reappears in the adult's situation. Naturalizing explanations of the adult person's being-in-the-world run up against mysteries at every turn. We have seen that over and over again in the critiques presented in Part I.

The implications and advantages of acknowledging and retaining the holistic paradox will be considered in Part III. For the moment I just want to summarize some of the broad advantages which I believe an ontogenetic perspective grounded in the UN can provide. First, it can integrate and unify the scattered paradoxes that dog attempts to understand the adult's Being-in-the-world. Instead of running into a set of apparently separate and diverse enigmas (about perception, consciousness, etc.) at every turn, one faces one fundamental and unifying paradox. Second, this paradox seems to be more grounded (if a paradox can be grounded) than those in what I have referred to as the scattered adultocentric set. Paradoxes pertaining to adult perception, etc., seem to float, to lack a conceptual center or focus. The holistic basis the UN provides seems conceptually and intuitively more satisfying. Third, the UN's holism can provide the means for maintaining or regaining a holistic aspect throughout the entire spectrum of human development, and it adds an ever-present dimension to later experience. In clinical work, it can illuminate every developmental phase and all aspects of a patient's situation. Whether and how it can be useful in other areas remains to be seen; in Part III I will explore that matter in several contexts. Fourth, keeping the mysterious origins of the adult's capacities and characteristics firmly in view can serve the kind of function Wittgenstein called therapeutic: it can be used in critiques to demonstrate the folly of many of the questions that have been, and continue to be, pursued in various disciplines; in other words, it can identify pseudo-questions (e.g.: How do electrical signals in the nervous system become subjective experiences? What "is" anxiety?). By performing such therapeutic functions an UN-based ontogenetic approach can clear a space in which new, novel, questions can emerge, questions that previously may have been obscured by the search for answers to the wrong kinds of questions. On all counts, it seems advisable not only to retain the UN mystery in one's conceptual framework, but to give it a prominent position.

There is a long tradition that maintains there are advantages to retaining rather than dismissing or obscuring mysterious bases:

> We answer a mystery by posing a mystery.[54]

> [*Explicitness*] leaves everything largely unexplained. Its aim, however, is to redefine the questions or to reinstate the mystery and so help ensure that the right questions are asked. These questions will not be asked so long as the idea of mental mechanisms, rooted in neural activity and serving an evolutionary agenda, hold sway as our model of human consciousness.... It is better to have an unsolved problem than a false solution.... When scientistic, as opposed to scientific, theories of the mind are proliferating at the present rate, it may be better to be fruitlessly illusionless for a while than fruitfully advancing deeper into confusion and untruth: 'to live', as Nietzsche says, 'off the acorns and grass of knowledge, for the sake of truth.'[55]

> Certain forms of perplexity... seem to me to embody more insight than any of the supposed solutions to these problems.[56]

I, too, am suggesting that identifying, acknowledging, retaining, and repositioning the right sort of mystery may be advantageous.

---

[54]  Barrett, 1986, p. 31.
[55]  Tallis, 1999a, pp. xv, 208, 250.
[56]  Nagel, 1986, p. 4.

# 10

# ANOMALOUS PRAGMATISM

It is one thing to recognize in principle the roles ontogenetic aspects might play in the adult's everyday life, but quite another to see how that insight might be put to work in various disciplines. To suggest some initial approaches I want to introduce and sketch out an idea, a position I label "anomalous pragmatism," a variant of pragmatism foreshadowed in Martin Heidegger's and Edmund Husserl's work.[1] The qualifier "anomalous" is intended to distinguish it from the more familiar pragmatisms associated primarily with the philosophers Peirce, James, Dewey, and more recently especially with Richard Rorty. The distinction is meaningful: "We must be careful not to confound Heidegger's pragmatism with, say, the American versions of pragmatism which move much more closer to common sense knowledge than Heidegger, and which are also overly optimistic as regards the comprehensiveness of scientific rationality."[2]

This anomalously pragmatic position is in contradistinction to the Pure Knowledge Paradigm position which assumes that disciplines just need to go about their usual work of pursuing the ideal of pure, "unapplied" knowledge, the attainment of a true, specifiable, accurate, verifiable understanding of reality. It is taken for granted without further ado that this presumably purist approach will result in asymptotically approaching that goal. (I say "presumably," because as numerous critiques have shown, and some of the earlier discussions also indicated, this "pure" paradigm is rife with covert metaphysical

---

[1]    And also adumbrated in some of my own publications: Berger, 1985, pp. 97, 111, 115-118, 125, 129-136, 159-170, 178-179; 1991, pp. 158-169, 175-183, 192, 224n10, 225n16; 2002a, pp. 14, 16n26, 39-40, 54, 71, 77n69.

[2]    Pylkkö,1998, p. 41.

presuppositions.) Furthermore, it is assumed that working within this paradigm will automatically lead researchers to develop the proper conceptual and empirical tools needed to carry out what is essentially an unspecific, open-ended task. Working in this way has a long and venerated tradition. The disdain for any departure from a purist position has a long history: "We are told the Greeks despised applications."[3] Let us first try to characterize the conventional pragmatisms, and then see how the proposed variant differs from these.

## STANDARD PRAGMATISMS

Pragmatism is a slippery, polysemous term. In its everyday meaning it refers to a matter-of-fact, practical treatment of things, and is often used as a contrast to an academic, ivory-tower, impractical, abstract, "theoretical" stance. In philosophy, however, the term is difficult to define formally: "The term... designates a variety of philosophical views all having a family-resemblance but in details quite different."[4] One definition that has been offered is "an American movement in philosophy founded by Peirce and James and marked by the doctrines that the meaning of conceptions is to be sought in their practical bearings, that the function of thought is as a guide to action, and that the truth is preeminently to be tested by the practical consequences of belief."

At the heart of pragmatism's American beginnings lies the fundamental maxim of one of its two founders, Charles Sanders Peirce:

> If one can define accurately all the conceivable experimental
> phenomena which the affirmation or denial of a concept could

---

[3]    Hersh, 1997, p. 185.
[4]    Potter, 1994, p. 124.

imply, one will have therein a complete definition of the concept, and *there is absolutely nothing more in it.*[5]

William James, the other founder of the American school of pragmatism, observes that

> the term is derived from the same Greek word... meaning action.... To develop a thought's meaning, we need only determine what conduct it is fitted to produce.... There is absolutely nothing new in the pragmatic method. Socrates was an adept at it. Aristotle used in methodically. Locke, Berkeley, and Hume made momentous contributions to truth by its means.[6]

Still, there are other conceptions of pragmatism. Another philosopher borrows "the term *pragmatic* from Aristotle's account of the way things (*pragmata*) are linked to words."[7] Yet another specifies pragmatism in terms of four complex central tenets.[8] And, William James himself gave "at least six accounts of what pragmatism is or contains.... [and Arthur Lovejoy in] a classic paper called 'The Thirteen Pragmatisms'... claimed that not only did 'pragmatism' stand for different doctrines, but that in some cases these doctrines conflicted.... There is no essence linking all pragmatist writers."[9] It seems that "the problem of giving an accurate brief characterization of the philosophical tendencies known as 'pragmatism' is far from trivial."[10] Giving such a description is made even more elusive when one takes into account the complex elaborations of the term developed in contemporary philosophers such as Richard Rorty.

Pragmatism approaches philosophical problems historically. Its "genetic method" is first to ask of a problem, "How did it get this way? What was its origin, its purpose,

---

[5]   Quoted in Dancy and Sosa, 1992, p. 352.
[6]   Quoted in Goodman, 1995, pp. 54-55.
[7]   Harris, 1996, p. 95.
[8]   Prado, 1987, 9-10; the particulars are irrelevant.
[9]   Goodman, 1995, p. 3.
[10]   Dancy and Sosa, 1992, p. 351.

its function?",[11] and to assume that "what counts as 'reality' or as 'knowledge' is a matter of historical context."[12] As one might anticipate from the positions developed in the preceding chapters, I shall recast this approach which is conventionally, adultocentrically historical into one that is historical in an ontogenetic sense.

Another familiar feature of the normal pragmatisms is that they address philosophical problems in ways that retain or highlight their ties to the problems of everyday living. Traditional pragmatisms are interested in seeing how a given problem can be addressed in a manner that will effectively serve human purposes, that, for example, can help people cope with the alienation brought about by a technological-industrial age. Pragmatisms put philosophical and scientific problems into behavioral and social contexts. Furthermore, they do recognize that human ties lurk behind apparently "objective" problems, a position expressed in William James's "humanistic principle: you can't weed out the human contribution."[13]

Incidentally, here there seems to be a distant link between American pragmatisms and Heidegger's thought. Heidegger makes a distinction between primarily ontologically focused approaches that retain the human connection to the outer world—a view in which "equipment" is seen as "ready-to-hand,"[14] where we see, say, a hammer in terms of its meaningful function as a tool "for humans"— and those scientific, technological-rational, primarily epistemological approaches that convert all objects including everyday ones into "present-at-hand" objects— neutral, independently existing entities severed from subjective aspects such as their origin, use, or meaning. The hammer is converted into an inert piece of material that

---

[11]   Kaplan, 1961, p. 20.
[12]   Prado, 1987, p. 10.
[13]   Goodman, 1995, p. 2.
[14]   Richardson, 1986, p. 17.

has such-and-such a composition, form, mass, hardness, velocity, trajectory, and the like, but that no longer has any natural meaning or visible human ties. The principal feature of Heidegger's thought, particularly of his early thought, that usually is identified as pragmatic is his rejection of the Cartesian quest for disinterested theoretical truth (I believe a position close to what I am calling working within the pure knowledge paradigm), together with his counterproposal to view *understanding* primarily as "a sort of practice, or... a sort of competence or ability."[15]

## ANOMALOUS FEATURES

As we have seen in the references to Peirce's and James' thought, one if not *the* major feature of pragmatism is its insistence that problematic issues or questions should have meaningful consequences in terms of everyday actions or beliefs. The scientific problems one poses, the questions one raises, are to be consequential for everyday life, or else they are to be set aside. (In spirit, this is close to the Logical Positivists' so-called verification principle, the maxim that in order for them to be meaningful and worthy of consideration, scientific questions must be operationalizable and if not verifiable, at least disconfirmable. In order for them to be sanctioned, scientific questions and projects must have tangible methodological and theoretical implications and consequences. If not, they are to be dismissed.)

I would transform this dictum about general usefulness to people in their everyday lives into a generalization pertaining to *disciplines*. I will not only be asking whether this or that issue or question is consequential in a given context, but asking much more generally, *What kind of a conceptual and methodological framework does this particular discipline require, and for what sorts of purposes?*

---

15    Blattner, 2000, p. 231; see also Rorty, 1991, p. 51.

This question is improper under the pure knowledge paradigm. There, the unquestioned goal of pure knowledge presumably makes such questioning not only unnecessary but illegitimate and unacceptable.

Against the background of the UN's unstructured, amorphous holistic condition this anomalously pragmatic question evolves further; it becomes: *To what degree, if any, does this particular discipline (e.g., physics, psychology) need to take the holistic origins of the human being into account?* When is it all right to take what from an ontogenetic point of view are actually Cheshire Cat residues as independent, objectively existing entities that are legitimate objects of a given discipline's investigation, and when is this kind of mainstream, traditional approach undesirable, detrimental? When does it introduce fundamental "innate constraints,"[16] that are crippling, making it desirable to reintroduce neglected, ignored, even denied holistic aspects and linkages into the picture? I trust that these global, abstract general questions will become meaningful as they are explored in specific contexts in Part III.

Once again there is an Heideggerian echo. One of his recurring points is that scientific thought is a special case, a frozen, "sedimented" residue, a remnant left over from true meditative, poeticizing philosophical thinking,[17] thinking that is centrally concerned with Being. Unlike my approach, however, Heidegger wants to leave the scientific (i.e., presumably nonphilosophical) disciplines alone. It always is risky to think that one understands the implications of Heidegger's thought, but it seems evident that he sees rational-calculative, technological thinking as appropriate when it is employed in the natural sciences. He seems to have no interest in exploring those disciplines'

---

16  Berger, 1978.
17  Heidegger, 1971.

ontological-epistemological needs. Furthermore, his position is overwhelmingly adultocentric; as far as I know, he never ties the grounds of Being to UN/ontogenetic aspects. In all these respects Heidegger's pragmatism differs fundamentally from the envisioned anomalous pragmatism.

## LANGUAGE

One of philosophy's principal concerns is language, and the usual pragmatism is no exception; indeed, it can be seen as "merely a method of ascertaining the meanings of hard words and of abstract concepts."[18] Perhaps the most prominent example is pragmatism's concern with the meaning of Truth, one of its central preoccupations. Furthermore, pragmatists—at least some—recognize the all-encompassing role of language. For example, Richard Rorty, the "most radical [and perhaps also the most prominent] of contemporary self-styled pragmatists,"[19] assumes that one is inextricably caught in the language web, attesting to the impossibility of "reaching out of language."[20]

Nevertheless, the usual pragmatic views concerning language remain entirely adultocentric; there is no sign of any concern with or even awareness of what Frederick Olafson calls "the ontology of language problem" (see chapter 7). *The nature of language itself* is almost never called into question. Neither is a related paradox, one that any investigation of language raises immediately:

> Every attempt to definitively say *what language is* is subject to a curious limitation. For the only medium with which we can define language is language itself. We are therefore unable to circumscribe the whole of language within our definition. It may

---

[18] Peirce, in Melchert, 1991, p. 530.
[19] Dancy and Sosa, 1992, p. 355.
[20] Rorty, 1982, p. xix.

be best, then, to leave language undefined, and to thus acknowledge its open-endedness, its mysteriousness.[21]

With respect to language, my proposed transformation to an *anomalous* pragmatism begins once again with a shift from an adultocentric to an ontogenetic perspective. As we shall see in the next chapter, the point of departure of the critique of language that I will develop is the baffling phenomenon of first language acquisition, an event whose utterly mysterious nature is almost universally ignored, or belittled, or explained away scientistically (e.g., as via Noam Chomsky's notion "that there is an innate set of linguistic principles shared by all humans"[22] that account for that phenomenon). Since whether or not one acknowledges it the presence and use of (adult) language is central and crucial for *all* disciplines including even those that are most mathematical, and thus seem to be non- or meta-linguistic (or, better, nondiscursive), I will begin my explorations of the implications that ontogenesis and anomalous pragmatism have for various disciplines with an examination of the all-encompassing subject of language.

---

[21]   Abram, 1996, p. 73.
[22]   Audi, 1999, p.138.

# PART III

## EXPLORING APPLICATIONS

~~~

## CHESHIRE CAT RESIDUES

*Academic disciplines are not immune from making quite fundamental mistakes about the field of their inquiries.*

> ~ Roy Harris, *The Foundations of Linguistic Theory*

*The influence of a fading paradigm goes well beyond its explicit domain. All paradigms include subterranean realms of tacit assumptions, the influence of which outlasts the adherence to the paradigm itself.*

> ~ Shimon Malin, *Nature Loves to Hide*

*That which is to be rethought must first, obviously, have become problematic.*

> ~ Jerry Gill, *Mediated Transcendence*

*Whenever a theoretical inquiry fails to begin by looking hard at the position inherited from common thought and practice, the most likely outcome will be a passive acceptance of that position followed by a desperate struggle to deal with its inconsistencies, which, however, never go away.*

> ~ John Ellis, *Language, Thought, and Logic*

# 11

# RESIDUE I: LANGUAGE

*'I am embrangled in words,' writes Berkeley at one point in his notebook, evidently with some annoyance; but then adds immediately, as if by way of consolation, 'tis scarce possible it should be otherwise.' Berkeley here speaks, if we are to be honest about it, for every philosopher who has ever lived. And, we might add, for every linguist too. Unfortunately, those in either discipline who have realized their own embranglement have been few, and those who admitted it with Berkeley's candour even fewer.*

> ~ Roy Harris, *The Language Connection*

*The study of language is one mode of contemplating a mystery, and a proper awe is a measure of the sense and depth of what goes on in the study of language. I mean, not that linguists should talk about their wonder and awe or use it to gain recruits to the profession... but that awe at language should be present in linguistics and inform it. Whatever is the discipline in the subject ought to be what leads the student up to a sense of wonder.... To get far in thinking about knowledge, meaning or thought, anyone has to wonder about language. Philosophy of language is wondering about how language and thought make each other possible.... Children begin to understand what is said to them and to talk. All children. That is a wonder of the world—of the specifically human world.... People are talking and we can understand them if we share their language: what more is being said? But the determination to demonstrate the existence of information previous to its 'encoding' in language goes deep into linguistics.... There is no further appeal in language beyond meaning, and until we get to meaning we are not studying language.*

> ~ Ian Robinson, *The New Grammarians' Funeral*

*It is worth remembering that theory of language is an
exceedingly intricate and subtle area of thought, full of
tricks and traps that seem benign until they have done their
damage, and that are difficult to spot even then. Small and
apparently insignificant differences of formulation can
make an enormous difference to the further course of an
argument.*

~ John Ellis, *Language, Thought, and Logic*

*If we grasp what we shall now try to say as a sequence of
assertions about language, it will remain a concatenation of
unverified and scientifically unverifiable claims. If on the
contrary we experience the way to language in terms of what
transpires with the way while we are under way on it, then
a kind of surmise could awaken, a surmise by which
language would henceforth strike us as exceedingly strange.*

~ Martin Heidegger, *Unterwegs zur Sprache*

*Language is an extremely mysterious phenomenon.*

~ Walker Percy, *The Message in the Bottle*

*It is important for people to understand that a great deal of
impressively authoritative modern theorizing about
language is founded upon a myth.*

~ Roy Harris, *The Language Myth*

## LANGUAGE: THE UBIQUITOUS AND PERENNIAL PROBLEM

Language is a huge, complex, controversial, obscure, paradoxical subject that has generated a huge, controversial, paradoxical, and often esoteric specialist literature over the course of Western thought: "In one sense, the whole debate about human knowledge in the Western tradition has always revolved round the relationship between words and the world, between language and reality."[1] Its importance is reflected in much of what has been presented in Parts I and II; some linguistic issues were raised in most of the preceding chapters.

Language occupies a special place in virtually all enterprises (although that fact is easy to ignore or even miss altogether in many circumstances and contexts):

> There is much that is unique about theory of language as a field of inquiry. Perhaps no other area of thought has its basic ideas so ever present in our ordinary everyday speech: we mention words, meanings, reference, grammar, ideas, and concepts all the time and in all kinds of contexts. Not surprising in view of this, linguistic theory is centrally involved in many branches of knowledge. Linguistics, philosophy, computer science, psychology, language teaching, anthropology and biology (to name only these) all have a vital interest in language and hence in the conceptual basis of our understanding of it, that is, in the theory of language.[2]

## THE RECEIVED VIEW AND ITS DIFFICULTIES

While there are of course numerous and often conflicting notions about the nature, characteristics, functions, origins, and other aspects of language, still, by and large these perspectives also share an underlying commonality, the

---

[1]   Harris, 1988, p. 8.
[2]   Ellis, 1993, p. 1.

belief system I began calling "the received view of language" in chapter 6. We recall that it is (1) enframing, (2) instrumental,[3] and (3) objectifying, reifying (treating language as a neutral, inert "object," as a free-standing, independently existing Cheshire Cat residue).

Another way of characterizing the received view is as the position the distinguished philosopher and linguist Roy Harris calls *segregational thinking*: "the notion that communication systems, including languages like English, exist independently not only of one another but of how they may—or may not—be used by those who use them."[4]

Segregational thinking assumes that although they may be related, in principle the three dominant constituents of the language picture (the semiotic communications system itself, its users, and the external world) are separately existing, segregatable domains. By insisting that material carriers of language do embody meaning, can carry information, can express judgments (e.g. in statements such as "this is a good *x*") and so on, segregational thinking creates a scene where "language in its semantic and constitutive aspects no longer has any essential conceptual linkage with human beings."[5]

This view entails a set of chronic, apparently inescapable difficulties, and there have been numerous attempts by various schools and theoreticians to develop viable, nonproblematic ameliorative approaches. Alternative frameworks that have been proposed and tried include such diverse stratagems as ordinary language philosophy, speech act theory, pragmatic approaches, behaviorism, logical-mathematical analysis, neurophysiological theory, and mathematical information theory.

---

[3] But to say in this context to say just what that means, even what a tool is, is by no means simple or straightforward—see Hunter, 1990.

[4] Harris ,1996, p. 12; see also 1998. Berman calls this "nonparticipatory consciousness" (1981, 1989).

[5] Olafson, 1995, p. 8.

Yet, ultimately linguistic theory reverts to the old standby framework, to what one critic calls "the default condition,"

> the theory with which we all start, the one that is virtually there in the language we speak. It is the default condition of linguistic theory to which everything reverts when all else fails, as it has seemed to do most of the time: we have a word for cats because cats exist and we need to talk about them and communicate information about them. We have words for the things we want to communicate about cats because the facts we are talking about exist too. Semantics is about matching words to what exists, and syntax and grammar is about a particular language's ordering and structuring the process of communicating these facts. The relation between the world and language is then simply stated. The world has a structure, and language adjusts itself to that structure. It does so imperfectly and untidily, largely because we are an imperfect and untidy species. This is the commonsense point to which we return, over and over gain, whenever any attempt to depart from it finally fails.[6]

The writer adds wryly, "And yet it never works very well either."

The apparently unresolvable and paradoxical difficulties that seem inherent in this default position are familiar and have generated a huge critical literature.[7] Here is a list of what seem to me the principal recurring and apparently unresolvable troublesome (and also interrelated) topics that arise in the course of default-oriented studies of language.

(1) *Meaning.* In philosophy, the general question about meaning is, "In virtue of what are certain physical marks or noises meaningful linguistic expressions, and in virtue of what does any particular set of marks or noises have the distinctive meaning it does?.... Philosophers have offered a number of sharply competing hypotheses."[8] W. V. O. Quine,

---

[6]   Ellis, 1993, p. 9.
[7]   See, for example, Stroll, 2000; Ellis, 1993; Rorty, 1967; Taylor, 1985; Audi, 1999, pp. 673-676; Harris, 1996, 1998.
[8]   Audi, 1999, p. 673.

a renowned American philosopher and logician[9] who has extensively analyzed the problems of the meaning-referring-naming constellation, refers to 'meaning' as "the baffling word."[10]

(2) *Reference.* "In virtue of what does a linguistic expression designate one or more things in the world?"[11] The identification and discussion of this problem dates back at least to Plato. As one contemporary philosopher put it, "How is it possible to use bits of language to speak about, mention, pick out, or refer to various kinds of things....? This query is the starting point for the philosopher of language."[12] Unorthodox critics, including Ludwig Wittgenstein, even have questioned the legitimacy of the very notion of linguistic reference: "Words in general cannot be made to refer directly to things; the counter-examples are too immediate, too accessible."[13]

(3) *Naming; Names.* For many workers in the field, names and naming are no less problematic than meaning or reference. As the epistemologist, linguist, humanist and novelist Walker Percy says, "What are we to make of this peculiar act of naming?... The longer we think about it, the more mysterious the simplest act of naming becomes.... Just what is this act of denotation?"[14]

It raises logical conundrums (e.g., concerning the existential status of at least some kinds of referred-to entities) that philosophers and linguists have attempted to resolve by, for example, contriving tortured distinctions "between ways of directly referring to features and processes in the world and ways of referring to them

[9] "Today's 'most influential philosopher'"—Hersh,1997, p. 12).
[10] Quine, 1961, pp. 47-48.
[11] Audi, 1999, p. 674.
[12] Stroll, 2000, p. 214.
[13] Davis, 2002, p. 143; re Wittgenstein's position, see Ellis, 1993, pp. 7, 11, 42; also Hunter, 1985, chapter 18 ("How sentences represent").
[14] Percy, 1953, p. 154.

indirectly or in a roundabout way,"[15] or by developing strategies such as Bertrand Russell's so-called theory of definite descriptions.[16] Such efforts have engendered all sorts of esoteric controversies, increasingly arcane, labyrinthine theories, and complex excursions into symbolic logic.

(4) *The structure of scientific language.* From time to time the natural sciences struggle with linguistic issues. A major episode occurred in the heyday of logical positivism when its advocates sought to reframe what they felt was too casual, imprecise, untidy scientific language to make it into a logical system that "formalized or regimented or 'gerrymandered' [language] to produce a transparent picture of its workings."[17] This linguistic project ran into insuperable obstacles and was eventually abandoned as untenable: "linguistics is seen as a science which explains how labels of things (grammatical subjects) and actions (grammatical predicates) can be organized to produce meaningful strings (sentences) which represent how things are in the world. Yet it is well known that this subject-predicate view cannot be developed systematically, and, among other things, it cannot explain how language is used even in science itself."[18]

(5) *Assertions of truth.* The apparently simple matter of what it is about an assertion that makes it true or false remains controversial and elusive in philosophy. There are various theories, the three most prominent types being correspondence theories (truth is a matter of language matching non-linguistic fact), coherence theories (truth is a property of an entire interlocking network of beliefs), and pragmatic theories (truth is what is in some sense good for

---

[15]   Stroll, 2000, p. 214.
[16]   Ibid., especially pp. 11-12, 20-25.
[17]   Bruns, 1987, p. 240; see also Carnap, 1966, chapters 24, 26.
[18]   Pylkkö, 1998, p. 38; see also Stroll, 2000, pp. 54-86; Berger, 1985, pp. 48-49.

us to believe).[19] The complexities and competing contentions regarding the truth value of assertions seem endless.

(6) *Relation to thought.* What is the nature of the relation between language and thought? Recurring, problematic, unresolved questions are: "Does language determine thought? Does thought exist independently of language? Is the character of our experience of the world... determined by the structure of our language?"[20]

(7) *Self-reference, reflexivity.* The capacity of language to refer to itself generates a host of paradoxes, some old and already known to the ancient Greeks, some more recent (e.g., contemporary mathematics' "limitative theorems" such as Gödel's).[21] Reflexivity (the quality, state, or capability of bending back, turning back upon itself) is also the dynamic behind a relatively new formal discipline, the so-called "sociology of scientific knowledge"[22] that examines the role of self-reference in scientific disciplines.

In that regard, one must also recognize that proposing and exploring language is *itself* necessarily a linguistic enterprise, a reflexive activity whose problematic nature typically remains unaddressed within language studies: "Philosophers and linguists in the Western tradition have always taken for granted that there is nothing paradoxical about using language as a tool for the rational description and investigation of language.... [But] the leap from asking questions about what was said to asking questions about the words uttered is a quantum leap."[23] For example, usually it is not even mentioned in standard texts,[24] most

---

[19] Audi, 1999, pp. 929-931; Stroll, 2000, especially chapters 1, 2, 7.
[20] Ellis, 1993, p. 55.
[21] See Lawson, 1985; Scharfstein, 1989; Roberts, 1992. Reflexivity and limitative theorems will be briefly considered in the next chapter.
[22] Ashmore, 1989; Blum and McHugh, 1984.
[23] Harris, 1996, pp. xiv, 31.
[24] E.g., BonJour, 1985; Kim, 1998; Dancy, 1985; Dancy & Sosa, 1992; Chomsky, 2000; Moravia, 1995; Crane, 2001; Melchert, 1995; Stroll, 2000; Audi, 1999, pp. 673-676.

likely because it is baffling and thus an embarrassment to the field. The problems entailed by such meta-linguistic use have not gone entirely unrecognized, however: "Language, symbolization, is the stuff of which our knowledge and awareness of the world are made, the medium through which we see the world. Trying to see it is like trying to see the mirror by which we see everything else;"[25] "What is spoken can only be explained in language, and so in this sense language itself cannot be explained."[26]

## WHY IS THE RECEIVED VIEW PERENNIALLY SO PROBLEMATIC?

When a central subject has constantly raised problematic issues that have been endlessly but unsuccessfully addressed over millennia, one might well suspect that there is something fundamentally wrong about the entire enterprise. In the case of language, we have had hints of what that might be. I have several times broached the idea that perhaps the perpetual difficulties encountered by the many and continuing attempts to understand language have a common core. Perhaps irresolvable difficulties necessarily arise when language is partitioned off, ripped away from its user(s) and from the "things" to which it refers and thus made into a pseudo-independently-existing, pseudo-self-sufficient entity. Perhaps when language is excised from user and world, reified, "dementalized,"[27] when intimate ties between user, world, and language become concealed or ignored, problematic issues follow automatically.

When language is said to have its own existential realm, then it necessarily follows that *the other two domains, world and person, must be non- or pre-linguistic* (or else the

---

25 Percy, 1954, p. 151.
26 Wittgenstein, 1958a, p. 40.
27 Olafson, 2001, p. 48.

assumed ontology becomes an indefensible muddle).[28] Is it not reasonable to expect that all kinds of questions will then be raised about *connections* between elements in these supposedly separate regions? With respect to the *self*, one is bound to wonder about the connection between language and thought, memory, perception, consciousness, to what it is that language about one's "inner state" refers. With respect to the external *world*, questions are raised about the nature of the "relation" between a linguistic statement and a nonlinguistic fact or state of affairs.

In general, what happens is that all the baffling kinds of general questions about connections and the nature of substances raised by the old Cartesian bifurcation into *res extensa/res cogitans* (e.g., How can the void between the mental and physical domain be crossed? Are there really two kinds of substances, or only one, and what are these, really?) reappear in the narrower linguistic context (e.g., how can language refer, link up with "things"? What is it?). In the course of Tallis's critiques of the usual conception of information (see chapter 3) he notes that "once information is uprooted from consciousness—and from an informant or from the experience of being informed and of wanting to be informed—then any kind of nonsense is possible.... Once the concept of information is liberated from the idea of *someone being informed* and from that of *someone doing the informing*, anything is possible."[29] This specific comment can be generalized and applied to all facets of language.

Two other general, and limiting consequences follow from the received, default, segregational view and further contribute to the confused and fragmented state of language studies.[30] First: within Cheshire Cat-laden,

---

[28] For an extended and highly unconventional critique of the premise that the existence and reality of non-linguistic "facts" is an obvious matter, see Heidegger, 2002, especially his Preliminary Considerations.
[29] Tallis, 1998a, pp. 100-101.
[30] That confused and fractured condition and its history are extensively

segregational, default-position-based Cartesianism position, language studies will be pushed inexorably in the direction of a pure knowledge paradigm; thus, Chomsky: "the task of linguistics is to provide a deep account of human language."[31] And second: invariably these studies and views will be approached from an adultocentric, synchronic, ahistorical, rational-calculative, fragmenting perspective.

If severing language from self and world might be responsible at least in part for the continuing, severe problems that plague mainstream language studies, it could be useful to explore how one might restore the severed or ignored ties, the ruptured primary holism and its traces in adulthood.

## ADULTOCENTRIC ATTEMPTS TO RECONNECT LANGUAGE AND PERSON

### Martin Heidegger

Heidegger's less enframing, more unitary conception of language has been introduced in Part I, particularly in the chapters that considered Bruns, Olafson, and Pylkkö. Heidegger distinguishes between two classes of language and corresponding language use: language as conceptualized within and used by the sciences and other formal disciplines, and language that is "the house of being," the proper environment for (non-metaphysical, in Heidegger's sense) philosophical, meditative thinking. Heidegger calls the former "apophantic": "predicative, objectifying, conceptual, methodical... in the form of a categorical statement... presuppos[ing] the Cartesian-Kantian axis of subject and object."[32] The second, contrasting vision is characterized as hermeneutic, poetic,

---

described and documented in Ellis, 1993, especially chapter 1.

[31] Maher and Groves, 1997, p. 4.

[32] Bruns, 1987, pp. 246-247.

figurative language, language that is intimately intertwined with authentic *Dasein*, being-in-the-world. Heidegger is not at all concerned with linguistic issues that might arise within or pertain to particular formal/scientific disciplines (e.g., linguistics, psychology, physics), other than their noxious consequences when apophantic language is used outside its proper domain of application. He seems to think that in the proper (i.e., scientific) contexts the use of predicative, objectifying language is appropriate and unproblematic. Therefore to my knowledge he does not address the kinds of linguistic issues I want to emphasize, namely, those pertaining to language as it is used professionally *in various disciplines*. ("New ideas in the theory of language do not simply have an impact on other fields, they can revolutionize them.")[33] Even so, Heidegger's work might be relevant in these contexts. We have seen one significant example of a plan to use it in just such an milieu, namely, Pylkkö's proposal to transmute Heideggerian thought about authentic language into a form that could be applied in his vision of an adogmatic, ametaphysical, yet still naturalized science.

## John Ellis

In his *Language, Thought, and Logic,* John Ellis after surveying the fragmented and unproductive history and state of language study identifies three "Initial missteps in the theory of language":

> The first... is the assumption that the purpose of language is communication... [the second is that] the movement of thought is assumed to be from simple to complex, where the simple will explain the complex but not itself be altered by what the complex shows. The third misstep is the assumption that the verbal categories of a language serve to group like things together.[34]

---

[33]  Ellis, 1993, p. 1.
[34]  Ibid., pp. 15-16.

His analyses are interesting and informative, and have two general points in common with the critiques I seek to develop: an awareness of the damaging fragmentation of language that is implicit in mainstream practices (those that he characterizes as predicated on the default condition of linguistic theory—see above), and an intuition that a genetic approach may be integrative. The concept he proposes to apply in the endeavor to achieve such an integration is *categorization*, for Ellis "the heart of language," the act logically prior to communication. He claims that one must first categorize one's experiences before one can communicate, and for him this is not a simple matter:

> Before either communicating or coding could occur something else must have happened, and that something must be fundamental to the nature of language: a framework that could allow operations such as coding and communicating to take place must first have been established. That framework must presuppose categorization and abstraction.... To say something about a situation is to place it among other possible situations, and this requires not a set of labels but a system of categories.[35]

Contrary to the received view, then, learning names of things, learning nouns and their referential meanings, learning grammar, are *not* foundational in learning language. They are conspicuous but superficial aspects and manifestations of much deeper and more complex underlying processes.

Though it furnishes valuable insights, Ellis's approach to integration differs fundamentally from mine. Since for Ellis categorization is logic-based, his restorative strategy is rational-calculative, epistemological rather than onto-logical, and remains adultocentric. His brief discussion of language acquisition is a telling example of that adultocentrism. At one point in his speculation he con-

---

[35] Ibid., pp. 27-28.

structs a hypothetical situation involving "two individuals who do not as yet have a language,"[36] but these prelinguistic individuals, the potential speakers A and B, are adults. He does not consider individual maturation; his approach is *genetic but not ontogenetic*; it remains "intralogical."[37] A second, related difference is that he implicitly adopts the usual assumption that the world can be partitioned into linguistic and non-linguistic elements (including besides "facts" or "states of affairs" the theorizer, speaker, observer, or communicator). His integration can be seen as the attempt to link what for him are separate elements or constituents.

It seems fair to say that Ellis believes the nature of language can be illuminated adequately without one's having to acknowledge or consider any mysterious, aconceptual, alogical, holistic aspects of origins including the origins of the self. In Heideggerian terms, Ellis takes for granted that an apophantic rather than an ametaphysical, poetic, meditative, hermeneutical approach to understanding language and restoring its ties to users will do in language studies.

## Roy Harris

For many decades Roy Harris, Professor Emeritus of General Linguistics, University of Oxford, has been presenting extensive, in-depth critiques of what he calls the "segregational" (see above) or "orthodox" position,[38] essentially the same as the received view or default perspective. Overall, his critiques echo the themes and objections we have already encountered: that linguistics and philosophy of language are fragmented fields with a fragmented subject, that they make wrong basic assumptions, pursue the wrong questions, and so on.

---

[36] Ibid., p. 27.
[37] Olafson, 1995, p. 6.
[38] Harris, 1981; 1986; 1987a and b; 1995; 1996; 2002.

However, his wide-ranging critiques reflect an expert linguist's specialized competencies, interests, and concerns. The fragmentations of language to which he objects include those created by the usual, familiar categorizations (e.g., the traditional "parts of speech," or structural hierarchies), but also by the linguist's or philosopher's more esoteric distinctions, such as those between types and token, use and mention, *langue* and *parole*, or direct and indirect reference.[39]

Harris's criticisms of various classifications that are commonplace in language studies are only one aspect of his critiques. He also objects to classifications that fracture the field of language study itself. He reports that the key events occurred in Athens in the fourth century BC. There

> we come to the first major crossroads that marks a professional parting of the ways between philosophers [also called "logicians"] and grammarians [also called "linguists"] in the ancient world. Roughly speaking, the grammarians opted for treating the parts of speech as mere word-classification.... The philosophers, on the other hand, opted for treating the parts of speech as reflecting operations of the mind.[40]

This basic dichotomy multiplied because it came to be believed that

> speech is an extremely complex business; far too complex to be dealt with from any single academic perspective. Consequently, it is not merely inevitable but essential that different disciplines should divide it up between them if any progress at all is to be made in its investigation. Thus while it is true that the rhetorician, the logician, the grammarian, the phonetician, the lexicographer, the conversation analyst, the speech therapist, etc. pay attention only to limited aspects of the subject, and ignore those which do not fall within their chosen province, this is

---

[39] Harris, 1996, chapter 1.
[40] Ibid., p. 29.

actually the best way of proceeding. Otherwise, we should have simply a muddle.[41]

Harris continues dryly, "The short answer to that is that we have a muddle anyway."

He also points out in passing that linguists and logicians have questionable motives for using this segregational approach:

> Segregational thinking has dominated modern linguistics and modern philosophy. This is no coincidence. For segregational thinking and segregational terminology are admirably suited to the academic politics of both disciplines. To the outside world, the linguist and the philosopher wish to present themselves professionally as authorities in charge of certain areas of investigation. For that is how academic disciplines are justified (and financed).... By treating—and constantly referring to— words, sentences, etc. as linguistic objects existing in their own right, it becomes possible to create the impression—and to convince oneself—that these objects provide materials for scientific investigation, just as physical objects do for the physicist and chemical substances do for the chemist.[42]

To survive well, to be respected and deemed scientific, a discipline must have its identified, sanctified, special orthodox objects of study and must vigorously defend their legitimacy. The presence of powerful sustaining motives suggests, then, that no matter how well reasoned or supported they may be, radical critiques of received views of language will find little support, particularly within the targeted professions, and are likely to fade away, sooner or later, having been defensively defused. (I reconsider motivational issues briefly in chapter 14.)

To counter all these kinds of fracturing processes and practices, Harris for some time has been developing and

---

[41]  Ibid., pp. 41-42.
[42]  Ibid., pp. 12-13; for analogous comments about similarly motivated defensive conservatism in mathematics, see Davis, 2002, p. 156.

advocating the alternative approach he calls *integrational linguistics:*

> The point of departure, in an integrationist perspective, is not the existence of complex cultural objects called 'languages' but, simply, the attempts by human beings to integrate whatever they are capable of doing into the various activity patterns we call 'communication'.... For the integrationist, we are starting from the wrong end if we suppose that linguistic communication presupposes languages. The right theoretical priority is exactly the reverse: *languages presuppose communication.*[43]

For the integrationist "communication is a much more complex matter than can be dealt with by saying that it requires the successful transmission of some message... from one individual to another..."[44] For Harris, it refers to an exceedingly rich, complex, multifaceted and multidimensional process that includes "biomechanical, macrosocial and circumstantial parameters of communication."[45]

Harris's integrationist approach is aimed at restoring the lost connections and distinctions, the many dimensions of variation that are suppressed in the segregationalist's desiccated and rupturing one-dimensional theoretical abstractions. His principal strategy is to place language studies into the rich fabric and context of actual living. Nevertheless, like Ellis's, his general approach remains adultocentric, intralogical, essentially epistemological rather than ontological let alone ontogenetic.

That to me seems like a significant shortcoming. I submit that any understanding of language that is truly integrational needs to attend to ontogenesis, because that is where the roots of the holistic ties are to be found. The undoing of fragmentation ought to begin at the beginning. Accordingly, I propose to start with a fresh look at how the

---

[43] Harris, 1989, pp. 4-5.
[44] Ibid., p. 5.
[45] Ibid., p. 41; Harris's "communication" is quite unlike Ellis's.

child acquires its first language. My premise is that insights into how language originates in a person could broaden and deepen our understanding of what language is—and also what might be equally important, of what it is *not*. I suggest that under the premise that we begin life as undifferentiated beings, it seems reasonable to suppose that revisiting this unitary starting point, the holistic phase before various ruptures and differentiations begin, might hold some clues about how one might go about restoring the rupturing that attends the default positions in language studies. To establish a context for this exploration of ontogenesis I will first outline the principal ways in which a child's first language acquisition is usually understood.

## MAINSTREAM EXPLANATIONS OF FIRST LANGUAGE ACQUISITION

### Cognitive-Behavioral Approaches

Chapter 9 outlined two mainstream conceptions of how children mature in general: cognitive-behavioral, and innatist. These general hypotheses become specific to language acquisition and development. The first type conceptualizes and explains that process in terms of standard learning theories. The basic idea is that in principle, learning one's first language is pretty much like learning anything else. No special explanatory mechanisms are called for: "most psychologists, at least implicitly, assume that some version of a 'behaviorist' account of the growth of vocabulary would suffice to explain how children learn their initial vocabulary."[46] Specifically, for most traditional theorists of this stripe learning one's first language is in all essentials just like learning a second language—a hypothesis often ascribed to Saint Augustine. It has been called into question by Wittgenstein, among

---

[46] Terrace,1987, p.127.

others.[47] Still, the premise is widely regarded as established fact. The well-known story of how the young Helen Keller, deaf and blind, came to "acquire" language is often cited as an example; I shall return to her story below.

This Augustinian view harbors significant difficulties, as I have said. In *second*-language learning, ostension, the act of pointing, either figuratively by means of language ("bachelor" means "an unmarried male"), or literally by means of a gesture of some kind, is the chief mechanism. The ostensive definition is the way one learns the meaning of words, phrases, sentences. Now, when one observes a child learning its first language, it is easy to think that the process is essentially the same. The young child seems to "learn" (itself not exactly an unproblematic term) the meaning of "words," usually of simple nouns, by learning that "doggie" or "daddy" means *that* (pointing). Almost invariably, parents will celebrate a child's first utterance, considering it to be a significant milestone, and teaching the meaning of individual words remains an important component in subsequent language education.

This scenario has major problems, however. First of all, as Ellis pointed out in his discussion of communication and categorizing, equating learning a language with learning the meaning and reference of individual words is suspect. He says that learning actually involves categorization, a much more complex, multidimensional concept and process. Ellis also is critical of the premise that simple models and explanations can be elaborated, that they can become the basis for explanations of complex phenomena (the second of his "three initial missteps"—see above). It is a mistake to think that "understanding" how a child "learns the meaning of simple words" will enable one to understand also how persons learn the complex aspects of language. (The principles remain the same.)

---

[47]   Harris, 1996, pp. 98-100.

These considerations raise difficulties for the Augustinian hypothesis, but there is an even more basic, more telling problem. The hypothesis relies heavily if not exclusively on the mechanism of ostension, presumably the prime device that enables the prelinguistic infant to link single terms and corresponding external entities. However, "as Wittgenstein saw, when we simply point to something, it is not clear what we are pointing at unless we accompany the pointing *with language*,"[48] "Wittgenstein, who wrote more extensively on ostensive definition than any other philosopher, held this picture of language to be profoundly misleading;"[49] he noted that "one might say: the ostensive definition explains the use—the meaning—of the word when the overall role of the word in language is clear."[50] In short, "an ostensive definition is of use only *within* a language-game, though superficially it looks like that elusive entity, a way to step outside language. It is no help in getting into the game in the first place;"[51] Ostensive definitions cannot explain how one's first language is acquired to begin with.

## Innatist Approaches

When we turn to innatist developmental hypotheses, in linguistics Noam Chomsky is their principal advocate, as was mentioned in chapter 9. He posits "the existence in every human being of internal mental structures that do not derive from experience."[52] Specifically, he has a *Theory of Universal Grammar*: "The human brain has an innate language faculty and part of the biological endowment is a system of principles common to all languages, which is the topic of the theory."[53] According to that hypothesis, the core

---

[48] Ellis, 1993, 128n1; see also Abel, 1976, pp. 227-229.
[49] Dancy & Sosa, 1992, pp. 315, 316.
[50] Wittgenstein, 1958b, §30.
[51] Melchert, 1995, p. 582.
[52] Stroll, 2000, p. 204.
[53] Maher and Groves, 1997, p. 3.

aspects of language, for example the nature of its composition (it is constructed from parts of speech taken from basic categories), or especially, its logical-grammatical, rule-bound structure, are common elements built into all humans and already in some meaningful sense present at birth. An important constituent of that machinery is the "language acquisition device," ("LAD")[54] a universal element that enables the child to acquire a specific first language.

Almost from its inception Chomsky's framework has been widely acclaimed but also extensively criticized from a variety of perspectives. The theory has been charged with harboring conceptual confusions—for example, with fallaciously equating language and sentences; with confusing what *speakers* (including language-acquiring children) actually do with what *grammarians* do with their observations (their interpretation of observations project their theories onto the phenomena); or, with conflating utterances and sentences (for example, automatically and without further ado treating and analyzing a young child's *uttering* "want!" as a rudimentary form of saying the *sentence* "I want *x*," thus gratuitously superposing grammatical structure).[55] The basis of the Theory of Universal Grammar has been called shaky: The universal rules are said to be stored inside, but

> where 'inside'? In the brain, we are told, where they are 'represented'. What form do these cerebral 'representations' take? That, it seems, unfortunately no one knows. Perhaps one day neurophysiologists will find out for us. Any simpleton who asks at this point how we can be sure about these rules in the brain if no one knows how they are 'represented' will be told that it stands to reason that the brain must have such 'representations' because otherwise no one could possibly have 'internalised' the rules, and unless the rules were 'internalised' a person could not have

---

[54] Robinson, 1975, pp. 69-73; Chomsky, 2000, pp. 81, 86.
[55] Robinson, 1975.

'mastered' them, and therefore by definition would not know languages. With this compellingly circular demonstration the simpleton is expected to rest content.[56]

## Mixed Models

There also are hybrid models that combine features of both types. A recent text claims that

> development of linguistic abilities is linked to maturation of cognitive processes.... Children learn language primarily through their own cognitive efforts utilizing the genetic potential that is part of their human endowment. Noam Chomsky has stated that a fundamental question in the study of language is to account for a 'speaker's ability to produce and understand instantly new sentences that are not similar to those previously heard.... It seems plain that language acquisition is based on the child's discovery of what, from a formal point of view is a deep and abstract theory—a generative grammar of his/her language'.... The first step in acquiring language is learning to differentiate and articulate sounds occurring in one's language.... Children are clearly able to understand language before they speak their own words.[57]

## PSYCHODYNAMICALLY INFORMED ONTOGENESIS AND LANGUAGE ACQUISITION

In chapter 9 I mentioned the developmental discontinuities inherent in the undifferentiated neonate model, and also acknowledged that the differentiations that appear in the course of maturation simply cannot be explained scientifically, formally, within that model. (I also pointed out that other models, too, cannot really explain this emergence, that they offer obfuscating pseudo-explanations and promissory notes that ultimately are just as problematic.) We have already encountered the claim (e.g.,

---

[56]  Harris, 1987, p. 131. Other critiques abound—see, for example, Hunter, 1973, pp. 146-169; Tallis, 1998b, pp. 87-90.

[57]  Bowman, 1993, pp. 243-245; similar explanation are offered in Golinkoff and Hirsh-Pasek ,1999; de Boysson-Bardies, 1999.

in discussions of Heidegger's thought) that one cannot *step outside* language, that one cannot have direct, non-linguistic sensual access to some non-linguistic domain or entities; the apparently reasonable, common-sense bifurcation of our universe into language and (non-linguistic) fact ultimately turns out to be highly problematic and fundamentally unsupportable.[58] One could say, then, that the puzzle of how the child acquires its first language is the inverse or mirror image or complement of that puzzle. Now the reverse problem is: Not having language in the first place, how is it possible for the neonate eventually to *step inside* it? The question of how the child acquires the "requisite linguistic proficiency.... [remains] the metalinguistic puzzle which underlies the perennial question of the 'origin of language' (at least as posed within the Western tradition from Plato via Condillac down to the present day)."[59] There is no logically viable, satisfactory way of conceptualizing the step from having no language to acquiring its rudiments—a major instance of what one thinker called an "ontological discontinuity."[60] If one is honest, one must admit that emergence remains a baffling phenomenon—a fact usually covered over by means of scientistic pseudo-explanations, or defused with the promise that scientific progress surely will provide the answers, some day (supposedly, by fiat, the only viable possibility, given the scientistic premise that all else would be mystagogy). Emergence is little more than a term, and its explanation is little more than a hope for the future.

I now want to return briefly to Helen Keller's story, because it illustrates how tempting it is to try to rationalize this transition, and how easy it is to think that one has done so. Several authors have maintained that the deaf and blind Helen Keller's often recounted luminous experience

---

58  Heidegger, 2002.
59  Harris, 1996, p. 98.
60  Schumacher, 1977, p. 17.

illustrates and explains a child's mysterious leap into language. Supposedly it was a particular combination of sensual experience (the flow of water over her hand) and her teacher's spelling of a word that one day, one moment, led to young Helen's sudden realization "that *the things around her had names.*"[61] The strong implication in such accounts is that this step shows and explains how the process of first-language acquisition works in general, that Helen's experience is a prototypical description and explanation of how the change from not having to having language occurs: To acquire one's first language is to link words and (non-linguistic) things, sensations, and this happens by some combination of sensuous perception and cognitive act. We have seen that in any case, the premise that such a linking constitutes the essence of first language leaning is itself suspect, but what these accounts specifically ignore are two critical and related further problematic aspects of Helen's situation that are obvious to any psychodynamically-informed clinician: first, Helen already was twenty months old when she lost her hearing and sight as the result of scarlet fever—interestingly enough, a fact not mentioned in the usual retellings of her dramatic moment, and second, she was eight years old at the time of her linguistic illumination.

Compared to the neonate a twenty-month-old child is already developmentally quite advanced of course, well on its way to being able to make all kinds of differentiations and discriminations. From an ontogenetic perspective a child that age is already in many ways "old," mature, certainly when compared to the neonate. It not only can navigate, elaborately relate to others, manipulate the environment, but has rudimentary language. What is most salient here is that by this time the child certainly has

---

[61]  Harris, 1996, pp. 100-101; also Gill, 1989, p. 115; Percy, 1954, pp. 34-39, 150-158.

already ("somehow") acquired the *idea* of language and thus has passed well beyond that first mysterious developmental step into language on which I have been focusing. Furthermore, at eight, when Helen's illumination is said to have occurred, she was able to build not only on the dormant, already previously developed pre- and post-linguistic and other experiential, differentiating achievements of a more or less normally developed twenty month old, but also was able to draw on the eight-year-old's multitude of structured experiences that occurred in the intervening years between the time of her catastrophic loss of hearing and sight and the moment of illumination. Helen's story does not at all resolve the key problem that "one cannot learn a language unless one has a language."[62] Her "aha" experience at the age of eight sheds no light at all on the fundamental problem of first language acquisition.

I have said that psychodynamic thought cannot furnish a "rational-calculative" explanation of language acquisition or, more generally, a viable scientific explanation of what language "is," although some varieties of psychoanalytic theory do claim to have explicative formal models.[63] In my view, it is not only more honest but more productive in the long run for a discipline to admit the presence of such basic mysteries. Even Freud, whose aversion to lack of structure I mentioned in chapter 9, while discussing dream interpretation made the remarkable admission that "There is often a passage in even the most thoroughly interpreted dream which has to be left obscure.... This is the dream's navel, the spot where it reaches down into the unknown."[64] His sound clinical intuition overrode his defensive and culturally-conditioned need to theorize. I believe that the potential for acknowledging and working with such imponderable aspects of psychological life is one of

---

[62]  Young, 2002, p. 99.
[63]  See Kovel, 1978; Loewald, 1980, chapter 12.
[64]  Freud, 1965, p. 564.

psychoanalysis' all-too-seldom appreciated strengths. At its best, it does not try to explain, or explain away, the inexplicable, but does try to take it into account and to work with it.

In the version of psychoanalytic thought I have in mind, the origins of language cannot be conceptually or intellectually separated from the origins of anything else that evolves with maturation, a position I already introduced in chapter 9. That does mean that under the proposed ontogenetic and holistic model, *all* aspects of adult being-in-the-world, *all* the so-called more adult faculties that become differentiated and apparent with maturation (e.g., cognition, perception, imagination, memory), are considered as having at one time been indistinguishable from one another. A further assumption is that after differentiations, these various faculties and competencies always still continue to carry traces of their common, unitary origin—*and that these traces matter in later life*, that they manifest in various and usually subtle but often important ways. These ontogenetic generalities hold for language in particular. It, too, in some deep sense remains "the same" as perception, consciousness, differentiation of self and other and of inside and outside, proprioception, sensuality; it, too, continues to carry traces of that common origin, and those traces have consequences in one's later life. For example, this haunting legacy may explain at least in part why in so many adult situations magical properties are ascribed to language (e.g., some words are evil and bad and must not be used in polite society; promises, or oaths, may be sacred; fights break out over some name calling).

## IMPLICATIONS FOR LANGUAGE STUDIES

As we shall see in the remaining chapters, the ontogenetically and holistically informed view of language that I have sketched can have implications for other disciplines, but what does it imply for those fields, primarily linguistics and philosophy of language, whose principal subject matter is specifically language itself?

If the critiques of the received view are valid, if the segregational/default positions cannot be relied on, then these fields would no longer have an obvious subject matter. If workers can no longer maintain that there are linguistic objects, meaningful, independently existing linear sequences assembled from independent basic building blocks according to structural-logical rules of grammar, then what ought to be the subject matter and goals of linguistics and philosophy of language? What might replace the old *raisons d'etre*: the study of linguistic objects, conducted within a pure knowledge paradigm? Roy Harris notes that "no one sat down and first asked 'How can speech best be studied?'"[65] Perhaps it is time that someone did ask, and not only about speech but about language in general.

Thus, one obvious consequence of the critiques is that it asks the fields of linguistic studies to reconsider their undertaking, their purposes, methodologies, and the ontology of their situation. This is a large order, and realistically I do not expect these entrenched, vested enterprises seriously to consider undertaking the kind of massive, baffling reexamination I am suggesting. Harris' proposal for an integrational linguistics[66] could be seen as a much tamer version of the revision I am proposing. If a relatively modest proposal for basic change coming from a prominent, highly qualified academician in the field is not enthusiastically welcomed, one can guess how a radical proposal like mine, and coming from an outsider, would be received. Nevertheless, the need for such a drastic

---

[65]  Harris, 1996, p. 42.
[66]  Harris, 1998.

reexamination and revision seems to be the prime implication of the work I have been outlining.

A second consequence comes into view. Anomalous pragmatism suggests that even though the received view of language may at bottom be deeply flawed and indefensible, still, there may be situations in which its study remains appropriate. One can draw an analogy with physics. It seems likely that in a fundamental sense the two major contemporary theories, relativity and quantum theory, displace their classical predecessors. Yet, it is well known and taken for granted that in many applications the old theories not only are adequate, but also the only ones that are viable. (Think of trying to calculate the path of a billiard ball quantum mechanically.) One continues to study and apply classical theory—but in its proper domains of application, and with a deep appreciation of its limitations. Thus, the second question raised by the linguistic critiques is: Are there situations in language studies where it makes sense, where it remains legitimate, to continue treating language along the lines of the standard received view, even when one knows that basically this old default view is wrong or at least seriously flawed? If so, what are these kinds of situations, how can they be identified and defended, and what would the goals of such studies be?

These two-pronged implications for language studies of the combined ontogenetic and anomalously pragmatic points critiques are prototypical and generalizable. In the chapters that follow I shall try to show the parallel implications in other fields. In those other contexts, too, I shall be questioning traditional missions, subject matter, and methodologies.

# 12

# RESIDUE II: MATHEMATICS

*Logic can be provided with a foundation only if the nature of the acting subject has been fully clarified.... [Heidegger] sees that the attempt to provide epistemological grounding for our beliefs and practices cannot avoid dealing with the ontological status of the entities posited in such grounding.*

> ~ Charles Guignon, *Heidegger and the Problem of Knowledge*

*Logic alone leads nowhere because it starts nowhere; sensing must be involved.*

> ~ Bruce Holbrook, *The Stone Monkey*

## PRELIMINARY CONSIDERATIONS

### The Subject and Its Objects

Mathematics is a huge and burgeoning discipline. In 1868 the field comprised 38 subcategories (e.g., algebra, probability, analytic geometry, theory of functions); by 1979 the number had grown to approximately 3400.[1] What, then, *is* this field? Reuben Hersh, the author of a recent book that asks this same question, reports in his Preface that many years ago he "discovered the classic, *What is Mathematics?* by Richard Courant and Herbert Robbins. They never answered their question.... I was still left asking, 'But what is mathematics, really?'"[2] Apparently although just about everyone has at least a vague idea about what mathematics

---

[1]  Davis and Hersh, 1981, pp. 29-30.
[2]  Hersh, 1997, p. xi. (This actually is the title of his book.)

"is," still, for mathematicians and philosophers there seems to be no simple answer.

Perhaps it would be more instructive to look at its "objects of study" instead. In a way these are easy to identify for the general public; they are such "things" as numbers, geometrical shapes, sets, and surfaces. Yet when one starts to look professionally it quickly becomes obvious that here, too, what they "are" also is problematic and controversial for the professionals: "As everyone who has followed it knows, the debate on the foundations of mathematics has never come to any generally acceptable conclusion."[3] There are a number of different positions on this issue, but it seems that there are three principal alternative views: Platonism, formalism, and constructivism. The *Platonist* regards mathematical objects as already existing in a separate, timeless, unchanging "third" realm,[4] neither mental nor physical. Consequently, mathematics is seen almost as an empirical investigation of natural phenomena: the worker in pure mathematics has something like a special visual ability to see into, and investigate the entities and relationships that exist in this realm. Under this position, mathematics is an exploration of the strange inhabitants of this strange realm. The *formalist* regards mathematics as a game that, much like chess, is played with freely invented objects according to contrived and arbitrarily imposed rules. The emphasis is on creation, on a certain kind of meaninglessness (in the same sense that invented games are meaningless outside their field of play). The *constructivist* "regards the natural numbers as the fundamental datum of mathematics... from which all meaningful mathematical notions must be

---

[3]  Scharfstein, 1980, p. 21. See also Hersh, 1997, chapters 1,10-13; Notturno, 1985; Klenk, 1976, especially chapter 1; Katz, 1998; Stroll, 2000, chapters 2, 5, 6, 7; Audi, 1999, pp. 681-684; Dancy and Sosa, 1992, pp. 270-276.

[4]  Notturno, 1985.

constructed."[5] Here the emphasis is on logical processes, on rules and assumptions that define the starting points (axioms, fundamental building blocks) from which constructions into more elaborate "objects" proceed.

Ontological/epistemological issues in mathematics are complex and remain controversial. Nevertheless, it seems that currently there is a broad consensus among working mathematicians: "Most writers on the subject seem to agree that the typical working mathematician is a Platonist on weekdays and a formalist on Sundays."[6] That is, on weekdays the assumption is that mathematical objects and rules have a separate, independent existence so that mathematics is a work of investigation and discovery of that preexisting reality, but when mathematicians are challenged by the philosopher this working position becomes embarrassing and hard to defend. The mythical aspects of Platonism are difficult to justify in an age that prides itself on hard-nosed scientific realism. It is difficult to take seriously and defend a belief in the existence of a realm that lies beyond ordinary perception and yet one whose contents (the mathematical "objects, laws, inferences) are somehow visible to the mathematician's inner eye and accessible to exploration. So, on "Sundays," the mathematician becomes a more scientifically acceptable, respectable formalist.

## Mathematical Segregationalism

Mathematical segregationalism, the notion that the objects of study of the field have a separate, independent existence from people and follow their own laws, exactly parallels the linguistic segregationalism that was a principal concern of the last chapter. The historical roots can be traced at least as far back as the era of the German mathematical

---

5    Davis and Hersh, 1981, p. 393.
6    Davis and Hersh, 1981, p. 321.

astronomer Johannes Kepler (1571-1630). He saw mathematical relations as "nearly physical manifestations of God's fully coordinated creation"[7] and therefore existing independently of humans. As a manifestation of God's presence, such relations (e.g., numerical aspects exhibited by the behavior of astral bodies) were even seen as causal agents.

Mathematical material is an object of study that is once again seen and treated by its field as severed from human beings:

> Mathematics consists of concepts.... [They] have their own life.... When once born they obey laws all their own.... 2 + 2 really is 4 in reality....
>
> From living experience we know two facts: Fact 1: Mathematical objects are created by humans. Not arbitrarily, but from activity with existing mathematical objects, and from the needs of science and daily life. Fact 2: Once created, mathematical objects can have properties that are difficult for us to discover.... Once created and communicated, mathematical objects are there.... *We can choose a problem to work on, but we can't choose what the answer should be.*[8]

It is evident that even the formalist believes that once some branch of mathematics has been invented, the inventor no longer needs to be—indeed, may be—kept in the picture. At any rate, in mathematics persons are seen as superfluous: "But what about the fact that two plus two is four. Surely, this fact does not depend on human beings;"[9] "everyone accepts the rules of arithmetic as valid in themselves."[10]

### Indifference

There is universal agreement that most working mathematicians do not care much about philosophical

---

[7]   Harvey, 1989, p. 14.
[8]   Hersh, 1997, pp. 15, 16, 140.
[9]   Grossman, 1992, p. 11.
[10]  Scharfstein,1980, p. 48.

questions or issues concerning their field:
"Mathematicians,... like other scientists, typically conduct
their professional business with little interest in the
philosopher's concern with the nature of numbers, sets,
propositions, sentences, and so on.... As I see it, philosophy
is not necessary to provide the underpinnings of
mathematical practice, but only to provide understanding of
it.... [there is] a general malaise about the philosophy of
mathematics that stems from doubts that any philosophical
position can provide an acceptable epistemology and an
acceptable ontology for mathematics;"[11] "Between the
philosopher's attitude toward the issue of reality and that of
the mathematician there is this essential difference: for the
philosopher the issue is paramount; the mathematician's
love for reality is purely platonic;"[12] "One can spend a
lifetime working on mathematics without ever having any
idea whether mathematical items exist, nor does one have
to care about such a question;"[13] "I know of no practical
consequence of this dispute [about the existential status of
mathematic's objects], nor any way to settle it.... on the
principles of mathematical proof they [formalists and
Platonists] have no quarrel."[14]

## Can/Should Mathematics Ignore Ontology?

In my view, the field of mathematics embodies and exhibits
precisely the same kinds of problematic Cheshire
Cat/adultocentristic aspects criticized in the language study
fields. That is hardly surprising, since mathematicians (and
most others) regard mathematics as a "formal language
made up of a vocabulary and a syntax."[15] Furthermore,

---

[11]   Katz, 1998, pp. 5, 119, xxx.
[12]   Dantzig, 1954, p. 231.
[13]   Rota, 1997, p. 161.
[14]   Hersh, 1997, pp. 179,180, 139.
[15]   Cryan, Shatil and Mayblin, 2001, p. 52.

> it is not just that mathematics is frequently compared to or seen as a language.... It is a language with an extremely important function, that of expressing patterns which correspond to an objective or external scientific reality.... By saying that mathematics is a language, what is the western tradition saying? That it is systematic. That it is symbolic. Neither of these properties would trouble most mathematicians or linguists.[16]

In mathematical work, the language of mathematics is treated according to the received segregational view of language. Consequently, one can expect the familiar kinds of difficulties to surface in that field. Its supposedly independently-existing inert objects, too, actually are Cheshire Cat residues and are dealt with according to the usual adultocentric, segregationalist, segmenting, reifying, alienating (Enframing) manner.

Anomalous pragmatism suggests that dealing with one's subject matter according to this view may be harmless or even productive in some contexts but not in others. The question is, when it comes to mathematics, which is the case? My wager is that there will be important instances where predicating mathematical work on the Cheshire Cat position is detrimental, limiting; then, reexamining and rethinking the subject from a novel ontogenetically-grounded holistic position could prove to be useful even for the working mathematician. I am not sure that this will be so, that there will be useful consequences for the mathematician, but I believe the possibility is worth exploring. What I plan to do, then, is to bring to bear an ontogenetically-based holistic critique on some aspects of two major mathematical areas: (1) *arithmetic* (not to be confused with the rote skill we learn in grade school), and (2) *self-referential logical paradoxes*. I hope thereby to raise some new kinds of questions and shed a different light on old ones.

---

[16] Davis, 2002, pp. 140-141.

## Are the Proposed Approaches Psychologistic?

For many, even most, mathematicians and philosophers, "psychologism" in mathematics has been anathema. A well known example is the case of Edmund Husserl and Gottlob Frege. Husserl was a thoroughly trained mathematician before he turned to philosophy, and his early approach to mathematics took subjective factors into account, attempting "to reconcile the objectivity of mathematics, and of all science in general, with a psychological foundation for logic."[17] When the prestigious logician Frege charged him with "psychologizing," (a notion very briefly introduced in chapter 1, meaning, very roughly, converting mathematics into a subdiscipline of psychology, explaining mathematics and its laws in terms of psychology's "laws of the mind") Husserl apparently was intimidated to the extent that he "faithfully avoided psychologism ever after."[18] The sanctioned anti-psychologistic view is that it is not only possible but mandatory to separate the notion of truth and falsehood from consciousness, under the dogmatic axiom that "truths may exist in the absence of anything—truth-speakers, languages, consciousness or even material objects"[19]—plainly a Cheshire Cat position on mathematics and its subject matter.

Since the ontogenetically-based holism I advocate does strive to reunite or reconnect persons with alienated Cheshire Cat residues, it may very well seem that I will be advocating and practicing some variety of psychologizing in mathematics; after all, in general I do want to bring psychological matters (back) into the picture. However, that is not at all the same as psychologizing if by that term one means replacing the laws of one (segregational) discipline, mathematics, with the laws of another, psychology (also a

---

[17]   Quoted in Tallis, 1999b, p. 59.
[18]   Hersh, 1997, p. 166.
[19]   Tallis, 1999b, p. 9; also p. 63n10.

segregational discipline, as we will see in the next chapter). I will be in a better position to consider this issue and criticism and the conclusion of this chapter, after I have outlined my proposed approaches and critiques.

## ARITHMETIC: THE RECEIVED VIEW

Although we all know and use arithmetic (mostly in the form in which we learned it in grade school), those who have not studied it in the context of advanced mathematics are unlikely to appreciate either the complex meanings it holds for mathematicians, or its far-reaching importance in that field: "all classical mathematics can be built from natural numbers....there's hardly any mathematics that doesn't depend on the real numbers."[20]

Let us take a brief look at what 'arithmetic' means to the mathematician, and at some of the different mainstream conceptions of the nature of the natural numbers (the whole numbers 0, 1, 2,...).

> Very roughly, 'arithmetic'... is high school algebra (but limited to positive whole numbers).... More technically, 'arithmetic' is defined as the set of truths and falsehoods expressible using a certain specified vocabulary: symbols for positive whole numbers (1, 2, 3,...), "plus," "times," "to the power of," parentheses, "equals," variables (x, y, z,...), and some simple logical concepts [not," "and," "or," "if-then," "for every (number)," and "for some (number)"]. [21]

Thus, according to this view arithmetic is a kind of theory, and "a mathematical theory consists of axioms, primitive notions, notation, and rules on inference.... [But] axiomatic presentations... may vary radically."[22] (Axioms are "principles [that] are just taken to be true.")[23]

---

[20]  Hersh, 1997, pp.142,155.
[21]  Gensler, 1984, p. 2.
[22]  Rota, 1997, pp. 109, 151.
[23]  Gensler, 1984, p. 2.

Arithmetic, then, like natural language, "has" syntax, grammar, meaning, reference. Numbers are its atomic constituents or elements, the basic building blocks that assemble into larger, meaningful concatenated units. We can readily recognize the close parallels between the received views of arithmetic and the received view of language discussed earlier, particularly in chapter 11. Therefore virtually everything that was said in the preceding critiques applies across the board to mathematics as well (e.g., it is segregational, adultocentric, has Cheshire Cat residues as its objects of study, follows the pure knowledge paradigm).

What about the numbers themselves? What "are" they? The views vary. Aristotle explained numbers as abstractions.[24] The prominent German mathematician David Hilbert believed that "all positive whole numbers can be constructed from two simple rules: '1 is a number' and 'any number plus 1 is a number'."[25] For the influential logician Gottlob Frege a number has some kind of objective reality; it certainly is not anything subjective, "no whit more an object of psychology or a product of mental processes than, let us say, the North Sea is."[26] For nominalists, numbers are arbitrary names: 2 + 1 is the *definition* of 3;[27] "the statement that 3 + 2 = 5, then, is true for similar reasons as, say, the assertion that no sexagenarian is 45 years of age. Both are true simply by virtue of definitions or of similar manipulations."[28]

For Wittgenstein (whose position seems to elude labeling),[29] arithmetic "is nothing but calculation, and the rules... are arbitrary.... Everything is algorithm and

---

[24] Hersh, 1997, p. 226.
[25] Ibid.
[26] Quoted in Hersh, 1997, p. 143.
[27] Hersh, 1997, p. 196.
[28] Hempel, 1945, p. 545.
[29] Klenk, 1976.

nothing is meaning."[30] The Swiss epistemologist and psychologist Jean Piaget believed that when a child physically handles and deals with its environment, that process leaves a trace in the mind-brain which, for instance, "would be the child's concept of two.... Piaget proposed that the concept of counting and natural number are acquired through activity. Real physical activity."[31]

In L. E. J. Brouwer's intuitionism mathematics is "an essentially languageless activity of the mind having its origin in the perception of a move of time,"[32] a free creation of the human mind, and numbers are objects that exist if and only if they can be (mentally) constructed.[33]

For Bertrand Russell, certainty, secure foundations, avoiding "metaphysics," are the dominant and valued criteria for doing acceptable mathematics. He believes that these can be met by constructing the natural numbers from sets, starting with a group of axioms (Dedekind-Peano), the empty set, and several undefined terms (e.g., "1"; "successor of"):[34]

> Two equally numerous collections appear to have something in common: this something is supposed to be their cardinal number. But so long as the cardinal number is inferred from the collections, not constructed in terms of them, its existence must remain in doubt, unless in view of a metaphysical postulate *ad hoc*. By defining the cardinal number of a given collection as the class of all equally numerous collections, we avoid the necessity of the metaphysical postulate, and thereby remove a needless doubt from the philosophy of arithmetic.[35]

---

[30] Hersh, 1997, pp. 201, 203. (Note the "view from nowhere.")
[31] Ibid., p. 226; this view has vague affinities with the position I will be developing.
[32] Ibid., p. 154.
[33] This still is segregationism, although now the "objects" are isolated in "the mind"—see Detlefsen, 1986; Heyting, 1971.
[34] Hersh, 1997, pp. 253, 256.
[35] Russell, 1916, p. 56.

(Cardinal numbers will be important in the discussions that follow. Roughly, they are the natural numbers before any structural relationship such as ordering or succession, notions that include "equal," "greater than," "less than," are imposed [or discovered?]. That is, cardinal numbers are just unrelated entities.) Russell's is the prototypical way of constructing arithmetic. One defines constituent elements, axioms that specify how these elements are to be concatenated into strings and define operations on those strings.[36]

In spite of this diversity, as mentioned earlier Hersh maintains that "most everybody seems to think the natural numbers exist in some sense, though they are infinitely many, and some people gag at anything infinite."[37] One consequence of this thinking is that arithmetic is seen as going its own way, almost automatically. Numbers have their own independent properties and implications; proofs or demonstrations (e.g., theorems about prime numbers) are somehow already there, waiting to be discovered by mathematicians.[38]

I believe enough has been said to support the claim that working mathematicians view, and deal with, natural numbers and their properties very much in the same manner that linguists and logicians of language deal with their subject matter. The Cheshire Cat elements and the segregational, logic-centered, adultocentric approach dominate unchallenged. Any holistic ties to humans which arithmetic or numbers may once have had have become erased, rendered invisible, or dismissed as relics of a more

---

[36] Lucid and accessible illustrations of such processes are given in Gensler, 1984.
[37] Hersh, 1997, p. 179.
[38] See Tallis, 1999b, pp. 77-80, and 1999a, chapter 4, for critiques of the ubiquitous and apparently self-evident (but nevertheless misguided) parallel belief that computers can and do calculate, that they, too, go their own way— i.e., that humans are nowhere in the picture.

naive age. We are in "a land of rigorous abstractions, empty of all familiar landmarks."[39]

## ARITHMETIC: RESTORING LINKAGES

### "Independent" Mathematical Objects

In formal mathematics the natural numbers are logically constructed from some underlying axioms and ingredients. The formalization proceeds in four steps: (1) A catalogue of signs, the vocabulary, is prepared; (2) rules (the system's grammar) are laid down for what "strings" of the signs constitutes legitimate "formulas;" (3) transformation rules that state how one may legitimately transform one formula into another are specified; and finally, (4) certain formulas are selected as axioms which by fiat are to "serve as foundation for the entire system."[40]

I already have cited Russell's set-theoretic approach as a prototypical example. What he required in order to construct arithmetic was a particular group of axioms (Dedekind-Peano), the notion of the empty set (roughly, our "0"), and several undefined primitive terms (e.g., "1"; "successor of").[41] Now, what is the nature of these basic ingredients? What "are" they? From what we have seen about mathematicians' indifference, I assume that Russell would consider this to be an improper, inadmissible question. He probably would see such ontological musings as irrelevant for the working mathematician, otiose metaphysical speculations that can be safely ignored and left to the philosopher. Well, if we do not know (or care) in any but a formalistic (and segregationalist) sense what a set is, what axioms are, what the undefined terms are, and if in addition we also have lost sight of the fact that Mr.

---

[39]   Nagel and Newman, 1958, p. 13.
[40]   Nagel and Newman, 1958, pp. 45-46.
[41]   See Gensler,1984, for lucid, accessible examples of the construction of arithmetic systems of various degrees of complexity.

Russell is the progenitor of all these ingredients and their products, is it any wonder, then, that starting from such entirely obscure, unstated, dessicated ontological foundations we arrive at an erected mathematical system, a collection of segregated "objects" (e.g., the natural numbers) and their complex extensions and elaborations (e.g., the integers [the positive and negative whole numbers, plus zero]; rational numbers; real numbers; imaginary numbers; or even more complicated types)[42] whose ontological status and apparently willful, human-independent behavior and logical properties are baffling, inexplicable to all? No wonder mathematicians are driven to being crypto-Platonists.

## The Pattern Sense

What would it take to reverse this Cheshire Cat procedure and its products? How could the holistic aspects of numbers and their behavior be restored? A clue may be found in Tobias Dantzig's classic *Number: The Language of Science*, first published in 1930. The cover quotes Einstein's opinion: "This is beyond doubt the most interesting book on the evolution of mathematics which has ever fallen into my hands." Its main topic is the history of number, but for the present purposes what is most pertinent are Dantzig's descriptions and brief discussions of what he calls the *Number Sense*.

Dantzig begins by pointing out that humans and a few (other) animals are able to discriminate among collections of objects on the basis of *something resembling numerosity*. He says that, for example, the behavior of crows monitoring the comings and goings of humans in a field indicates that they can tell the difference between the presence and absence of 1, 2, 3, or 4 people, but that they lose track when there are more than four persons.

---

[42]  See Hersh,1997, pp. 268-286.

That does not mean that the crows are *counting,* if we take that label to mean that they are doing something like what adult humans do when they count. For one thing, that process is impossible without human language (as we will soon see):

> An individual without a milieu, deprived of language, deprived of all opportunity to exchange impressions with his peers, could not construct a science of number. To his perceptual world arithmetic would have no reality, no meaning.[43]

To maintain that since crows do differentiate between the size of small groups on the basis of size they *must* be counting is to commit the same kind of error I briefly discussed earlier about observation in child studies (chapter 9). There I claimed that studies of "the competent infant" make a conceptual/methodological mistake when they cite competencies like first language acquisition, or the ability to discriminate between mother and others as evidence that the "competent" infant must have a set of internalized *logical-structural rules or mechanisms* (e.g., Chomsky's Language Acquisition Device, Harris's "Language Machine"[44]). For adultocentrically, scientistic, cognitive-behaviorally oriented investigators, of course that is *by fiat* the only kind of framework that can explain ordered, meaningful behavior.[45]

To return to the crows, then: I doubt that one can legitimately take their behavior as evidence that they are counting, and therefore I don't like Dantzig's use of term "number sense" in this context. Furthermore, he tends to conflate what crows do with what people do when they discriminate between the sizes of different groups. People often do rely on formal, mathematical operations such as actual counting, and/or employing the principle of

---

[43] Dantzig, 1954, p. 244.
[44] Harris, 1987.
[45] See Harris, 1990, chapter 10 ("Must monkeys mean?").

correspondence—i.e., pairing up or matching members of different groups;[46] I very much doubt that crows do. Incidentally, in material added in a later edition Dantzig shows that he appreciates the issue I am raising, because he asks, "How can one discern that the number of objects in a collection has changed, without recourse to actual counting?",[47] and also uses the less adultocentric, anthropocentric term "pattern reading" instead of the more "number sense."

This notion of pattern sense is the starting point and core of my proposed approach to generating arithmetic. I submit that from an ontogenetically informed perspective this pattern sense can be viewed simply as one of the numerous different discriminating functions and capacities that emerge from the undifferentiated unitary state, mysteriously, like languaging. It is impossible to account for pattern sense scientifically, to explain it in by means of some more fundamental notion (e.g., in neurobiological terms). I submit that one simply needs to accept as a given that the child (and adult) "just can tell the difference" (up to a point) between ▢, ▢ ▢, ▢ ▢ ▢ and so on, *without counting*. Formal mathematics has its basic primitive *logical* premises (its axioms, vocabulary, formation and succession rules); one might say that accepting the fact that humans (and some other animals) have a pattern sense simply is one of my basic ontogenetically-informed, holistic primitive axioms.

## A Sensuously-Linked Arithmetic

### Naming

Let us say that these objects are pebbles observed by the members of some tribe. Since persons can tell the difference

---

[46]  Dantzig, 1954, p. 8.
[47]  Ibid., p. 253.

between these collections, at some point it may occur to them to *name* these—say, Arthur, Betty, Charles,... (In order to avoid further complexity in an already highly complex subject, I will simply ignore the pragmatic dimension—i.e., any consideration of why the tribe would bother to give their perceptions names.) Now note: we are not (yet) talking about numbers or counting, just about telling differences and naming (something). However, let us remember from the discussions of chapter 11 that naming is not at all a simple matter. We can imagine the name-giver saying, "that is Charles"—but, according to the discussions on language segmentation in chapter 11, it would be a mistake to immediately interpret such a saying as "having" a subject/predicate structure, or exhibiting a referential notion of language, or being understandable as based in ostension, or covertly referring to the number 3. As Tallis puts it in another context, that kind of analysis begins too far down stream. Naming is a mysterious process, a reflection of ontogenesis.

In the case of our hypothetical tribe, it is not obvious what its adult members are actually naming. Is it the pebbles as a group? The "inner experience" (Collins's mental content) resulting from the pattern sense? Just as in other fields, the obscurity and elusiveness of naming is not generally recognized and appreciated in mathematics. If naming is considered at all, it is treated as a mundane, unproblematic act of verbal labeling; for example, in one discussion of geometrical shapes we read that "one of the most fundamental uses of language is to assign names to things. Naming is a primitive concept.... Naming is the first step toward knowing, whether it is the name of a person or the name of a shape."[48] Perhaps the approach to mathematics which I am outlining ought to be called "naming theory."

---

[48] Senechal, 1990, p. 145.

Very well, the tribe has named the pebbles-sense pattern experiences. From here we can branch out in different directions. For one thing, since the pattern sense is not confined to one kind of object, persons discriminate between patterns not only in groups of pebbles but also, say, in groups of trees. They notice the difference between /, //, ///, etc.,—again, up to a point, until there are too many trees or the tribe runs out of names—and again can name these tree groups, say, Adele, Bob, Cora,... So far nothing really new has been added.

But now we make a second elaboration that *is* new. We can conjecture that at some point and again in an utterly mysterious way this tribe dimly recognizes some similarity or identity between the two naming situations (pebbles and trees), and begins to *generalize*. A member decides to capture this as yet unrepresented *commonality* among patters of different kinds of objects by a slightly different kind of naming. To distinguish these kinds of generalized names from the kinds of names given to groups of specific kind of objects, they may call the new name type, say, A, B, C. Arthur and Adele become subsumed under the "super-name" A, Betty and Bob under B, Charles and Cora under C, and so on. (The tribe may have to make up some new type of names if they do not already have suitable terms in their vocabulary.)

This step is far from simple; Bertrand Russell writes that "It must have required many ages to discover that a brace of pheasants and a couple of days were both instances of the number two."[49] From the experiential-perceptual point of view whereas before, persons used a name to name a concrete sense experience of a specific perceived pattern in a group of specific kinds of objects, and therefore the name types or vocabularies used to name pebble patterns and tree patterns were different, now we have introduced

---

[49]  Dantzig, 1954, p. 6.

an imponderable generalizing, almost abstracting, step, and it becomes even more difficult to say just what the "names" A, B, C,... are "naming." This class of "super" names no longer refers directly to the experience of pattern sense; individually the new kind of names refer to an "abstraction"—a concept that can easily be explained superficially, in terms of facile cognitive models, but that on deeper examination is yet another elusive phenomenon that defies scientific understanding. In contemporary terms, what exactly is it that we do when we move from "three apples" to just "three"? We can glibly say that we are abstracting or generalizing, but I suggest that here we have an important source of the bewilderment that arises when mathematicians and philosophers ask themselves what it is that numbers "name," what they "really are." They do not take the ontological problems inherent in the moves that lead to such abstractions or generalizations nearly seriously enough.

At any rate, we essentially have now created the *cardinal* numbers, *a collection of named number-like entities* that 1) is still intimately connected to pattern perception and naming, 2) yet no longer refers to a direct perceptual experience, 3) but so far does not involve counting or any other arithmetic manipulation, and 4) has no internal structure (e.g., there is no notion of "successor of," or "greater than," or "equal to;" the entities/names are formally/structurally unrelated to one another).

Let us remember that this is *not* the usual way mathematicians construct cardinality. The standard approach is grounded in the (abstract) concepts of sets and their members, in using matching or the "one-to-one correspondence" between members of different sets, and assigning all these matched sets the mysterious general property we call "cardinality." After all that, we can define a (cardinal) number as that property which all sets of the same cardinality have in common. The abstract notion of *threeness* is that property which a certain set, A, consisting of a star, a dream, and a monkey, has in common with all other sets whose elements can be placed in a unique one-to-one correspondence with the set A.[50]

## Sensual Manipulations

Returning once more to our tribe, let us next begin to consider *operations* performed by means of their new super-numbers (e.g., A, B, C,...) and their more concrete precursors (e.g., Arthur, Betty, Charles,...). Let us assume that the members of our hypothetical tribe now notice that there are certain internal relationships that can be identified within each type of group. They see, for example, that Betty (the *name* we had given to the experience of "2 pebbles") can be arranged into Betty groups of Arthur (our "1 pebble") and, alternatively, that Betty Arthurs (two ones) can be assembled into Arthur Betty (into a single "two"). (In less contrived terminology: twos can be segmented into two ones; two ones can be brought together to form one two.) Eventually this insight, too, becomes generalized; the tribe sees that it holds for the "super names" A, B, C, etc. I.e., B's can be separated into B A's; B A's can be conjoined into A B. This is another momentous step—actually, two; manipulation (aggregation and separation of pebbles, and the employment of super names). We have the dawning of something very like the notion of size, comparison, ordering, equivalence.

Let us next assume that for some pragmatic reason (say, for reasons of commerce) the people find it convenient to *memorize* these discovered relationships. As long as the naming remains oral, the grouping and assembling relationships become increasingly difficult to remember (or even to conceptualize) as the groups get larger. So does the reliability, even the viability, of the pattern sense. (Here

---

[50]  Jones, 1982, p. 26).

from another perspective we again speculate that we are witnessing the dawning realization that there is a something like *size*.)

## Writing

As I have said, with increasing size and complexities, memorizing becomes difficult. To remember that for example George and Laura can be assembled into Sandra, or Irene and Henry into Quentin, or, in terms of the more general names, F and J into P, and to remember such relations for very many other names obviously becomes laborious, unwieldy, clumsy, and, ultimately, untenable. So, it is time for another set of major advances. First, the tribe hits on the happy solution of *writing,* an apparently innocent step that actually is a momentous but easily down-played advance: mathematics "could not have evolved to its modern state *without* writing."[51]

From an *ontological* perspective writing in general is a complex, poorly investigated, poorly understood phenomenon.[52] Yet, its role and functions ought to be a major focus in all those disciplines where language is important (and we know that mathematics has become a linguistic discipline):

> The advent of writing was the cultural development which made the most radical alteration of all time to man's concept of what a language is.... [writing is] a milestone in the cultural history of any community. Once its member become literate, their notion of 'speech' will never be the same again.[53]

The central place that writing has come to take in virtually every endeavor has not only obscured but displaced the role of speech. In important respects speech had, and has, precedence. Historically and culturally it came first. It is

---

[51] Harris, 1995, p. 134; written mathematics dates back at least to 2000 B.C. in Egypt (Bunt et al., 1976).
[52] Harris, 1990; 1995; 1998, chapter 5.
[53] Harris, 1990, p. 185; 1998, p. 124.

learned first by all children, automatically, without formal schooling; it serves more purposes than does writing. It is also "ontologically prior," foundational. (We can have speech without writing, but, as Harris points out, we cannot have writing without speech.) Now, a curious, virtually invisible, yet critically important *reversal* in our conception of language has developed gradually over millennia: *scriptism,* "the assumption that writing is a more ideal form of linguistic representation than speech."[54] This reversal or inversion of the genesis of speech and writing is a specific and major example of a very important and all too often destructive *general phenomenon,* namely, the move Husserl called the *"ontological reversal"* (see chapter 6): What had originally been a derivative phenomenon has become foundational; the end results of a process come to be seen as primary, originary, causal, and that heavily distorts— actually, inverts—one's ontology.[55]

What is true of writing and language in general holds specifically for mathematics. There, too, scriptism and the subsequent primary role ascribed to writing remain virtually unexplored, except for historical considerations.[56] As far as I know, the only beginning investigations of the ontological reversal in mathematics brought about by scriptism are Roy Harris's "Non-glottic writing: mathematics,"[57] and Davis's "The Language Myth and Mathematical Notation as a Language of Nature."[58]

Writing shifts naming from the aural to the visual mode—a momentous shift indeed. Acoustic events are linear in time, nonspatial (at least in most of our experiences, except for directional localization), transient, elusive, difficult to segment, compare, manipulate (e.g.,

---

[54]  Harris, 1990, p. 185.
[55]  For important discussions see Harvey, 1989.
[56]  E.g., Dantzig, 1954; Swetz, 1987; Bunt et al., 1976.
[57]  Harris, 1995, chapter 12.
[58]  Davis, 2002.

transform, assemble), remember accurately and reliably, reproduce. When one speaks a name, that act's holistic ties to a person, time, place, are still obvious. In contrast, writing binds time, allows spatial manipulations (e.g., writing numbers in columns) and the invention of different kinds of notations, and so on. It easily becomes an agent of segregationalism with the concomitant loss of human ties. These features of writing facilitate the illusion of seeing mathematical entities as independent, having lives of their own.

## Steps Facilitated by Writing

Having taken this momentous step of recognizing that spoken pattern names can be notated, the natives now can visually summarize and add to their previously gained insights. First they need to find some way of graphically symbolizing the process of putting together, assembling, the entities. Let us assume they choose the simple notation of placing a comma between two number names to denote such an assembly process or act. We will show this practice only for the first few super names. The results for A to H are shown in Table 1.

|   | A | B | C | D |
|---|---|---|---|---|
| A | A, A ➔ B | A, B ➔ C | A, C ➔ D | A, D ➔ E |
| B | B, A ➔ C | B, B ➔ D | B, C ➔ E | B, D ➔ F |
| C | C, A ➔ D | C, B ➔ E | C, C ➔ F | C, D ➔ G |
| D | D, A ➔ E | D, B ➔ F | D, C ➔ G | D, D ➔ H |

TABLE 1

Now the tribe can take another momentous step. We recall that members had difficulties discriminating between patterns when assemblages became too large. With the capacity to notate, they are able to invent another generalization. Let us assume that their pattern sense begins to run into difficulty when it has to discriminate between D and E (our 4 and 5). They hit on the idea of batching. They realize that E (our old "5") could be considered as, somehow renamed as, an A ("1") of something new—a super-group, a group either D, A, or C, B, or B, C, or A, D. All these are now "A" (one) of E. The tribe can make do with four names (almost—as we shall see shortly). With batching they discover the notion of hierarchies or levels of numerosity.

To put this insight to use requires a further invention. The tribe needs to find a suitable notation to show the difference between A when it is functioning in its original sense as a super *name* (A pebbles *or* trees) and when it is used as the name of a super *group*—that is, the people need to find a way of indicating when the writing means just plain A ("1") and when it is functioning as an "A" of "E." The members hit on the *Principle of Position*, another considerable conceptual advance.[59] To re-write E as A of a supergroup, they use the *position* of A to indicate in which of the two capacities it is serving in any given instance. They have intuited a cardinal number system that has the "base" E. Note that this step would have been almost impossible as long as the tribe remained in an auditory mode; the device rests on the spatial modality, on position. The change of modality is yet another mysterious element of mathematics' ontology.

This process creates another new problem. If the tribe wants to capitalize on the Principle of Position, it must invent a new sign so that they can show when "A" means just A (our "1"), and when it means "one" in the sense of "one super-A," or one E (our "5"). In the latter meaning and

---

59   Dantzig, 1954, pp. 256-257.

using the associational convention shown in Table 1, E becomes "A, (nothing)." In other words, they need a positional symbol, essentially an empty place-holder (our "0", of course). They decide on "_", and E becomes A_, F becomes AA, and so on.

We see that to put the Principle of Position into play required not only its invention in the first place, but also created the need to invent a unique name/concept: a place-holder, a name that may look and act like one of the old number names but actually is an entirely different (and obscure) kind of an entity. Unlike the other names, it has no direct or indirect experiential counterpart in pattern perception and discrimination. We can see why zero has always been conceptually problematic and special in number theory. Ontologically it is a horse of a different color. Still, the foundations of the mathematics I am developing remain the pattern sense and naming, albeit now elaborated in several important directions.

With the basic patterns sense, naming, and considerable conceptual advances and refinements—batching, creating hierarchies of name use, inventing the position principle, and inventing the empty place holder—the tribe can now rewrite Table 1 in terms of its new positional notation and the new symbol for nothing:

|   | A | B | C | D |
|---|---|---|---|---|
| A | B | C | D | A_ |
| B | C | D | A_ | AA |
| C | D | A_ | AA | AB |
| D | A_ | AA | AB | AC |

TABLE 2

Here we now have the basis for an arithmetic of addition, a system that has the "base 'E'" (for us that would be the base 5). All that remains to make it familiar to us is to substitute our familiar (but arbitrary, *and in themselves meaningless*) *visual* squiggles (e.g., 5 and 9) for super-names letters (e.g., E and I), and the squiggle "0" for "_":

|   | 1  | 2  | 3  | 4  |
|---|----|----|----|----|
| 1 | 2  | 3  | 4  | 10 |
| 2 | 3  | 4  | 10 | 11 |
| 3 | 4  | 10 | 11 | 12 |
| 4 | 10 | 11 | 12 | 13 |

TABLE 3

We can enlarge of this table slightly by adding one column and one row, treating "_" as though it, too, were a pattern name (which we know it isn't). Although the step looks innocent enough, in fact it is another major but obscure conceptual move. It is major and obscure because we have taken a squiggle, a visual element that does not stand for names like Arthur or "B," one that initially does not name, refer to, or correspond to any experience that is intimately tied to the pattern sense, and treated it as though ontologically it were just like those names. We have taken an unwarranted step of assigning a (numerical) name function or role to a place holder. Table 4 displays this seemingly trivial elaboration.

|   | 0 | 1 | 2 | 3 | 4 |
|---|---|---|---|---|---|
| 0 | 0 | 1 | 2 | 3 | 4 |
| 1 | 1 | 2 | 3 | 4 | 10 |
| 2 | 2 | 3 | 4 | 10 | 11 |
| 3 | 3 | 4 | 10 | 11 | 12 |
| 4 | 4 | 10 | 11 | 12 | 13 |

TABLE 4

Continuing the same process we get Table 5:

|    | 0  | 1  | 2  | 3  | 4  | 10 | 11 | 12 | 13 | 14 | 20 | 21 |
|----|----|----|----|----|----|----|----|----|----|----|----|----|
| 0  | 0  | 1  | 2  | 3  | 4  | 10 | 11 | 12 | 13 | 14 | 20 | 21 |
| 1  | 1  | 2  | 3  | 4  | 10 | 11 | 12 | 13 | 14 | 20 | 21 | 22 |
| 2  | 2  | 3  | 4  | 10 | 11 | 12 | 13 | 14 | 20 | 21 | 22 | 23 |
| 3  | 3  | 4  | 10 | 11 | 12 | 13 | 14 | 20 | 21 | 22 | 23 | 24 |
| 4  | 4  | 10 | 11 | 12 | 13 | 14 | 20 | 21 | 22 | 23 | 24 | 30 |
| 10 | 10 | 11 | 12 | 13 | 14 | 20 | 21 | 22 | 23 | 24 | 30 | 31 |
| 11 | 11 | 12 | 13 | 14 | 20 | 21 | 22 | 23 | 24 | 30 | 31 | 32 |
| 12 | 12 | 13 | 14 | 20 | 21 | 22 | 23 | 24 | 30 | 31 | 32 | 33 |
| 13 | 13 | 14 | 20 | 21 | 22 | 23 | 24 | 30 | 31 | 32 | 33 | 34 |
| 14 | 14 | 20 | 21 | 22 | 23 | 24 | 30 | 31 | 32 | 33 | 34 | 40 |
| 20 | 20 | 21 | 22 | 23 | 24 | 30 | 31 | 32 | 33 | 34 | 40 | 41 |
| 21 | 21 | 22 | 23 | 24 | 30 | 31 | 32 | 33 | 34 | 40 | 41 | 42 |
| 22 | 22 | 23 | 24 | 30 | 31 | 32 | 33 | 34 | 40 | 41 | 42 | 43 |

TABLE 5

## Noticing Invariances and Obtaining a "System"

After all these advances and refinements, the tribe is now in a position to note some useful general visual patterns among the named entities. It is obvious from the diagonals that most names can be obtained from several different pair combinations (e.g., there are five different ways of obtaining "4"). It is also obvious from the table that the order in which a pair of names is associated does not matter—names "commute." We are deriving several "laws" of our simple arithmetic without needing to use formal logic. With some further thought and effort one can also arrive at a mechanistic, rote method (it tells us to "carry" a name forward) that automatically gives us the single name for the association of any two names—a law of addition, a rote rule that tells us how to add numbers. The inferences one draws from patterns discerned in Table 5 are limited only by one's ingenuity and inventiveness. (I note, again, that these kinds of advances and insights would be nearly impossible as long as one did not write and only spoke.)

The first major point is that all this has been accomplished without any formal-axiomatic developments such as Russell's. We even have managed without introducing ordinals, integers. Every step has remained visibly tied to a basic human action or perception. Secondly, I see no reason why analogous processes—that is, steps that remain closely tied to basic human presence, perception, awareness, and action—should not lead also to more elaborate arithmetics. For example, it is not difficult to imagine how the tribe might next develop an arithmetic that included what we would call multiplication. My hypothesis is that the start grounded in perceptual experience (pattern sense), naming, invention, observation of regularities, and so on, which led to the operation we would call addition can also be extrapolated so as to lead to any other kind of operation—clumsily, to be sure. In short: *I propose that in principle, the apparently independent (segregational) status of mathematics and its objects is a Cheshire Cat illusion that raises a host of pseudo-questions and pseudo-problems; it severs and thus obscures the ever-present ties between that discipline and its human progenitors.* Furthermore, although I have not attempted a proof, I strongly suspect that there is a corollary, that we could invert the construction process. I suspect that we could take any portion of our present mathematics and painfully retrace its genesis, reconnecting it to holistic, personal fundamentals such as the pattern sense.

I repeat an observation made previously in other contexts: I have not removed mysteries (in this case, from mathematics) but merely suggested how to relocate them. Now, instead of appealing to, say, a mysterious third realm of pre-existing objects and truths, instead of saying that outcomes and truths of arithmetic somehow magically and inevitably inhere in its subject matter (e.g., that 2 + 2 necessarily and eternally "is" 4, that we have no say in the matter, that this is an abiding "fact" discoverable in the third, Platonic realm), I point to the mysteries of the pattern sense, of the materiality of pebbles and trees, of naming, inventing, abstracting, writing, appreciating positional factors, languaging, discriminating between one's internal and external worlds, and so on. And underlying all *these* mysterious matters is the unfathomable undifferentiated neonate state, the genesis of adult phenomena that when one attempts to nail them down scientifically, disappear into Freud's "navel of the dream."

## LOGIC AND ITS PARADOXES

### The Nature of Logic

We ask another version of our by now familiar generic question—in this case, what *is* logic? The renowned American philosopher and logician W. V. O. Quine whose work we have previously encountered introduces one of his books on the subject with a short quotation from Lewis Carroll's *Alice* (Carroll was a logician) in which Tweedledee purports to say what logic is. Quine continues, "If pressed to supplement Tweedledee's ostensive definition of logic with a discursive definition of the same subject, I would say that logic is the systematic study of the logical truths. Pressed further, I would say to read this book [i.e., his *Philosophy of Logic*]."[60]

Here are some other definitions: "Logic is quite simply the study of *truth-preserving arguments*."[61] "Logic might be defined as the science of inference; inference, in turn, as the drawing of a conclusion from premises.... Logic, then, is primarily concerned with arguments."[62] "Logic can be defined as the study of consistent sets of belief."[63] "Logic can be defined as *the analysis and appraisal of arguments*."[64] The implications of such definitions seem straightforward enough, but we also might do well to remember Wittgenstein's admonition to the English philosopher G. E. Moore: "logic isn't as simple as logicians think."[65]

Whatever else logic may be, ever since its beginnings in classical Greece language has played a central role. Aristotle discussed sentences, their subject-predicate structure, and how truth or falsity of one sentence affected the truth or falsity of other, related sentences, using his "square of oppositions" to formalize the relations of premises to conclusions in the syllogism.[66] Early logic was about, and used, ordinary language, but more than two millennia later, logicians were busy formalizing language because by then, ordinary language was considered by them

---

[60]  Quine, 1986, p. vii.
[61]  Cryan, Shatil and Mayblin, 2002, p. 3.
[62]  Audi, 1999, p. 679.
[63]  Hodges, 1977, p. 13.
[64]  Gensler, 2002, p. 1.
[65]  Quoted in Stroll, 2000, p. 89.
[66]  Cryan, Shatil and Mayblin, 2002, pp. 5-6.

to be much too imprecise, sloppy, ambiguous when it was an object of formal study or employed (self-referentially) as an analytical tool.

Logic and its language became mathematized, axiomatized, transformed into specialists' arcane symbolic system, the prototypical example being Russell and Whitehead's famous 1910 *Principia Mathematica*. The aim was to produce an ideal, transparent, logically perfect semiotic system whose structure and workings would be clear, as would its relationship to corresponding facts.[67] In this enterprise anything in language that was deemed to be other than central to its pure logical structure was removed.

The resulting pared-down logical systems are probably the most extreme examples of a Cheshire Cat residue. The always problematic ties of language to world and person became even more obscure when the "language" consisted of basic axioms, arcane, invented squiggles, and abstract logical rules governing their various combinations and transformations. That pure language and its workings then did seem to take on a life totally its own, to become totally independent of its human caretakers and practitioners, manipulated by an invisible, unobservable subject. It was a depersonalized view from nowhere that had its own truths and inner dynamic.

A major landmark in this program, and an even more extreme case of generating Cheshire Cat residues, was Kurt Gödel's work. In the early twentieth century he produced a set of foundation-shaking proofs that demonstrated the existence of fundamental limitations in any sufficiently rich mathematical system. He showed that such systems either led to inner contradictions (they were inconsistent), or else were unable to prove some of the truths inherent in the systems (they were incomplete). These proofs were

---

[67] Stroll, 2000, especially chapter 2.

accomplished by reducing even the symbolic language to numbers, by cleverly coding the already stylized, abstract symbolisms into numerical equivalents and then demonstrating the problematic nature of a system of these so-called "Gödel numbers." As I understand it, others extended Gödel's proofs along similar lines.

I am in no position to offer a direct critique of Gödel's or similar work. Pure mathematics is entirely outside my areas of mathematical competence. When Gödel's proofs first appeared they were unintelligible to most mathematicians, and even now "the details of Gödel's proofs in his epoch-making paper are too difficult to follow without considerable [and highly specialized] mathematical training."[68] The proofs did involve highly sophisticated and novel manifestations of so-called self-referential paradoxes, statements that seem to say something about themselves, so what I intend to do here is to consider several old and relatively simple examples of such statements in order to demonstrate through ontological considerations that there may be good reason to be critical of the ways in which formal logic handles these old self-referential paradoxes. My point is that if it can be shown that holistic approaches have something to offer in these simpler cases of self-reference or reflexivity, if we see that the approaches can raise questions and doubts about the legitimacy of the usual logical analyses of this class of paradoxes, then these ontological critiques may also be applied to, and may also raise doubts about, highly complex proofs such as Gödel's.

## Paradoxes

Let us begin with Bertrand Russell's well-known "Barber Paradox." It is assumed that there is a village in which a barber lives who shaves only those who do not shave themselves. Does he shave himself? The paradox is readily

---

[68]  Nagel and Newman, 1958, p. 7.

apparent. If he shaves himself, he may not shave himself because the barber does not shave that group of inhabitants (selfshavers). If he does not, then he must, by stipulation (because now he would be a non-selfshaver).

Russell's expectable reaction, and those of other notable mathematicians such as Hilbert, Brouwer, and Zermelo, was to try to resolve this paradox within his own field, logic. It is exemplified by Russell's development and use of the so-called theory of types, a step taken within set theory that constructs logical hierarchies of sentences along the dimension of self-reference together with rules specifying or forbidding their use. Others, such as Hilbert and the formalists, assumed that this class of paradoxes could be avoided by devising arcane logical rules that specify how an "object" (e.g., a sentence) was to be constructed, and what permissible, "absolutely certain" rules of inference could be used in logical arguments.[69] The discussions and critiques of this and related paradoxes bristle with arcane logical notations and procedures. The paradoxes are to be resolved, it is presumed, by further applying rigidly formalized deductive demonstrations. In the case of Russell's barber, it is claimed that such logical manipulations will ultimately lead to a logical contradiction, a *reductio as absurdum,* which shows that such a barber cannot exist.[70]

One of the main points I want to make about this and several other, similar paradoxes is that such heavy-handed formalistic machinery of symbolic logic simply is unnecessary, that what one might call *ontological* considerations will do just as well. I now will begin to call these *"ontic"* rather than ontological, employing Heidegger's distinction between, roughly, ordinary inanimate objects (their being, their existence, is ontic) and the ontological, the global, mysterious, unfathomable "Being" (capitalized)

---

[69] Irvine, 2004; Quine, 1968.
[70] Quine, 1968, p. 200.

that is not any *thing* or *attribute*, but the unsayable ground within and out of which ontic entities and persons [his famous *Dasein*] both arise.

In the case of the barber, the ontic consideration is very simple: The barber in our hypothetical village either shaves himself, or he does not. That ontic "fact" comes first; it is (or should be) logically prior to any more convoluted logical considerations involving ponderous logical machinery, arcane notation, special rules (e.g., Russell's theory of types). *In either case, whether he does or does not shave himself, we simply cannot assume that there is a village in which there is a barber who....* That *stipulation* is obviously untenable, incoherent, *right from the start:* If in fact he *does* shave himself, we can't say that there is a village in which... (etc.) because according to that stipulation he would not shave himself. The parallel proscription holds if the barber in fact does *not* shave himself. So, a simple ontic scrutiny, considerations of real, human situations, of what Wittgenstein famously referred to as that "which is the case," show us that we simply must not posit Russell's barber.[71] This is demonstration via simple linguistic and ontic reflection that restores the previously invisible ties between sentences, persons, ordinary (but, as we need to remember constantly, ultimately utterly mysterious) language, and real-world situations. By refusing to treat a premise as a viable, separate object we resolved a self-referential paradox and reversed the Cheshire Cat phenomenon, and did so without any but the simplest common-sense argument.

Let us next consider "the ancient paradox of Epimenides the Cretan, who said that all Cretans were liars. If he spoke the truth, he was a liar."[72] Quine says that this paradox is untidy, and to clean it up he switches to another ancient

---

[71]   Much the same point is made by Hodgson, 1991, p. 27.
[72]   Quine, 1961, p. 202.

paradox with the same idea, "the *pseudomenon*, which runs simply: 'I am lying.'"[73] Before pursuing the latter, I want to comment on the Cretan version, again subjecting it to a simple ontic analysis. Looking at the Cretan population from the outside as it were, we find that *in fact* either they all are liars, or always speak the truth, or are a mixed bag. In the first and second situation, the sentence "All Cretans are liars" simply must not be uttered, just as if, for example, in the first case (they all lie) a Cretan must not, by hypothesis, say "the sun rises in the East" (we will not quibble about whether the sun does actually does rise at all), and in the second case (they all are truthful) a Cretan must not say "the sun rises in the West." That is dictated by the world, not by arcane logic. By hypotheses *and by a consideration of ontic fact*, such sentences simply are inadmissible; under the stipulated assumptions, it is impossible for the two classes of Cretans to utter them.

The third, mixed case is more interesting. If we happen to encounter one of the truthful Cretans, then she is a Cretan who must not say that all Cretans are liars. But if we encounter a liar, and he says "all Cretans are liars," then this is a lie, and permissible under the stated hypotheses. So, if we meet a Cretan who does speak the sentence, and, we know immediately that the person is a liar *and* we can infer that as far as truth telling is concerned, Cretans are a mixed bag.

Before moving on, I want to note a linguistic oddity that is seldom considered, as far as I know: This kind of paradox arises because in the sentence "All Cretans are 'X'", X is "liars." Suppose X stood for "truth-tellers" (or, for that matter, "ten feet tall"). Then there would be no problem! Should the Cretan whom we meet be a liar, he could say the sentence because he would be lying; were he a truth-teller, he could say it also, because he would be telling the truth.

---

[73] Quine, 1968, p. 202.

Therefore, *self-reference as such cannot possibly be the crux of the difficulty of this class of self-referential paradoxes. The problem must issue from a specific posited attribute, in this case, lying.* Lying must have some idiosyncratic feature that most other descriptors do not have. In any case, we have seen that one can deal ontically with this type of paradox, that once again no massive logical machinery is needed.

Let us next consider the version of this paradox that Quine thinks is less messy: "I am lying." Viewed ontically in one way, this is just a collapsed version of the more general Cretan claim. The speaker we meet either is a liar, or a truth-teller, or a sometime truth-teller/liar. Now, no matter whether in fact she always lies, or always tells the truth, or tells the truth only at times, it is easy to work out that "I am lying" is one of the sentences that she is prohibited from uttering, *by hypothesis, and not because of arcane logical reasons.* There is no paradox here. The sentence must not be posited of a speaker. However, an ontic approach raises a second consideration: Normally when one says that about someone that they are lying, one implicitly means, lying *about something.* In this case, what is the speaker lying about? In the usual dyadic situation were a person to say to you "I am lying," the natural response would be, "about what?" So, an ontic approach raises doubts about the coherence of the posited situation (which comprises a Cheshire Cat residue). (One could try to tinker with the hypothetical situation to make it more viable by changing it to "I always lie.")

Now I want to introduce what I see as another major consideration, one which as far as I know does not seem to have been considered by logicians. Furthermore, its implications remain elusive; I, at least, cannot make much progress in this area. The ontic consideration I want to introduce is *writing.* We already had an intimation of its importance in the earlier discussions concerning arithmetic, and I am convinced that its potential importance for logic also is great. I will approach the topic in small steps.

Consider again the person who wants to maintain that he or she is lying. This time I have said "maintain," not "say." Suppose now that the person is wearing a sign that says "I am lying." What is the ontic situation now? So far all the examinations of the paradoxes have been made with the unstated assumption that we are dealing with the spoken word. Now with writing, the statement and its implications and claims become even more complex; the situation begins to be obscure and ambiguous. First: is "lying" something that one can do only verbally, or at best in clear situations when writing something directed to someone (e.g., signing an oath)? Is it something that can occur only synchronically? (Writing removes the temporal dimension.) If it is, then the sign may be meaningless. Did the person write the sign herself, or was it perhaps hung around her neck as a joke, or as a part of some initiation ritual? The apparently simple change in modality to writing already seems to introduce a certain amount of confusion and ambiguity that was absent in the case of the spoken message. The change in modality is not innocent.

Let us go on. Another well-known paradox is (the written!) sentence "this sentence is false." Quine again analyzes its problematic roots logically; he considers grammatical matters, such as what a sentence may, or may not refer to. One line of analysis, he reports, raises the logical-referential question of just what it is that the phrase "this sentence" refers to. I would begin an ontic exploration by asking, what would the situation be were that sentence spoken rather than written? This change of modality seems to introduce a world of uncertainty. How would one take it if a speaker were to *say* the sentence? If someone were to say to us "this sentence is false," I think most of us would be puzzled: "What are you talking about? What do you mean to say? Which sentence?" Presented in the auditory mode, such an assertion seems to produce an incipient state of vertigo; at least it does so for me. So, writing seems to introduce a drastically new and different, but elusive, element. For one thing, it changes a statement that would be nonsensical when made in the oral mode to an apparently acceptable statement.

I will consider just one more paradoxical case, outlined by Bertrand Russell: "We give a person a piece of paper on which is written: 'The statement on the other side of this paper is false.' The person turns the paper over, and finds on the other side: The statement on the other side of this paper is true. '"He adds: "It seemed unworthy of a grown man to spend his time on such trivialities, but what was I to do? There was something wrong...."[74]

I will not try to resolve this apparent paradox, but merely comment again on the matter of writing. It is obvious but, again, never identified in logic as a problematic issue that may merit and repay close study, that the posited situation has no simple counterpart in speech. We need the spatiality, the two surfaces, a certain timelessness, an ability to revisit the two sentence—the Cheshire Cat, distancing, impersonal, alienating, segregational mode so readily supplied by paper and ink. The tacit assumption among logicians seems to be that modality has no particular significance, that it is merely an extraneous, irrelevant feature of the posed problem. Here, language looks as though it were acting in an apparently quite straightforward referential manner, but when we contemplate the written sentence, we see that persons, subjective intentions, context, temporality, intended meaning, no longer are present. We now are in the domain of the received view of language, where, among other things, written linear, segmented, segregated sentences composed of grammatically arranged individual words have

---

[74] Russell, 1967, p. 311.

referents or logical functions that can be either true or false. (Sentences have a "truth value.") The Cheshire Cat process creates an arid, unpopulated, innately paradoxical, rationally untenable universe of written, person-less discourse that, it is maintained, somehow has a life of its own. A sentence by itself can, for example, express truths or falsehood, or beliefs, or carry "information"—and refer to itself.

All of these assumptions have been strongly questioned in much of what has been presented in all the preceding chapters. I will only mention a few points: Tallis's critique of the idea that truth and falsity can exist without "explicitness;" the many kinds of difficulties raised by the idea that language is a linear array of building block elements; simplistic notions concerning reference and naming; untenable notions about content (e.g., information, truth-value); and most particularly, the problems raised by the overriding idea that once freed from the immediacy and context of an utterance, language can be written down, stored, analyzed, and wend its separate ways without our having to keep in mind its genesis and residual human ties.

## Gödel's Proofs

As I see it, this writing step raises what potentially may be an extremely important issue for logic in general. I have shown that at least some paradoxes concerning spoken language can be dissolved by means of ontic considerations. Specifically, I have shown that these paradoxes *deal with the matter of inadmissible sentences*. In speech situations, because what is postulated about the speaker (typically, whether she or he always tells the truth, sometimes elaborated by what is postulated about the speaker's group in general—e.g., "all Cretans...") clearly implies what sentences are forbidden under the hypothesized situation.

We saw that this ontic examination was a straightforward matter when the posited modality was auditory, and when there was a progenitor of the language under consideration in the picture. We were able to counter the paradox ontically. The question now, however, is: *What is the counterpart of this ontic examination when one is dealing with writing?* Severed from any considerations of persons, mysteriously altered ontologically in profound ways, writing is a situation where the question of what sentences are forbidden by postulated conditions eludes clear formulations and clear replies. Simply put, there are no apparent constraints on speakers because there no longer are any, nor on the writers, because they, too, have vanished from the picture. *There are no ontic restrictions on writing "This sentence is false," or on writing paradoxical sentences on opposite sides of a piece of paper.* Anyone can write anything at any time. One may run across any sentence, an apparently found, separate, independent object. So, somehow, writing by its nature as a Cheshire Cat residue has removed the possibility of applying the kind of simple ontic, life-connected critiques offered in the preceding examples.

What, if any, are their implications for such critically important paradoxical enterprises as Gödel's proofs? Even though my understanding of these proofs is rudimentary at best, I believe they are centrally predicated on the legitimacy of formulating paradoxical Cheshire Cat statements and translating them into an equivalent numerical code, their so-called Gödel Number. It does seem incontrovertible that such proofs rely entirely on manipulations presumably performed by a "person from nowhere" (with due apologies to Thomas Nagel). We now have an inkling of the kinds of complications these practices may introduce into logic. Even though I do not know how to carry my critique forward, I am suggesting that by relying entirely on writing, on purified, isolated, cast adrift language, on a segregationalist view of the subject matter, on a stilted, person-independent, entirely notated conception of number, pairing, coding, referring, Gödel's and similar proofs of so-called limitative theorems that are predicated on self-referential written statements thus may actually rest on fallacious, shaky, and ultimately untenable grounds. Perhaps ontological analysis would ultimately demonstrate that the self-referential sentences that provide the start for this class of proofs somehow violate the very conditions of acceptable language. Perhaps it is as though the entire enterprise were based on accepting as legitimate the premise that a Cretan may say that all Cretans are liars. We have seen that such sentences are forbidden basically not because of some arcane logical considerations about sets, but because they violate ontic basics, the simple facts that govern languaged life in the real world.

There is yet another issue which an ontic position brings up. If I understand the essentials of Gödel's proof correctly, since it pertains to the question whether systems exist that are complete (*every* true formula—roughly, equation—can be derived from the axiomatic base), or internally consistent (i.e., *no* mutually contradictory formulas can be derived from that basis), the proof necessarily entails the premise that one can tell *by inspection* whether a given arithmetical formula is true or false:

> Gödel's theorem states that in any consistent system which is strong [i.e., rich, complex] enough to produce simple arithmetic there are formulae which cannot be proved-in-the-system, but which we can see to be true.[75]

"We can see..." That contention raises once again the question Tallis challenges (see chapter 3): can it be legitimately said of inanimate items such as formulae or sentences that they *by themselves* are true or false, or is explicitness (i.e. roughly, the presence of persons, active ties to a human being) a vitally necessary component? If Tallis is right, saying that a sentence or formula is true (or false)

---

[75] Lucas, 1964, pp. 43-44.

is at bottom just as incoherent and meaningless as saying that by itself, a rock is true or false. In his terminology, *explicitness* must have become manifest. That consideration introduces yet another ontic/ontogenetic dimension into the critique of the Cheshire Cat aspects of Gödel's proof.

There is an alternative way of raising the same question about the existence of independence of truths of arithmetical formulae. We have seen in the development of the rudimentary arithmetic in the first half of this chapter that its "truths" are not somehow Platonic truths existing self-evidently, eternally and independently in some third realm, but rather "truths" whose basis can be traced back to a fundamentally human experience that followed from the pattern sense. I have posited that such an ontic tracing back could, in principle at least, be done for any apparently independent truth of more complex arithmetics (such as those that, say, include exponentials and square roots).

On both ontological counts, then—the questions raised by a critique of writing and language, and by the assumption that truth can be a property of inanimate, severed, independent linguistic objects—there are reasons for being wary of Gödel's proof and its implications. Since this class of proofs and of (limitative) theorems in general apparently occupy a central position in contemporary mathematics, the doubts raised by the ontic critiques I just outlined also may be very important. However, since this subject matter falls outside my professional competence, as I have noted, the ontological critiques I have offered need to be evaluated by mathematicians. Given the way professions work, though, I do not know whether the field of mathematics has the capacity to seriously entertain a radical critique by an outsider, and to explore its merits. As Thomas Kuhn famously argued, in formal fields and academic enterprises defenses against radical thought— even thought developed by insiders—usually win out, at least for some time; history tells us that almost inevitably,

214 * *Residue II: Mathematics*

annoyingly troublesome critiques somehow disappear from view.[76] Be that as it may, I obviously believe that a study of the issues I have identified would be worthwhile.

## SOME COMMENTS ON PSYCHOLOGISM

In philosophy, psychologism has always been a pejorative term:

> Philosophers have long been cautioned against 'psychologism,' which appears to repel them much as sin repels (and attracts) theologians.... Intimations of warnings against it appear as early as Plato.... Following Kant's lead, philosophers such as Lotze, Frege, and the Neo-Kantians, Windelband, Rickert, Cohen, and Natorp, all take psychology to be irrelevant to philosophy.[77]

On the whole, the term is treated as if it had a straightforward meaning: "the doctrine that reduces logical entities, such as propositions, universals, and numbers, to mental states or mental activities,"[78] "the theory that attempts to reduce all semantic and syntactic organization to the mental contents and operations of empirical subjects,"[79] the ideology that "attempts to conceive the subdisciplines of philosophy as branches of empirical psychology,"[80] "the theory that the subject-matter in question can be reduced to, or explained in terms of, psychological phenomena: mental acts, events, dispositions, and the like."[81]

Matters are not quite that simple, though. Careful explorations of the term and its history reveal problems; for example, an entire monograph has been devoted primarily to unraveling and analyzing its complex and obscure

---

[76]  Silvers, 1995.
[77]  Scharfstein, 1980, p. 45.
[78]  Audi, 1999, p. 404.
[79]  Welton, 2000, p. 260.
[80]  Smith and Smith, 1995, p. 5.
[81]  Dancy and Sosa, 1992, p. 401.

implications;[82] psychologism's core assumption is that the psychologizer proposes to explain via the laws of psychology (of the mind?) instead of remaining within the confines of a particular (non-psychological) science or other discipline, but as the author of the monograph notes, the idea that there is an identifiable body of psychological laws on which psychologizers can call is questionable:

> For the past one hundred and fifty years, "psychologism" has been used as an umbrella term to cover a multitude of philosophical sins, both metaphysical and epistemological. As a result, the meaning of the term has remained systematically obscure, and even today there is little clarity as to exactly what is being charged when an author labels a theory "psychologistic." There is, of course, little doubt that "psychologism" is intended to connote, and to denigrate, the use of psychological methods in philosophical and scientific investigations. But far from clarifying matters, this simply contributes to the elusiveness of the charge. For the various methodological perspectives adopted by the different schools of psychology are so diverse that any reference to psychological methods itself suffers from the same obscurity as "psychologism." [83]

A second problem is that as some thinkers have pointed out, "an 'apsychologistic' epistemology would be one that completely ignored or excluded psychological considerations,"[84] and that would be a most peculiar epistemology: "For centuries philosophers have been anxious to avoid what they call 'psychologism'—that is, confusing questions of logic with matters of psychology. For the pragmatist, logic is either inseparable from psychology or else it has nothing to do with thinking: thought, after all, is inescapably a psychological process."[85] So, logic/mathematics is either in some way thoughtful and has psychological ties (to persons), or "it has nothing to do with

---

[82]  Notturno, 1985; also Scharfstein, 1980, pp. 45-48; Rosen, 1980, pp. 4-33; Tallis, 1999b, pp. 8, 13, 60.
[83]  Notturno, 1985, p. 5.
[84]  BonJour, 2002, p. 245.
[85]  Kaplan, 1961, p. 32.

thinking." The latter would seem to be a peculiar and difficult position to sustain. Does mathematics write itself? As a matter of fact, a noted mathematician even has said (or rather, written) that "all mathematics is mental."[86] In any enterprise or field that involves thought, awareness, use of language, and so on, can one really maintain that at the same time it also is independent of psychological ties?

As I see it, rejecting as I do the notion that any field of endeavor actually can be independent of human ties (obviously a major thesis of this work) is a quite different matter from claiming to reductively explain a field's phenomena in terms of some presumably existing psychological "scientific laws of the mind." For one thing, for years I have been critical of the premise or claim that psychology can be formalized into a science-like, law-like discipline.[87] In any case, I am not aware of here having appealed to "psychological laws" as I have been developing the holistically- and ontogenetically-grounded ideas in my attempt to vivify the Cheshire Cat residues, the "independent objects of study" of mathematics. Perhaps a critic might say that phenomena such as the pattern sense I invoked earlier, or the appeal to ontic matters in the critique of logic, invoke "psychological laws," but I believe that would be stretching a point. The arguments surely involved psychological considerations, but not laws.

Furthermore, I have emphasized throughout the earlier chapters that I am not seeking to "explain" anything in formalistic terms. On the contrary. I have been at pains to stress the derivative nature of adult phenomena (such as language, or mathematics) and their ultimate ineffability—

---

[86]  Rota, 1997, p.160. In general, Rota, an MIT mathematics professor, was refreshingly unorthodox, often unsettling and angering his more conventional colleagues. A prime example is his important paper "The pernicious influence of mathematics upon philosophy," reprinted in Rota, 1997, pp. 89-103. Apparently it "was taken as a personal insult by several living philosophers" (Ibid., p. xxi).

[87]  See, for example, Berger 1978; 1985; 2002a; 2002b, Parts I, II, IV.

their roots in an unfathomable, utterly mysterious domain of the merged, undifferentiated state—and arguing that therefore there are stringent limits on the degree to which one can legitimately claim to explain or understand virtually anything in the adult's world. In any case, as I have insisted *ad nauseam,* my intent is to productively relocate and ground the paradoxes arising in the various disciplines within an unfathomable but unified and unifying ontogenetic framework rather than explaining them away piecemeal and in some facile, scientistic, pseudo-psychological manner. The point is, the issue being explored here is whether or not one needs to consider the person in the apparently impersonal discipline of mathematics, so it seems to me that it would be a plain case of begging the question were one to dismiss these critiques of Cheshire Cat residues on the basis that they bring human ties into the picture.

# 13

# RESIDUE III: PSYCHOLOGY AND PSYCHIATRY

## GENERAL PSYCHOLOGY

### A History of Critiques

The British psychologist Donald Bannister opens his paper (of which more later) by noting that originally it had been titled 'Was Psychology Ever a Good Idea?' He adds that "on reflection such a title seemed both undignified and doomladen, and was discarded."[1]

I think he should have stayed with his original title; it raises a question worth asking and pondering. Mainstream psychology's views, practices, values, aspirations, presuppositions, belief systems, dogmas, methodologies, philosophical grounds, and self-understandings are alarmingly trivial and disingenuous. Here is a glib definition of the field from a standard text: "Psychology is the study of the mind, behavior, and the relationship between them.... Psychology is both a natural science and a social science."[2] What about the phenomena psychology claims to deal with? "Thinking involves the representation and processing of information in the mind.... An emotion is a psychological feeling, usually accompanied by a physiological reaction.... For example, happiness and sadness are emotions."[3]

I see general psychology as a shadowy discipline that ever since its 19th-century beginnings as a supposedly autonomous scientific discipline that split off from

---

[1]   Bannister, 1966, p. 21.
[2]   Sternberg, 2001, p. 27.
[3]   Ibid., pp. 275, 410.

philosophy of mind has been zealously defending its claim to being a legitimate science against skeptical criticisms not only within the field but also from many workers in the natural (i.e., the "real") sciences, hard-nosed (typically, analytic) philosophers, and humanists who objected to the very idea of a reductionist, materialist-physicalist psychology modeled after those sciences (see chapter 1).

General-experimental psychology does not evidence any substantial growth. (I suspect that not all will agree.) Instead, in its driven quest to achieve recognition and status as a real, respectable and respected science it appears to have opportunistically fastened onto whatever the dominant intellectual *Zeitgeist* happened to be in any given era. As mentioned in chapter 1, its beginnings coincided with the heyday of classical physics, so it became *psychophysics.* In the early part of the twentieth century it allied itself with educational efforts such as those of William James or John Dewey, and that association readily lead to its becoming a behaviorally-oriented discipline, dedicated to empirical studies (mostly animal studies) of *learning* and *habit* supported by formalistic, pseudo-scientific, pseudo-mathematical stimulus-response theorizing (Watson; Skinner). Later, in the middle of the last century, it allied itself with the burgeoning computer age and became primarily a cognitively-focused discipline, structuring much of its subject matter in terms of computational or similar mathematical-formalistic models; the buzzword became *artificial intelligence* (AI); mathematical psychology was born. The latest phase has come about with the explosion of drug treatment in psychiatry and clinical psychology and with the dramatic rise in brain studies facilitated by new and sophisticated scanning and other bioneurological monitoring technologies; psychology cast its fortunes with the neurosciences.

All along, there has been strong but minority opposition to this poorly grounded, mechanistically-oriented, reductionist enterprise. In its early days that opposition came mostly from humanistic philosophers (see chapter 1). Later it also came from within the ranks of the discipline itself; a prominent early example is the 1950's critique of general-experimental psychology by Sigmund Koch, one of the most respected members of that community.[4] Criticisms and calls for basic reform continue, reflected in books such as *Psychology: Designing the Discipline*,[5] *Reconsidering Psychology*,[6] *The Myth of Psychology*,[7] *Re-Visioning Psychology*,[8] *In Defense of the Soul*,[9] or *Coming to our Senses*.[10]

## Two Major Issues

The subject matter and rationales of this steady stream of appraisals range over a broad spectrum of often interlocking topics such as: the field's autonomy (e.g., from the natural sciences; from philosophy), methodology, pathological motivations, conceptual foundations, relevance and significance of investigations, interpretation of the experimental outcomes, and neglect of important but difficult to formalize topics and phenomena.[11] I wish to focus briefly and comment on two topics that are seldom included in this body of criticism: psychophysics (a subset of the physical-material reductionist practices rampant in general psychology), and self-reference or reflexivity.

Consider Tallis's arguments against the claim that so-called psychophysical laws have an explanatory force, one

---

4    Koch, 1961, 1974, 1985.
5    Manicas et al., 1986.
6    Faulconer and Williams, 1990.
7    Newman, 1991.
8    Hillman, 1975.
9    Machuga, 2002.
10   Berman, 1989. I myself have also published numerous critiques of general psychology—see Berger, 2002b, especially Parts I and IV.
11   The books mentioned above, especially Manicas et al., 1986, and Faulconer and Williams, 1990, give good overviews.

aspect of his general critique of psychophysiology,[12] the field that claims we "have made considerable progress in explaining how 'the diversity of working [i.e., of the world impinging on our bodies] produceth the diversity of experience'."[13] In chapter 3 I outlined his critique of the unwarranted and duplicitous energy transformations used by physiologists in their pseudo-attempts to "explain" our experience, transformations that slide over the conceptual gap between, say, electrical energy transmission in the nerves and the stimulation of the brain, and one's experience of seeing, or hearing.

Psychophysical laws claim *mathematically* to relate physical and subjective events. A prototypical example is the Weber-Fechner law according to which "there is a correlation between the intensity of the energy incident on the sense ending and the magnitude of the corresponding subjective experience."[14] Now, correlation is a statistical-mathematical manipulation, and therefore to correlate these two domains (the physical and the experiential) one obviously must first find a way of quantifying or at least mathematically structuring the phenomena arising in the latter; otherwise there would be no possibility of mathematical treatment, manipulation. What Tallis shows in a closely-reasoned, extended and as far as I can see incontrovertible analysis is that this process, this scientific step of producing an equation, is predicated on a built-in, conceptually indefensible circularity: "The scales on the 'objective' measuring devices used to generate the relevant scientific data [i.e., the instruments that quantify or mathematize the subjective experience] are not [I would say: cannot be, *in principle*] validated independently of the

---

12   Tallis, 1999a, especially pp. 51-82. These pages merit, and would repay, careful study.
13   Ibid., p. 51.
14   Tallis, 1999a, p. 51.

subjective experience."[15] That is, the mathematical representation of the experiential side of the equation already is *derived*; it is not the experience. The latter remains elusive, not at all captured by the identities that psychophysical laws seem to express. The apparently *psycho*-physical laws merely equate one set of *physical* measurements to a second. Tallis extended analysis[16] calls the entire psychophysics project into question.

The other problematic aspect of general psychology to which I want to call attention is its covert, unattended-to reflexivity. We have already encountered this issue, especially in Frederic Olafson's critiques of naturalizing the human being (chapter 7). He pointed out repeatedly that this move involves a strange sleight of hand, a magic act where the observer, theorizer, reporter, disappears, leaving only what I came to call Cheshire Cat residues, Thomas Nagel's View from Nowhere, a body of independently-existing theories, observational data, records, proposals for future study, and the like. There is a double rupture and disappearing act: The scientist is severed from the scene, and so is the person who stands behind experimental psychology's beloved "subject"—for example, the middle term in stimulus-response models.

For Bannister, the British psychologist mentioned at the beginning of this chapter, a major problem for the field is that "we have not yet faced up to the issue of reflexivity and the need for reflexivity in psychological thinking.... Psychologists share the privilege of scientists in being outside the range of convenience of such theories."[17] At the very least, ignoring reflexivity leaves a large conceptual (epistemological-ontological) gap in psychology's theoretical frameworks.

---

[15] Ibid., p. 52.
[16] Ibid., pp. 51-88.
[17] Bannister, 1966, p. 21.

## Contributions from Holistic and Anomalously-Pragmatic Critiques

The first obvious issue that the critiques developed in the previous chapters raises for psychology involves the linked difficulties concerning its objects of study and associated language problems. What are general psychology's "objects of study"? Unless one wishes to biologize/naturalize psychology entirely (i.e., omit all considerations of and references to the subjective realm), one has to admit that the field presumably concerns itself to some degree at least with "mental contents" (preferably rigorously operationalized, turned into supposedly equivalent objectively measurable data), behavior, interactions, personal meanings—with thoughts, feelings, perceptions, cognitive acts, dreams, wishes, goals, beliefs, and the like. Obviously, right from the start the present work has raised all sorts of doubts about the legitimacy of seeing this collection of entities as independent, even existing, objects that can be objectively (or even not so objectively) studied. We only need to recall Collins' critique of the idea of mental contents that could be legitimately reified and studied, Tallis's critique of all sorts of supposedly objectively and independently existing entities such as "information," Loy's and Olafson's critiques of the inside/outside distinctions and models, Pylkkö's critique of fields that neglect the aconceptual realm, and mine of adultocentrism.

Closely intertwined with the difficulties concerning psychological entities or objects are those subsumed under the label "ontology of language problem." The activities of psychologists themselves (theorizing, observing, referring to [what?], reporting) are one dimension of this problem; the activities of their human subjects (self-reports [of what?]; responding to structured "psychological instruments," performing cognitive-linguistic tasks) are a second dimension.

If we do not go along with the field's indifference to the ontology-of-language problem and its easy assumption that *nameable* psychological entities/objects exist in some sense (i.e., can be studied objectively), we are left with the strong impression that the field lacks a defensible subject matter. While parallel problems do arise in fields such as mathematics or, as we shall see in the next chapter, physics, nevertheless they seem to do less mischief in these fields; at least they have managed to evolve and mature in significant ways. Perhaps when the Cheshire Cat objects themselves are not intended to represent psychological entities specifically, the effects of philosophically suspect beliefs, dogmas, methodologies, etc. are less noxious in a discipline. My wager is that in the case of psychology, the epistemological/ontological flaws cannot be tolerated because of the nature of its identified subject matter and domain. The difficulties inherent in the concepts it has of its objects of study severely subvert psychology's project from the start.

Here is where the anomalously pragmatic question comes into play. If a conception of psychology as a pure knowledge enterprise whose mission is to obtain such knowledge about its objects is untenable, where does that leave the field? It seems obvious to me that this should be the central question for the discipline, and it seems likely to me that no defensible answer can be offered. Thus, returning to Bannister's old title question, 'Was Psychology Ever a Good Idea?', perhaps the sad answer is, no, it was not.

I doubt that my line of argument, premises, and conclusions will have an impact on the field. Its workers are too skillful at employing defenses to maintain the status quo. Any radical stand against naturalizing the person is rejected out of hand. In chapter 3 I quoted Raymond Tallis's lament that his critique of biological reductionism in his own field, geriatric neurology, has fallen on deaf ears.

From a logical (as against a psychodynamically-informed) point of view, it is truly remarkable how totally ineffective the long string of well-considered, deep criticism of mainstream scientistic psychology has been. It is almost never thoughtfully rebutted in the mainstream but just ideologically deflected and/or scornfully dismissed as unscientific or uninformed. In my view, there is a complex constellation of motives and defenses that maintains the status quo.[18] How one might productively address these kinds of effective defenses deployed in the various disciplines is an interesting and important question, and I will comment on it in the conclusion of the next chapter.

## THE MENTAL HEALTH FIELD

Much of what I have criticized about general psychology applies to the mental health fields as well. They display obvious and major parallel problems devolving from the combination of treating their subject matter (e.g., thoughts, wishes, beliefs, "mental disorders") in accordance with the Cheshire Cat residue paradigm and totally ignoring the ontology-of-language Issues.

I have been developing critiques, some quite extended, of clinical psychology and psychiatry along these lines for three decades now.[19] Furthermore, in more recent work I have gone beyond critique and begun to develop proposals for alternatives, primarily an approach to psychotherapy I call *praxis-based*.[20] Given that numerous others have also already offered much criticism, given that most the critiques and alternative proposals are in print and readily available, given the mental health field's dynamics that

---

[18]  I have discussed this at length in a mental health context, particularly in Berger, 1991, and 2002a, chapter 6.

[19]  See the three monographs (Berger, 1985, 1991, and 2002a), and published papers (mostly reprinted in Berger, 2002b). These works also contain voluminous references to and citations of related critiques.

[20]  Berger, 2002a.

defensively maintain the status quo (the subtitle of my 1991 book is *A Psychoanalytic Critique of Treatment Approaches and the Cultural Beliefs that Sustain Them*), and given also the total lack of impact that critiques offered by prominent, respected workers as well my own have had on the field, it seems futile and pointless to offer yet another Don Quixotic-like extended critical disquisition that covers familiar and thoroughly worked-over territory.

Accordingly, I want to conclude this chapter with a reprint of "Psychotherapy, Biological Psychiatry, and the Nature of Matter: A View from Physics."[21] The paper summarizes many of the criticisms that have been raised against the naturalizing physical reductionism that characterizes the mental disciplines' treatment of their subject matter, but from a somewhat different perspective. It sheds additional light on the material in the preceding chapter and also provides a convenient bridge to the chapter on physics that follows.

# PSYCHOTHERAPY, BIOLOGICAL PSYCHIATRY, AND THE NATURE OF MATTER: A VIEW FROM PHYSICS

## ABSTRACT

*Biological psychiatry has marginalized psychotherapy, and it is difficult for psychotherapists to counter its hegemony. The reductionist/materialist position seems incontrovertible and self-evident. An important factor in maintaining this stance is the belief that the physical world is understandable, solid, unproblematic, especially when compared to the realm of the psychological. Developments in quantum and relativity theories, however, cast doubt on that belief. They show the fundamental nature of the material world to be problematic, enigmatic, paradoxical, impossible*

---

21   Berger, 2001; I have made a few trivial updates in the references.

*to understand or conceptualize in terms of everyday
experience. This insight weakens the prima facie case for
privileging the material over the psychological, and
alternative (i.e., non-neurobiological) approaches to mental
health matters should therefore be able to compete on an
equal footing. However, the materialist-reductionist stance
is kept in place by powerful forces and is well defended;
rational arguments alone are unlikely to have an impact.
This pervasive ideological resistance to rational, often well
founded critiques of physical reductionism continues to be a
major impediment to changing the present materialist
climate. That resistance should be addressed before any
significant shift in orientation can be expected to occur.*

A major concept that has channeled thinking, research, and
practices within and on the periphery of the mental health
fields is the polarity of the mental or psychosocial against
the physical/material or neurobiological. It is the legacy of
Cartesian mind/body dualism which is "so marked a feature
of our spiritual and moral landscape."[22]

While a wide variety of positions and associated
practices reflecting differences in the relative weight given
to each pole are found among mental health clinicians and
researchers, few would quarrel with the conclusion that the
positions that privilege material, neurobiological pole
virtually have won the day. As Elliot Valenstein, Professor
Emeritus of Psychology and Neuroscience at the University
of Michigan reports,

> now it is widely believed by most authorities and the public alike
> that the cause [of mental disorders] is a chemical imbalance in the
> brain.... Brain chemistry is believed to be not only the cause of
> mental disorders, but also the explanation of the normal
> variations in personality and behavior.... Today, the disturbed
> thoughts and behavior of mental patients are believed to be
> caused by a biochemically defective brain, and symptoms are not
> "analyzed," but used mainly as the means of arriving at the

---

[22] Luhrman, 2000, p. 6.

diagnosis that will determine the appropriate medication to prescribe. Almost all current chairmen and the majority of the staffs of psychiatry departments are committed to a biochemical approach to mental illness.[23]

The dominance of neurobiological or biomedical orientation has brought with it a marginalization of psychotherapy. It has even "fueled speculation that one day soon all forms of talking therapy will be obsolete.... [C]onsumers increasingly rely on insurance companies and health maintenance organizations, which prefer cheap pharmacology to expensive psychotherapy."[24]

Is this marginalization justified? The answer will depend on one's position on a number of issues, including, for example, how one judges the efficacy of various psychotherapies, what one considers to be the goals of treatment, or what importance one places on simple economic considerations. Another major factor is one's position on *materialism* or *physicalism*—roughly, on the premise

that everything in the world is physical, or that there is nothing over and above the physical, or that the physical facts in a certain sense exhaust all the facts about the world.[25]

If one believes this premise, one will naturally tend to reduce mental domain to the physical:

Everything mental or spiritual is a product of material processes.[26]

[O]ne can explain *everything* in terms of the motion of elementary particles moving inexorably according to the rules of mechanics— there is nothing else.... [I]n principle one can envisage a chain of analysis in which sociology is analysed into psychology, psychology into physiology, physiology into biology, biology into chemistry and chemistry into physics. This view of science is

---

[23] Valenstein, 1998, p.1.
[24] Lear, 1998, p. 17.
[25] Chalmers, 1996, p. 41.
[26] Tolman, 1987, p. 214.

called "reductionism" by those who don't like it and "the unity of science" by those who do.[27]

For the reductionist, once all the facts about the brain are in, then the facts about mind "are a free lunch."[28] Describing mental phenomena will simply be redescribing facts about the brain.

## THE CREDIBILITY OF THE MATERIAL DOMAIN

It is apparent that in the mental health fields, both advocates as well as critics of physical (neurobiological) reductionism see the material domain (especially the brain) as having a major role. I know of no clinician who would deny that, who would seriously hold to an extreme idealistic position, one that maintains everything is mental. Rather, mental health professionals are either strict physical/material/biological reductionists or, more commonly, dualists who believe that both poles of the Cartesian dyad are needed in the field: "The reality... is that all of what are termed diseases (in either psychiatry of physical medicine) have a combination of mental and physical characteristics."[29] Thus, even those who would challenge the hegemony of a neurobiological, material/reductionist position usually support a dual approach to the conception and treatment of mental disorders that would integrate, or at least draw on, both Cartesian poles. Examples are a neuropsychodynamic model,[30] organic unity theory,[31] a biopsychosocial model,[32] or a so-called double aspect model that would use theories based on neuroscience or on the mind as needed, depending on the particular situation, problem, context, or clinical

---

[27]   Squires, 1990, pp. 12, 14.
[28]   Chalmers, 1996, p. 41.
[29]   Woolfolk, 1998, p. 37.
[30]   Miller, 1991.
[31]   Goodman, 1991.
[32]   Engel, 1977.

application at hand: "Biomedical, neurobiological, and psychosocial perspectives... are all necessary."[33]

However both groups, reductionists as well as dualists, apparently do not question the nature of matter. The ubiquitous unexamined assumption is that, essentially, the physical realm is uncontroversial, incontrovertible, tangible, scientifically well established and respectable, tangible, understandable, quantifiable, measurable, directly observable. Both groups accept at face value, without question, the existence and reality of, for example, brain tissue, nervous system, hormones, neurotransmitters, genes, or electrochemical events. Both groups broadly agree on what such "things" and phenomena "are", even when they disagree on their role and function in, say, the etiology and treatment of "mental disorders". Unlike the inner, psychological domain, the domain of the solid, measurable, objectively observable, predictable well-studied material world has enormous scientific credibility. It is seen as essentially straight-forward, conceptually and ontologically essentially unproblematic.

I submit that here, in this face validity and seeming incontrovertibility of the material domain, lies a major and compelling reason for the appeal and hegemony of reductionist neurobiopsychiatry. (I will mention and comment on other factors that support this hegemony in my concluding discussion.) It is easy to privilege the brain and marginalize the psyche when matter has such enormous, apparently unchallengeable credibility.

## OUTLINE OF THE ARGUMENT

If a belief in materialism sustains the biological stance which marginalizes and devalues non-psychopharmaco-logical approaches, then the hegemony of that stance will be

---

[33] Wallace et al., 1997, p. 68; see also Gabbard, 1994.

challenged if the belief is shaken. But how can that be done?

The argument of the body of this work is one response to this question. Of course, numerous arguments have been advanced against material/biological reductionism from various perspectives (e.g., clinical, sociocultural, ethical or spiritual). In philosophy, its legitimacy has been extensively (and inconclusively) debated for centuries under the general rubric of "the mind-body problem." The debates in the vast literature typically have centered about the question of how events in the physical domain—specifically, in the brain— could possibly explain the events in the domain of inner experience (consciousness, perception, affect, meaning, personhood, and the like). Thus, we find, for example, the following typical argument against reductionism:

> How could a physical system such as a brain also be an *experience?*... Present-day scientific theories hardly touch the really difficult questions about consciousness. We do not just lack a detailed theory; we are entirely in the dark about how consciousness fits into the natural order.... Neurobiological processes... can also tell us something about the brain processes that are *correlated* with consciousness. But none of these accounts explains the correlation: we are not told why brain processes should give rise to experience at all. From the point of view of neuroscience, the correlation is simply a brute fact.[34]

The argument which I will present against reductionism will rely altogether on another rationale, however. I have already mentioned my premise that a major factor in establishing and maintaining the hegemony of the biological is a belief in *the apparently unproblematic nature of matter.* I want to argue that this faith in the material world is poorly founded: our conviction that we more or less "understand" what the physical world "is", is without a sound basis. To support this point I will draw on the insights and implications of contemporary physics—

---

[34] Chalmers, 1996, pp. xi, 115.

quantum and relativity theory. Thus, if the material domain turns out to be just as problematic as the mental/psychological, then the convinced belief that a biological reductionist approach should predominate in the mental health field because the material domain is unproblematic while the realm of the "mental" bristles with difficulties, becomes less defensible. The limited objective of this paper, then, is to demonstrate the poverty of our understanding of the physical realm.

Because discussions of quantum mechanics and relativity theory constitute a large portion of this paper, it would be easy to infer that I am arguing for a psychology, psychotherapy, or psychiatry grounded in contemporary physics. That is *not* so. Quite the contrary, and in the concluding sections I will refer to previous publications which explicate my position: I do *not* believe that eventually progress in physics will (or can) "explain" consciousness.

I re-emphasize that the main points I will be making from the perspective of physics are one, that the belief that we understand the material domain well is unwarranted, and two, that therefore our faith in reductionism is on shaky ground.

## PHYSICS AND ONTOLOGY

### The Conflation of Two Levels

What can, what does, physics tell us about ontology, about what exists in the world? The received view is, a great deal. I submit, however, that in an important sense that is not quite the case. To see why this is so let us consider two distinct levels of conceptualizing existence. The first is the domain Wolfgang Smith calls the *corporeal*—the realm of everyday objects, movements, events, what we know through our perceptions, through our normal experience of our world.[35]

The second domain is the level of *physics*. I will be using this latter term to refer to the realm of abstractions in the natural sciences. Its "objects" are various mathematical entities (e.g., variables, equations), symbols, operations, and theoretical laws. (I will not address the issue of how these two levels are connected. The connection between abstractions and "raw data" which involves perception and thought has posed daunting, apparently insuperable philosophical problems and paradoxes that continue to elude understanding and clarification.)[36] Obviously, the two domains are very different from one another ontologically - that is, as far as their nature, being, existence are concerned. It seems beyond question that their respective constituents—roughly, material, observed objects and events in one, mathematical objects in the other—are drastically different from one another.

If these two domains are so different ontologically, how is it that according to the received view, the understandings achieved on the plane of (theoretical) physics *do* tell us what the "real" nature of objects in the corporeal plane is? I believe that this misperception arose because during the long reign of classical (i.e., pre-relativistic, pre-quantum-mechanical) physics, it so happened that the mathematical formalisms and findings which obtained at the *physics* level seemed to have obvious meanings and corresponding counterparts at the *corporeal* level. That is, there was a close and conceptually apparently unproblematic fit between the formal characteristics of the world of mathematical objects and those of the experiential world of macroscopic objects. Take, for example, the familiar

---

[35]   Smith, 1995.
[36]   Smith, 1995; Griffin, 1998; McGinn, 1993; Olafson, 1995; Lockwood, 1989; Nagel, 1961.

Newtonian formula, **F=ma**. It seemed easy and natural to identify its three mathematical variables with our corporeally-based, experiential ideas of physical force, massiveness, and accelerated movement, respectively.

During that classical era this kind of analogizing was possible across a wide range of phenomena. Various mathematical entities in the physics domain could be readily identified with springs, pulleys, water waves, colliding billiard balls, orbiting planets, clocks, and other apparently corresponding objects in the corporeal domain. It was relatively easy to "understand" this abstract aspect of physics in terms of corporeal experiences, and this fostered the illusion that physics was telling us what the world was "really" like. The two levels were conflated, and it became natural and easy to *reify* the level of physics, to clothe its "mathematical entities with imaginary forms and thereby in a way 'corporealize'" them.[37]

Consequently, a curious synergism was established between the two domains: the solidity of the corporeal world gave an apparent solidity to the mathematical world, and, in turn, the established truths of the mathematical laws gave a privileged status to phenomena at the corporeal level. Under those circumstances it became tempting and easy to become convinced that the material world was essentially unproblematic, well understood, and—by extrapolation—capable of explaining all phenomena. This mirroring relationship between classical physics and corporeal "confirming" experience was a major factor in establishing and maintaining the hegemony of a positivist, physicalist, reductionist world view, one where all general knowledge would be contained within the boundaries of physical science and especially of physics, and where any other belief would be dismissed either as metaphysical or as mystical obfuscation.

---

[37]   Smith, 1995, p. 138.

The fallacy in this line of reasoning is that it failed to take into account the step of *interpretation* in science, the process of moving from mathematics to statements about "what there is" in the world. One always *must* "interpret" the formalistic findings achieved at the level of the physics plane in order to impute physical meaning to the mathematics. The mathematical formalisms by themselves leave ontological questions open, as we shall see. Interpretation may be explicit or implicit, visible or concealed, but it always is in the picture when one draws ontological conclusions from physics, when one moves from the realm of mathematics to speaking about "what there is," "what the world is like." In other words, one always has to clothe the mathematical formalisms and experimental outcomes in material meanings, and as we shall see more clearly below, this step of clothing is speculative, creative, uncertain. It is *not* a step that can be taken deductively, that would lead by logical inference from theory to solid, unambiguous conclusions about ontology, about what the material world is like.

During the classical era of science, the ready conflation of the two realms—appealing and possible for the reasons discussed above—tended to push questions of interpretation into the background. They were of interest mostly to philosophers of science.[38] The problem of interpretation became more visible and pressing, however, when quantum mechanics and relativity theory became the master theories in physics. The ontological implications of the mathematics became highly problematic; interpretation became controversial. The very nature of the material domain became obscure and uncertain. What matter "is" could no longer be conceptualized in terms of familiar, ordinary models and objects drawn from the corporeal realm. The

---

[38] See Nagel, 1961, for discussions concerning the problems with so-called "coordinating definitions" or "correspondence rules."

mathematical formalisms of quantum theory and relativity simply do not lend themselves to such concrete modeling.

## The Ineffable in Contemporary Physics

I want to demonstrate that the characteristics of the mathematics have no conceivable counterpart in the characteristics of our corporeal world. One such discrepancy concerns

> the problem of understanding what, in quantum-mechanical terms, happens when we observe a physical system. Popular understanding of the theory would have it that, according to quantum theory, observation invariably involves a physical interference with the system being observed; and that is why the observer comes to play an active role in the theory. But, this... is a gross misconception (albeit one that many physicists, who really ought to know better, have had a hand in perpetuating). The apparent "entanglement", within quantum mechanics, of observer with observed, is a far subtler and far more mysterious affair than the popular account would suggest. It cannot in general be understood in terms of any (ordinary) physical effect that the activities of the observer may have on the objects of observation.[39]

A second peculiarity is the "holistic awareness" displayed by a "particle" (but quantum-mechanical "objects" are not really like the kinds of material particles we know in the corporeal world) in so-called "two-slit" experiments. When a single particle is projected through one of two slits in a screen, quantum mathematics tells us that the path it actually will take (better: the position at which it is likely to land) after passing through that first slit will depend on whether the other slit had been open or shut. Somehow the particle "knows" the status of that second slot.[40] That kind of effect makes no sense in terms of our experiences on the corporeal plane; in classical, common-sense terms the condition of the second slit should not have any influence on

---

[39] Lockwood, 1989, p. x.
[40] Smith, 1995, pp. 115-119.

a single particle's path. In terms of its path pattern, the "particle" will behave like a particle when the second slit is closed and like a "wave" when it is open. The usual explanation that this paradoxical behavior arises from something called "the wave-particle duality" actually explains nothing; the term is "a collection of empty words that indicate only that we really do not understand [i.e., cannot meaningfully *interpret*] quantum theory."[41] Interpreting the experimental results in such terms only serves to trivialize and obscure the strangeness of the physical domain that contemporary physics implies.

Another phenomenon that is inexplicable in terms of our macroscopic experience is the well-known interpretation of Heisenberg's uncertainty principle. Quantum mathematics says that when measuring the values of two particular kinds of related variables of a system (so-called "conjugate observables"), the more exactly one is measured, the less accurately can the other be known.[42] In our usual world, measurements of system parameters are not coupled in this strange kind of inverse relationship, and we cannot make sense of this phenomenon in terms of our experiences at the corporeal level.

Perhaps the strangest feature of the quantum world is the uncanny holism, the unbroken wholeness, implicit in Bell's so-called "interconnectedness theorem."[43] Quantum theory predicts that when two originally proximal and interacting particles separate they continue to retain a close connection: making an observation on one has an instantaneous effect on the other, even when their separation is very great. We no longer can assume locality,

---

[41] Squires, 1990, p.180; see also Smith, 1995, pp. 117-118.
[42] Smith, 1995, p. 50.
[43] Ibid., pp. 68-71; this theorem, its experimental verification, and its uncanny implications are widely discussed.

that we can study what happens in some small region of space, over a small time, without having to worry about what is happening in regions of space very far away.[44]

Some have called this so-called "failure of locality" the most important discovery made by physics, ever. At any rate, it again exemplifies a counterintuitive phenomenon that seems to have no corresponding experiential counterpart at the corporeal level. That is, we cannot conceptualize it or understand it in terms of any macroscopically meaningful and familiar model.

Furthermore, the failure of locality implies that "the fundamental process of Nature lies outside space-time... but generates events that can be located in space-time;"[45] "reality as such is neither space, time nor matter, nor indeed can it be contained in space or time."[46] A consonant finding comes from relativity theory:

> The unsettling feature... [of the theory is that] the geometrical and temporal aspects of things as we ordinarily conceive of them get mixed up.... If one accepts the view that the true character of physical reality is captured by the theory of relativity, then one must be prepared to deal with something that is neither spatial nor temporal but more fundamental than either spatiality or temporality.[47]

Here, too, there are no lived experiences at the corporeal level, the level at which time and space seem utterly distinct, that could make sense of this kind of space-time "mixture."

In this sense, then, physics *cannot* tell us anything meaningful about the fundamental nature of our physical world. What its "thin", mathematical formalisms say is unintelligible in experiential terms. We can find no understandable macroscopic *interpretation*, no way of

---

[44] Squires, 1990, pp.167-168.
[45] The physicist Henry Stapp, quoted in Smith, 1995, p. 69.
[46] Smith, 1995, p. 69.
[47] Jones, 1986, pp. 280, 281.

making (ontological) sense of the information which exists at the physics plane:

> the basic laws of physics... do not tell us what *is*, but instead they tell us about what will happen when we *make an observation*. In fact they only do this in a probabilistic way, i.e., they tell us the probability of certain outcomes of observation.... The basic problem of quantum theory is that there is a gap between what the theory says about the world, and the experience we have of the world.[48]

There is no consensus about the ontological implications of contemporary physics. It "confer[s] a logical structure on physical reality",[49] but that is all it can do. In a fundamental sense, *we do not know what "matter" is*. That is why we now have *the multiplicity of interpretations of quantum theory*,[50] different and mutually incompatible ontological speculations, extrapolations, best guesses about what the implications of the mathematical findings at the level of physics might be for the experiential, macroscopic, corporeal domain:

> When... we ask how the theory *explains* what is happening, or enquire what it says about the external world... we meet only confusion and controversy! This is the interpretation problem of quantum theory.... [W]e have only a very vague idea of what the external world really *is*. Perhaps the only thing of which we can be confident is that we do not understand it![51]

If physics could provide direct and unambiguous ontological information, there would be little room for competing and incompatible interpretations of quantum or relativity theory.

In other words, the levels of physics and corporeality can no longer be identified with one another. We no longer can claim to "understand" the basic constituents of the material

---

48   Squires, 1990, pp. 20, 21.
49   Janik & Toulmin, 1973, p. 142.
50   Squires, 1990, chapter 13.
51   Ibid., pp. 177, 225.

world in terms of our naive everyday macroscopic understandings. The world toward which physics points is vastly more problematic, mysterious, strange than is generally recognized within and without the mental health field. Its nature is largely unknown and apparently unknowable. The mathematics cannot be conceptualized, interpreted, or modeled in terms of familiar, common sense concepts, mechanisms, phenomena, or events—forces, waves, particulate objects, definite paths in space, straightforward measurements—that characterize our experience in the macroscopic world. Consequently, we can no longer claim that the material world is less mysterious and elusive than the inner world, the realm of the psyche. I submit, therefore, that if one takes physics seriously, it has to be admitted that the material domain can no longer claim to have a privileged conceptual status over the "mental." Fundamentally, the material is no less intangible and elusive. Therefore, physicalist "explanations" given in terms of the material domain (e.g., the brain) ultimately dissolve, disappearing into an unknown and unknowable realm.

## THE QUESTION OF RELEVANCE

### The Issue of Scale

It is still widely believed, and particularly by non-physicists, that classical physics and its ontological views continue to describe the macroscopic world in a fundamental way. Of course, in many practical situations one can safely operate on that assumption. For example, in most routine scientific or engineering applications one can—indeed, usually *must*—use classical rather than contemporary science.[52] Consequently it is widely believed that whether or not classical physics gives the "correct"

---

[52] Note the implicit reference to anomalous pragmatism.

picture of the world in a given instance is a question of *scale* (for quantum mechanics) or *velocity* (for relativity theory). However, from a deeper, ontological perspective, that is false: *In a fundamental sense, quantum theory is valid not only in the microworld, and relativity not only in the range of very high velocities.*[53] In the early part of the twentieth century

> [i]t was still possible to escape with some vague feeling that big objects did not obey quantum theory. From a later-20th-century viewpoint, such an escape no longer seems to be available.[54]

This point is echoed by the philosopher Michael Lockwood:

> There is a widespread belief about quantum mechanics, as also about relativity, that it is something that one is entitled to ignore for most ordinary philosophical and scientific purposes, since it only seriously applies at the microlevel of reality: where 'micro' means something far smaller than would show up in any conventional microscope. What sits on top of this microlevel, so the assumption runs, is a sufficiently good approximation to the old classical Newtonian picture to justify our continuing, as philosophers, to think about the world in essentially classical terms. I believe this to be a fundamental mistake.... [T]he world is quantum-mechanical [and relativistic] through and through; and the classical picture of reality is, even at the macroscopic level, deeply inadequate.... [Q]uantum mechanics is not to be regarded as just another scientific theory. To the extent that it is correct, it demands a complete revolution in our way of looking at the world.[55]

This is an extremely important point. It implies that whether the old or the new physics is relevant and appropriate for a given application is *not necessarily* a question of scale and may not be self-evident, since from the perspective of physics the conceptual bedrock and ruling theory *always* is ultimately postclassical. In any given field

---

[53]   Smith, 1995, pp. 62-65.
[54]   Squires, 1990, p.181.
[55]   Lockwood, 1989, pp. 177-178; see also Smith, 1995, pp. 62-65.

of work, then, the question may be: Can that fact be ignored with impunity? *In that specific situation*, is it appropriate, adequate, productive, to predicate one's thinking on a classical ontology?[56] It is safe to say that there are no absolute ground rules for deciding that question, although in many application and contexts within the natural sciences the answer seems obvious and considerations of scale and velocities do play a deciding role. But that may not always be true.

## Contemporary Physics and the Mental Health Field

I have shown that physics suggests one cannot conceptualize the basic aspects of the material domain in terms of the familiar concepts, perceptions, ways of thinking that we use to deal with the everyday corporeal realm, that in its own way, then, the material domain is just as elusive and baffling conceptually as is the domain of the psyche. Can one still maintain, against this understanding, that in the mental health field the material should be privileged over the psychological because the former is somehow solid, substantial, unproblematic? Can one continue to argue that the insights of contemporary physics are irrelevant? In other words, do we know whether in the mental health fields one can safely ignore the conceptual/ontological implications of post-classical developments in physics and continue to privilege a materialist approach based on the earlier conceptions of matter, particles, waves, energy, fields, and the like?

I submit that *no one* can be sure of the answer. We saw that one cannot argue for valorizing materialism simply on the basis of scale alone—that is, on the basis that the insights of contemporary physics have a bearing only on microscopic, not the macroscopic, domains, or on situations

---

[56] Another reference to what I now am calling the anomalously pragmatic perspective.

involving very high speeds. All that can be said about this question of relevance is that opinions are divided. The situation is ironic: mainstream psychiatry seems to assume that the classical framework will do and that it is justified in privileging "ordinary" physicalism (as even a cursory look at the mainstream psychiatric literature will demonstrate), while many important physicists and mathematicians who are knowledgeable about quantum mechanics and relativity theory think otherwise. Members of this latter group tend to appreciate more acutely the conceptual limitations inherent in classical ontology and tend to surmise that the concepts of contemporary physics are likely to be relevant in those fields that deal with person, consciousness, subjectivity.

It seems, then, that a deeper understanding of contemporary physics has led a number of its prominent practitioners to conclude that dealing with persons as material entities conceptualized in classical terms can never significantly advance our understanding of the domain of consciousness or subjective experience—the very domain that ought to be the focus of mental health professionals' concerns. These scientists have concluded that the brain as conceived along traditional material lines can never explain the psyche: The laws and frameworks of classical physics are "too simple and narrow to account for even the lowest processes of life."[57] A much more radical framework seems to be needed:

> The foundations of quantum theory... imply a world-view much more hospitable to resolving the mind-body problem, or the relationship of consciousness to physical reality, than classical metaphysics.[58]

---

[57] The prominent nineteenth-century physicist Heinrich Hertz, quoted in Janik & Toulmin, 1973, p. 141.
[58] Kafatos & Nadeau, 1990, p. 10.

The list of physicists, mathematicians and philosophers who broadly agree with these views includes such luminaries as Wolfgang Pauli, Werner Heisenberg, Heinrich Hertz, Alfred North Whitehead, David Bohm, Erwin Schrödinger, John von Neumann, Eugene Wigner, Ludwig Wittgenstein, and Henry Stapp, as well as numerous less familiar names.[59] Let me emphasize that no while one has *proved* that post-classical physics needs to be taken into account when one is working in the mental health field, *neither has anyone proved that conventional views of the brain, and a physicalist approach to psychopathology and its treatment can suffice.* Therefore, the self-assured certainty of those who would privilege classically-based neurobiological approaches rests on questionable ontological assumptions.

### Could the Psychological Domain be Grounded in the New Physics?

What I have said so far might be construed as a recommendation to conceptually ground psychiatry and clinical psychology in contemporary physics. David Chalmers lists and documents a number of proposals that have been made along this line which assume that "that the key to the explanation of consciousness may lie in a new sort of physical theory."[60]

Although I have drawn heavily on post-classical physics in my discussion I am *not* advocating a quantum-mechanical approach to mental health research and treatment. Quite the opposite. As I have argued elsewhere in some detail,[61] I do not believe that even the most exotic or esoteric advances in physics can *ever* lead to a deeper understanding of the phenomenal/ experiential/

---

[59]  Squires, 1990; Griffin, 1998; Lockwood, 1989; Stapp, 1993.
[60]  Chalmers, 1996, p. 118, also pp. 119-120, 153, 333, 357; Griffin, 1998; Lockwood, 1989; Protter, 1988; Hodgson, 1991; Shalom, 1985.
[61]  Berger, 1985, 1991, 2002a, 2002b, chapters 1, 2, and 11.

psychological domain. I have argued at length, primarily via critiques of the use of what I have called "state process formalisms", that at least as long as physics remains a mathematical discipline as we know it, one that deals with "the structure and dynamics of physical processes",[62] it will remain unable to address the mental domain adequately: "No set of facts about physical structure and dynamics can add up to a fact about phenomenology.... The explanatory gap is as wide as ever."[63] In a nutshell: My critiques of state process formalisms (the generic, underlying mathematical structure on which *all* formal sciences rely) demonstrate that mathematics does not have "in it" the potential to adequately capture the phenomena that are central in mental health work.

Thus, a reminder: I did not present the material about quantum and relativity physics to suggest that future psychiatries or psychologies should be grounded in such a framework. I have had a different purpose in mind. I wanted to provide a science-based argument against an apparently invulnerable biological reductionist stance. The discussions and arguments about post-classical science which I presented were designed mainly to challenge and undermine the hegemony of that world view. The point was to show that the material domain is itself most mysterious and conceptually highly problematic and that therefore there is little justification for the presumption that it is the royal road to understanding and treating psychopathology. That is to say, if we have to admit that apparently ultimately we are unable to conceptualize or understand the material domain in terms of macroscopically meaningful models, ever, then the commonsense, compelling argument for privileging that domain in the mental health field is weakened, undermined.

---

[62] Chalmers, 1996, p. 118.
[63] Ibid., pp. 118-119.

I also noted earlier that in addition to the critiques from philosophy of science, other kinds of critiques of physicalism, particularly of reductive physicalism, have been offered from a variety of other positions and perspectives. For example, significant flaws can be identified in the interpretation of data, research methodology.[64] Questionable ethical practices and the impact of economic interests motivate a physicalist approach.[65] Crosscultural studies have provided another kind of critique.[66] Yet other critiques are based on the demonstrated influence of psychological factors on material events in the brain.[67]

Still, there are no signs that this body of criticism has had any impact on the dominance of neurobiology on theory, research, or clinical practices in the mental health field. The mainstream psychiatric and psychological literature continues to be steeped in biological approaches, and in my own experience, few clinical colleagues are even aware of the existence of these critiques let alone affected by them.

Biological reductionism thus displays an uncanny resilience, apparently being immune to the steady stream of criticism. It seems highly unlikely, however, that reductionism persists because *all* criticisms are flawed; surely, at least some are solidly grounded and deserve to be taken seriously. Yet, "the pro-materialist positions have become so forceful that any claim to refute them... appears naive."[68] I will conclude by briefly commenting on this state of affairs.

---

[64]   Luhrmann, 2000; Valenstein, 1998; Ingleby, 1980; Kirk & Kutchins, 1992; Lewontin et al., 1984; Szasz, 1996.

[65]   Valenstein, 1998; Kirk & Kutchins, 1992; Lewontin et al., 1984; Hubbard & Wald, 1993; Eagleton, 1991.

[66]   Ingleby, 1980; Kleinman & Good, 1985; Marsella & White, 1982.

[67]   Valenstein, 1998, pp. 126-132.

[68]   Hubbard & Wald, 1993, p. 13.

## THE PROBLEM OF IDEOLOGY

I believe that the apparent immunity of neurobiological reductionism to criticism can be understood from a restricted as well as a wider perspective. Both pertain to *ideology*—roughly, the covert promulgation of false or deceptive beliefs, of "false consciousness," typically in the service of powerful interests and often "securing the complicity of subordinated classes and groups."[69]

I have mentioned that reductionism serves the interests of many groups involved either directly or peripherally in mental health matters. For example, consider some of the gains derived from biological explanations and treatments of addictions, depression, or attention deficit disorders. Such explanations encourage patients—and often their families—to defensively disclaim responsibility for their difficulties, to avoid looking at problematic psychodynamics, and to dismiss out of hand any need for deeper and costly psychotherapy. Of course, it is readily apparent that these biological explanations provide other gains as well. For instance, obviously they advance the financial interests of drug and insurance companies; they rationalize the need for profitable research programs; they allow nonspecialists to treat "mental disorders", and so on.[70]

These are ideological aspects of material reductionism in a narrow sense, in that they manifest specifically the context of mental health issues. In a wider sense, they can also be identified in the very wide context. They are an aspect of the ideology of *modernism* whose roots can be found in the Enlightenment era.[71] (Some would trace the roots back to the age of Plato.) This vast ideology and its pathological symptomatology has been articulated and addressed in various critiques by major thinkers, such as

---

[69] Eagleton, 1991, p. 30.
[70] Valenstein, 1998; Berger, 1991.
[71] Pippin, 1991; Smith, 1996; Toulmin, 1990.

Nietzsche, Marx, and Heidegger, and elaborated in a large secondary literature. The critics broadly agree on the major symptoms: an overvaluation and overapplication of science, objectivity, and rationality ("scientism"); a priority given to control, prediction, manipulation ("a kind of technological self-assertion");[72] the devaluation of subjectivity, tradition, history, context. As one philosopher has put it, The "heart of the modernity problem" is

> the intrusion of market considerations into every aspect of life, the effects of a mass, eventually media-dominated society, or the narcissism and impatience created by modern institutions, each or all signal[ing] some vast decline in the moral sensibilities or taste....[73]

The value given to physical reductionist views concerning the nature of psychopathology and its rational treatment can thus be seen as but a manifestation in the microcosm of the mental health field of a much broader, culturally pervasive condition. Both expressions of materialist, physicalist ideologies are maintained by powerful, complex and often poorly understood socioeconomic, cultural, psychological, material, scientific, and political factors. Both are deeply embedded and demonstrate an uncanny homeostasis. They are virtually immune to criticism, no matter how well conceived and compelling it might be.

One must ruefully conclude, therefore, that, by themselves, rational critiques of biological reductionism based on logical arguments cannot be expected to alter the prevailing orientation of the current mental health scene. The homeostasis of ideology in both the narrower as well as in the wider context will maintain the *status quo*. Proposals for radically different alternative clinical approaches[74] are unlikely to receive serious consideration under these

---

[72] Pippin, 1991, p. 5.
[73] Ibid., p. 84.
[74] E.g., Griffin, 1998; Berger, 2002a; Barratt, 1984.

conditions. One might well ask whether it is even possible to alter the ideological climate within the narrow, restricted clinical domain as long as the larger, general cultural materialist ideology remains in place. The ideologies are well and rigidly defended.

What *would* make an impact on this climate? How could one begin to counter the ideologies and their effects? These are baffling yet vitally important questions. Perhaps what some clinicians see as effective ways of dealing with individual maladaptive behaviors which are maintained by potent defensive needs and beliefs[75] could somehow be generalized and put to use in this wider application and context. I hope to explore that possibility in future publications.[76]

---

[75] In this context, see especially Gray, 1994.
[76] To some extent I have done so—see the remarks at the conclusion of the next chapter.

# 14

# RESIDUE IV: PHYSICS

*Uncritically adopted foundations fall easily into
inaccessible obscurity. The standard scientific attitude still
views the world as a set of external things, language as a set
of labels for the things and actions, and the human mind as
a mechanism which handles the labels and related concepts
in order to say something about the things.*

> ~ Pauli Pylkkö, *The Aconceptual Mind*

*Russell, after rejecting Descartes' fundamental Cartesian
dualism, pointed out that those who reject Descartes'
doctrine often retain a number of the underlying logical
beliefs, which subsequently influence their thinking. He also
noted that many philosophical debates center around
scientific questions "with which science is not ready to
deal".... Is science ready today?*

> ~ Karl Pfenninger and Valerie Shubik, *The
> Origins of Creativity*

## Mainstream Physics and Philosophy

We have seen that the polarizing bifurcations that
grounded Enlightenment natural science introduced
apparently irresolvable and by now familiar conundrums
into that science: "Problems started when Galileo suggested
that the... primary qualities were objective, while...
secondary qualities were mere subjective experiences not at
all inherent to the things themselves;"[1] the total separation
of the two drastically different domains predicated by a

---

[1]   Harvey, 1989, p. 21.

Cartesian substance dualism "permits no knowledge of the outer domain;"[2] we do not know to this day "how to combine the perspective of a particular person inside the world with an objective view of that same world, the person and his viewpoint included."[3] Other, less familiar kinds of difficulties inherent in a Cartesian-based natural science were identified in the course of the unorthodox analyses sketched in the earlier chapters. This class of difficulties can be characterized as deriving from the adultocentric, segregational approaches that create Cheshire Cat residues as a field's objects of study.

Accordingly, the conceptual foundations of physics are suspect not only because of their Enlightenment/Cartesian heritage but also because physics assimilates the belief systems and practices implicit in what I have labeled the received views of descriptive language, of mathematics, and of psychology (especially the causal theory of perception). It is a discipline dominated by Cheshire Cat residue "objects."

## Physicists' Indifference

Do the difficulties that bedevil the field's philosophical foundations matter to physicists? Given its three-hundred-year history of apparent successes and continuing progress,[4] it should come as no surprise that within mainstream physics the consensus clearly is that such difficulties are peripheral and insignificant:

> Bohr's so-called Copenhagen interpretation of quantum mechanics [of which more below], in spite of its strange overtones, is actually the 'official' view among professional physicists. In the practical application of quantum mechanics the physicist rarely needs to confront any epistemological problems. So long as the quantum rules are applied systematically, the theory does all that can be

---

[2]  Keller, 1979, p. 719.
[3]  Nagel, 1986, p. 3.
[4]  I say apparent, because these "successes" are marred by the major noxious end results Holbrook ironically called "side effects" (see chapter 4).

expected of it; that is, it correctly predicts the results of actual measurements—which is, after all, the business of physicists.[5]

Physicists display an extraordinary confidence in the status of quantum mechanics coupled with general reluctance to discuss its implications…. The strong positivist ethos surrounding contemporary science makes it possible for some, perhaps most physicists, to limit the definition of reality to the body of theoretical and empirical knowledge at our disposal, and to declare as meaningless all questions about the actual nature of the systems being studied, and our relation to those systems.[6]

There is little interest among physicists in foundational questions although there certainly have been notable exceptions—Einstein, for one. I think it is fair to say that most physicists just want to go about their professional business, undistracted by philosophical considerations they consider to be irrelevant frills, amateurish, metaphysical speculations and indulgences at best. It seems that most physicists are content with their simplistic epistemologies and ontologies, scarcely aware of any philosophical difficulties, certain that their field has done well and will continue to do so no matter how imperfect, problematic or unsatisfactory its bases might seem to its philosophical critics. There are, however, indications that for very practical reasons the field may be forced to change its position on the relevance of philosophical matters, so the issue merits further consideration.

## What Can Physics Tell Us About The World?

Physicists theorize and experiment (and the boundaries between these are by no means always clear), but what are they learning *about*? After all, *all* their thinking originates and terminates in acts of quantification, measurements. Still, I believe that in spite of their distancing from matters philosophical, most physicists would say that they are

---

[5]   Davies and Brown, 1986, p. 26.
[6]   Keller, 1979, p. 720.

learning about *something*—elementary particles, fundamental forces, black holes, the big bang. Now, to go from mathematics and experimental data to their meaning require the speculative act of *interpretation,* and that step takes us into difficult, muddled territory—into matters concerning the nature of reality, into questions concerning the referents of their mathematical and descriptive language, and so on.

Nevertheless, physicists usually take philosophically simplistic, naive positions with respect to that interpretative step. Two broadly distinct attitudes can be identified, represented by the two giants of recent physics, Niels Bohr and Albert Einstein. A physics professor labels these as "'ontic'... relating to being," and "'epistemic'... relating to knowledge"[7] respectively. While both physicists "agreed that the task of their science is to describe nature,"[8] they had what appear to be drastically different views about what such a description is and means. *Bohr's* idea of description is based on a complex but conservative notion of experience that divides it into an objective and a subjective pole:

> Every ordinary experience has this "subject/object structure." The objective pole is that which is experienced. The subjective pole is that which makes the experience possible, and it includes the experiencer.... The demarcation line between subject and object can be fluid.... [it] can even cut across the distinction between the animate and the inanimate.[9]

Under the Bohr-type model, description, then, is "epistemic:" "It is wrong to think that the task of physics is to find out how nature is. Physics concerns what we can say about nature."[10] Physics' job is the description of the *objective* pole, although the boundary between the two poles

---

[7]   Malin, 2001, p. 38.
[8]   Ibid.
[9]   Ibid. To me, this epistemology seems rather muddled, even cavalier.
[10]   Bohr, quoted in Malin, 2001, p. 38.

is fluid and the "objective pole may include myself... [and] the subjective pole may include objects, such as a hammer."[11] This essentially outlines the Copenhagen interpretation referred to above.

On the other hand, according to the *Einsteinian,* ontic, view, "the task of science is to describe nature as it is."[12] It assumes that nature is knowable, that the nature of that nature should and can be known and described by humans. It assumes that there is such a thing as true, independent reality (what some philosophers have ironically called "the really real"), and that although physics may never get to describe it quite completely and accurately, at least it will approach ideal knowledge asymptotically. The ontic view seems to be essentially that of folk psychology, a naive realism—we see what is out there, and that's the end of it. Apparently that is acceptable to most physicists; the Oxford physicist Sir Rudolph Peirls does "not think there are so many physicists who are worried about this [Einstein's view]."[13]

Be that as it may, the lay public assumes that physics is about *something,* that physicists can give us arcane and startling insights about how the world really is, what is beneath and beyond our understandings of macroscopic surface phenomena. Correspondingly, many physicists do venture interpretations, telling us what their theories and data imply about reality. (Physicists do not only report about tracks in bubble chambers but speak of them as the discoveries of new particles.) Interpretations are underdetermined by the field's data, however. Often, physicists do offer and champion numerous and mutually conflicting alternative interpretations or inferences of the results of their work. For example, one book cites eight

---

11  Ibid.
12  Malin, 2001, p. 39.
13  Davies and Brown, 1986, p. 76.

possible interpretations of "quantum reality,"[14] "conjectured alternatives, competing with one another,... to fill the ontological void;"[15] another book refers to twelve.[16] Although they may differ in their intuitive appeal, these various interpretative "explanations" apparently are equally supportable by the same body of mathematical theory and experimental data, even by "the same [Cartesian] ontological presupposition."[17]

My impression, however, is that the question of interpretation is much more of an issue for philosophers than it is for physicists.[18] My sense is that on the whole, physicists' often sensationalist interpretations of their findings are more of a playful public relations gesture than a serious professional concern with ontology. And, from their mainstream perspective such an indifference makes sense; if the theories and data of physics cannot adjudicate between imagined alternative world interpretations, then as far as working physicists are concerned, interpretations are idle indulgences. They may be good fun, good for calling the lay public's attention to the field and its wonders, but I submit that for the typical physicist who does not yearn for deeper philosophical understanding, questions of interpretation are frills, and at bottom otiose. So, I submit

---

[14]  Herbert, 1985, pp. 156-197, 240-245.

[15]  Smith, 1995, p. i.

[16]  Ibid.

[17]  Ibid. A large popular literature has evolved that illustrates and tries to "explain" the numerous baffling phenomena in quantum physics ranging from the wave-particle duality to Schrodinger's Cat problem to non-locality, and in relativity theory, such as the highly anti-intuitive merger of space and time—see, for example, Lindley, 1996; D'Espagnat, 1989; Albert, 1992; Kafatos and Nadeau,1990; Malin, 2001; Blakemore and Greenfield, 1987; Jones, 1982; Hodgson, 1991; Zukav, 1979; McTaggard, 2002. See also my critiques of the entire interpretational project in the paper reprinted in the previous chapter.

[18]  There certainly have been important exceptions, physicists such as Einstein, Schrödinger, Heisenberg, David Bohm, John Wheeler, Geoffrey Chew, Fritjof Capra, Roger Penrose, who seemed deeply concerned with philosophical implications.

that even in the matter of interpretation, mainstream physics is essentially indifferent to philosophy.

## Theory and Observation in Physics

The relationship between theory and observation is notoriously difficult. One can treat it simplistically, of course, confining the first to the blackboard and the second to the laboratory. If it is considered in any depth, usually the focus is on epistemological issues (e.g., the logical structure of scientific language); few serious efforts are made to understand the issue at an ontological level.

For example, mainstream physicists do not worry much about the conceptual discontinuities between quantum and classical physics:

> Most physicists do not pursue the logic of the quantum theory to the ultimate extreme. They tacitly assume that somewhere, at some level between atoms and Geiger counters, quantum physics somehow 'turns into' classical physics, in which the independent reality of tables, chairs and moons is never doubted. [Niels] Bohr.... left it vague as to exactly what this act ['an irreversible act of amplification'] entails.[19]

Neither do they seem to worry that "quantum theory is all about measurement but it never clarifies what a measurement actually is;"[20] "measurement, in the Copenhagen interpretation, is... a magical, unexplained happening."[21] While apparently physicists do seem to concern themselves with consciousness (these days, mostly in the context of the so-called "collapse of the wave function" that the act of observation precipitates), actually "references in physics to consciousness are often a matter of lip service.... [It is] the rare scientist who is concerned with such matters."[22] Unlike most reductive neuroscientists,

---

19  Davies and Brown, 1986, p. 31.
20  Penrose, 1995, p. 21.
21  Sheldrake, 2003, p. 11.
22  Jones, 1982, p. 16.

psychiatrists, brain researchers and others who zealously argue and claim that physics will ultimately be able to explain the nature of conscious experience, most physicists seem to casually acknowledge that they "can admittedly find nothing in physics or chemistry that has even a remote bearing on consciousness,"[23] that "the standard theory has no explanation for your most immediate and direct experience."[24] These views have been echoed by important scientists such as Einstein, Eugene Wigner, Henry Margenau, and Gerald Feinberg.[25] Most physicists do not seem particularly interested in subjectivity, nor driven to explain it scientifically, nor do they promise that future fundamental advances in natural science will be able to do so; they just casually accept the puzzling fact of consciousness.[26]

A notable exception to physicists' indifference to ontological issues is the work of Wolfgang Smith, a mathematician, physicist and philosopher. He wants to investigate ontological issues that go beyond the Cartesian dualism. To begin, he demonstrates that although it may remain unacknowledged or even denied, actually Cartesianism does silently underlie even the most radical of contemporary physics frameworks, quantum theory.[27] He wants to change that. He argues convincingly against segregationalism in physics, the usual decoupling of primary, quantifiable from secondary, qualitative attributes, of the perceiver from the perceived, a step that he recognizes has introduced basic conundrums into physics and continues to do so. His detailed and complex analysis of the problem of perception in physics draws on the

---

23   Niels Bohr, quoted in Dossey, 1999, p. 79.
24   Sheldrake, 2003, p. 11. For a highly radical view of perception, see Harding, 2002.
25   Dossey, 1999, pp. 78-82.
26   In that they seem much wiser and more realistic than their counterparts in the behavioral disciplines, as I pointed out in the last chapter.
27   Smith, 1995; also Kafatos and Nadeau, 1990, p. 77.

distinction he makes between the "corporeal world" ("the sum total of things and events that can be directly perceived by a normal human being through the exercise of his sight, his hearing, and his sense of touch, taste and smell")[28] and what he somewhat confusingly calls "the physical universe," the physicist's special domain, a realm seen through the artificial "eyes" of instrumentation and mathematics, "a strange new world comprised of [sic] quantities and mathematical structure."[29]

Smith's is a laudable, interesting, informative effort, but in my view one that is bound to fail. Despite his close and knowledgeable criticism of the Cartesian bifurcation(s), when all is said and done Smith continues to predicate his analyses on the perceiver/perceived basic distinction: "the world exists and is known in part... [it is] something that can and must on occasion present itself to our inspection."[30] From my point of view, what is missing of course is the ontogenetic dimension; he continues to operate in an adultocentric, fragmenting mode, hoping to explain the inexplicable via normal rationality, hoping that logical analysis will adequately resolve the paradoxes inherent in the perceptual process. I see that as a vain, scientistic hope.

## LANGUAGE AND NON-LINGUISTIC FACTS

One basic duality, however, whose legitimacy apparently must be assumed in physics (indeed, in all the natural sciences) is the partitioning of one's universe into word and object, linguistic/mathematical description and raw fact. Although in our time it has become commonplace to acknowledge that observations are, as fashionable jargon would have it, "theory-laden" (i.e., one's theoretical framework and basic assumptions inevitably cast a

---

[28]  Ibid., p. 19.
[29]  Ibid., p. 22.
[30]  Ibid., p. 3.

distorting, limiting, prejudicial template over one's observation of supposedly objective "facts"), nevertheless within that limitation it is taken as a matter of course that there *are* facts, and that there are, separately, observations, reports, theories, symbolic and mental representations, of these facts. That distinction is taken as incontrovertible, self-evident, basic, necessary for science: There is a fundamental, radical and obvious difference between the actual cat on the mat (the non-linguistic fact) and saying (or writing, or mathematizing, or asserting) "there is a cat on the mat."

Yet, we have had intimations that the referential aspect of language is not a straightforward matter; we have seen the ontological illusions a segregational view of language introduces. Heidegger, especially, calls the commonplace, apparently incontrovertible, dogmatic belief that there are non- or pre-linguistic facts into question. He makes a valuable excursion into this subject in the Preliminary Considerations to his *The Essence of Truth.*[31] He first states the received view of truth (one that he will strongly contest, or at least heavily qualify). Truth (and falsity) is a property of assertive propositions: "*correctness.... correspondence, grounded in correctness, between proposition and thing.... The proposition corresponds with that about which it speaks.*"[32] In this view of truth, linguistic reference is taken for granted, at face value, as the obvious (but not further explicable!) "relation" between something linguistic and something else *that is nonlinguistic.* The assumption of course is that one *can* directly experience, perceive, that non-linguistic something else. Western common sense supports this belief, and supports the assumption that it cannot be challenged.

---

[31] Heidegger, 2000.
[32] Heidegger, 2000, pp. 1 and 2.

Heidegger goes on to show that this notion of the non-linguistic element or component of the dyadic truth- and/or reference relation is at least highly problematic if not altogether incoherent. His remarks are worth quoting:

> 'Here in the room a light is on.' That about which something is said in this proposition, that *towards which* it is directed, must already be *given* as the measure [i.e., the standard, or criterion] for the proposition, for how otherwise could the proposition be directed towards it? So we must already know what and how the thing is about which we speak. We know that a light is on here. Such knowing... can only arise from knowledge..., and knowledge grasps the true.... And what *is* the true? The true is *what is known*. It is just what corresponds with the facts. The proposition corresponds with what is known in knowledge; thus with what is true. The true? So does the correspondence of the proposition amount to correspondence with something corresponding? [I.e., if truth is correspondence, and a fact is true, it corresponds to... what if it itself is to be true?] A fine definition! Truth is correspondence with a correspondence, the latter [the fact] itself corresponds with a correspondence, and so forth.[33]

Here Heidegger is calling attention to the difficulties that arise when one posits a world of facts that is supposedly separate from language and related to it via correspondence, reference: "What,... asks Heidegger, tells us what the facts are to which propositions are to be compared for correspondence?"[34] He shows that this position leads to a vicious circle. The relation between language and fact, the relation we call "reference, "depends on a something more 'primordial'," Heidegger says.[35]

There is good reason, then, to suppose that we ought to be cautious about glibly speaking of external facts, naming, and linguistic reference—whether direct or indirect—as self-evident, relatively unproblematic and straightforward entities and actions that we can take for granted. Thus,

---

[33] Ibid., p. 2.
[34] Young, 2002, p. 6.
[35] Heidegger, 2000, p. 7.

although it goes against common sense and seems like a untenable belief, important thinkers have concluded that "there is no 'fact of the matter' outside language":[36]

> Language is the air in which our minds breathe, the very space in which our consciousness is deployed. There is, consequently, no place outside of language from which we can see it.... Facts are neither purely intra- nor purely extra-linguistic: so the truth of declarative utterances is not grounded in a simple external relationship between the intra-linguistic meaning of strings of symbols and facts understood as entities existing independently of language.[37]

The question is, if this unorthodox claim has merit, does it need to be taken into account by physicists? Should the possibility that the fact/description dichotomy (ultimately, also the inner/outer dichotomy) is fundamentally untenable matter to practitioners and theoreticians?

## IS A NEW, DIFFERENT PHYSICS NEEDED?

### Some Opinions

Even though physics has had a history of successes, some have expressed the opinions that a new kind of physics *is* needed. The reasons given in support of this contention fall mostly into two groups: (1) physics needs to widen its vision so that it can become able to encompass the domain of subjective experiences (a realm that so far had been deemed to fall outside physics' legitimate and circumscribed domain of inquiry), and/or (2) a different physics is needed because it has come to the point where its framework impedes further progress as traditionally defined. Not surprisingly, recommendations based on the former rationale are more likely to come from philosophers while proposals based on the latter, traditional natural science criteria are more likely to come from physicists themselves.

---

[36]   Abel, 1976, p. 84.
[37]   Tallis, 1999a, p. 189, and 1999b, p. 18.

An example of recommendations of the first kind is David Ray Griffin and Christian de Quincey's advocacy of panexperientialism. I mentioned this ontological position in chapter 1, where I characterized it as an updated, arguably more scientifically respectable, defensible form of panpsychism—itself a position that has been generally disparaged and dismissed and usually is not even included in standard lists of acceptable ontological positions. These panexperientialists believe first, that the subject matter of natural science ought to include consciousness; "We have an atomic physics…, but we don't have a qualitative-character-of-experience physics at all,"[38] and that lack ought to be corrected. Second, panexperientialists (and others) maintain that the usual evolutionist-physicalist-materialist premise and explication that consciousness "somehow" emerged out of inanimate matter (generally regarded as incontrovertible dogma) is untenable, baseless, scientistic, wishful thinking. No one has the slightest idea how that evolution might be explainable within a physicalist natural science, a discipline that is quite unable even to conceptualize the entity it is trying to explain. The evolutionary explanation is a dogmatic promissory note. The third premise these advocates of panexperientialism hold is that in order to bring subjectivity into physics' domain of study, natural science will have to introduce some kind of rudimentary form of consciousness even at the most fundamental levels of material-physical existence.

A second example is Pylkkö, who also wants a natural science that is able to encompass subjectivity. For him that means a science that can also account for the entire spectrum of *a*conceptual phenomena and experiences, the foci of his work. Like Griffin and de Quincey, Pylkkö argues that because of its inherent structural limitations (see chapter 8), traditional, "onto-theo-logical," "dogmatic,"

---

[38] Quoting the philosopher Galen Strawson, Griffin (1998, p. 86).

metaphysical, enframing, reifying, dichotomizing naturalized science is necessarily unable to do so—either now, or in the future.

Let us next consider examples of proposals motivated by the traditional values and goals of natural science. Although Pylkkö is mainly interested in reconceptualizing science as a framework capable of encompassing aconceptual phenomena, still, he calls for a new kind of natural science also for less experientially-oriented, more traditional, reasons. He thinks that without a drastic conceptual shift in its framework, physics will be unable to resolve its currently stymying problematic dichotomies—for example, the embarrassingly "irreconcilable contrast of the microphysical and the macrophysical."[39] Also, he sees ontotheological (metaphysical, Cartesian, what he calls "dogmatic") physics as constricting and limiting our knowledge in principle because it excludes an entire aspect of the world. He believes that continuing along traditional lines will lead to "a gradually shrinking area of the reality... distancing us from the true picture of the so-called reality."[40] In other words, Pylkkö believes that without fundamental revision, physics is heading in the wrong direction, is misleading us about the nature of our world.

Pylkkö's contention echoes the view of Wolfgang Pauli, one of the major figures in the early development of quantum theory, who claimed "that the research program of natural science which was launched in the early seventeenth century has, with the invention of quantum theory, come to the end of its road... [because] nature has eventually disclosed its *irrational* face which had been covered for about three hundred years under the thin mask

---

[39] Pylkkö, 1998, p. 46.
[40] Ibid., p. 31.

of exaggerated rationality."[41] A call for a radically new program is implicit in this contention also.

Wolfgang Smith calls for a reconceptualization of physics because interpretations of quantum physics imply that nature is an "unbroken wholeness" and yet this is an aspect that the usual physics simply cannot encompass. He says that physics' most striking findings concerning this strange wholeness are Bell's interconnectedness theorem and the associated empirical confirmations, but that physics as presently constituted cannot take this finding further, or even make sense out of it:[42] "the concrete results cannot 'on principle' disclose this wholeness... that reality is not itself, in fact or in principle, disclosed."[43] Other physicists who champion a new holistic science for similar reasons are David Bohm whose proposals center around the notions of "implicate order" and "holomovement," and Geoffrey Chew, whose holistic approach is via the so-called bootstrap theory.[44]

Yet another similar example is the view expressed by Shimon Malin, a physics professor. He says that "the central quest of present-day physics is the search for 'a theory of everything,'[often simply "TOE"] a set of equations that contain, in principle, solutions to any and all problems," adding that "true unification must be based on a transcendence of the principle of objectivation."[45] That latter term is the renowned physicist Schrödinger's label for the practice "that a scientific inquiry always starts by removing the 'Subject of Cognizance', that is, ourselves, from the domain of nature that we endeavor to understand... and [by] treating its subject matter as a lifeless object.... [We begin physics with] the removal of life

---

[41] Ibid., p. 39.
[42] Smith,1995, pp. 68-69.
[43] Kafatos and Nadeau, 1990, p. 121.
[44] Capra, 1988, p. 64; also Bohm, 1976, 1980; Holbrook, 1981, p. 42.
[45] Malin, 2001, p. 189.

from nature."[46] (In my terminology: Schrödinger clearly is recognizing and articulating the Cheshire Cat residue problem.)

## Some Proposed Approaches

It is understandable, indeed expectable, that regardless of their motivation, those who advocate a new science would have great difficulty in going beyond their general critiques and aspirations to formulating specific recommendations about how such a science might look. Trying to envision a truly new alternative framework and approach is daunting; everyone knows it is much easier to recognize and criticize a framework's shortcomings than it is to offer a viable alternative. Thus, for example, Malin only repeats that Schrödinger's principle of objectivation (see above) needs to be set aside if the unificationist goal of physics is to be achieved: "It is possible that *the integration of the objective and subjective domains within the context of the scientific endeavor will be the next decisive step in the evolution of science.*"[47] He says nothing about how to set that principle aside, or in general how one would go about achieving this integration, or how such an alternative science might look.

We have seen that Pylkkö wants a physics that is "otherwise," a "genuine" naturalism that is *a*-dogmatic, *a*-onto-theo-logical, *a*-metaphysical, and so on. When it comes to specifying what such a genuine naturalized physics would look like, however, Pylkkö's arguments also become amorphous. He presents a collection of desirable criteria and goals for such a science; he suggests that dogmatic science could be avoided by the *way* in which we talk, say, about quantum phenomena, or by *reinterpreting* the implications of contemporary theory;[48] and, he suggests, vaguely, that an adogmatic science might possibly be

---

46 Ibid., pp. 87, 203.
47 Malin, 2001, p. 230.
48 Pylkkö, 1998, pp. 53, 69.

developed via the use of a properly modified (perhaps "noncomputational") mathematical neuroscientific model.[49]

One can find a few more specific proposals. For example, David Bohm and Geoffrey Chew both want to express their insights and realize their visions via mathematical innovations: "both use matrices to represent change and transformation, and topology to classify categories of order."[50]

Another example of a more concrete recommendation is the approach proposed by Christian de Quincey, one of the above-mentioned advocates of panexperientialism:

> I believe we do need a radically different physics. This is not to say that current physics is all wrong—that, indeed, would be absurd.... It may be, however, a *limit* case of a more complete physics, analogous to Newtonian physics being a limit case of relativistic physics. The new physics hinted at here would include not only the four currently known forces (electromagnetism, strong and weak nuclear, and gravitation) but also data and theories that account for the panpsychist notion of inherently sentient, subjective, and self-agented matter-energy. It would be a physics compatible with true psychology because it would include both matter and mind."[51]

Under this vision the new physics would include new kinds of forces; what else might be needed in order to be able to include mind in the physicist's domain of study remains obscure, however.

These more tangible proposals are predicated on the possibility of making significantly different kinds of advances while retaining an essentially mathematized, quantifying science. Can one retain such formalizing ingredients and yet have a really (qualitatively) new kind of science?[52]

---

[49]  Ibid., p. 53 and chapter 3.
[50]  Capra, 1988, p. 64.
[51]  de Quincey, 2002, p. 201.
[52]  In my own field of psychoanalytic psychotherapy, I have attempted to go beyond criticism. My *Psychotherapy as Praxis* (2002a) offers an outline (see

## AN ONTOGENETIC/ANOMALOUSLY PRAGMATIC RESPONSE

Most proposals for a new physics (such as those just outlined) tend to be presented and discussed in a vacuum. That is, both types of proposals discussed above adopt a Pure Knowledge Paradigm position rather than first exploring the implications of what I have been calling anomalous pragmatism. The needs for revision are addressed immediately, without first considering the question of what the field's goals and aspirations ought to be; they are taken as givens.

A host of critiques, including most of those presented in this work (see especially chapters 4 and 10), question the viability of the pure knowledge paradigm and its presumptions. It conceals a multitude of unexamined foundational assumptions, so actually it is not a question of choosing between working toward pure vs. applied, practical, vulgar, biased, or otherwise tainted and limited "un-pure" knowledge, but rather a question of under what *kinds* of limiting assumptions one is working. There *is* no pure knowledge paradigm. Any position is always grounded in usually covert but nevertheless central and consequential *metaphysical foundations*.[53] The premise of ungrounded initial assumptions is a mirage, as for example logical positivism was to discover much to its embarrassment when it sought to purify science of what it considered metaphysical nonsense. (Logical positivism's *verification principle*, a key tool in its purification efforts, according to its own criteria had to be classified as such a piece of unscientific nonsense—a victim of sefl-reference.) I hold that the question of whether a new physics is needed

---

chapter 5) of an alternative to what I call "technotherapies," those grounded in naturalizing, scientistic approaches.

[53] See, for example, Burtt,1954.

and if so, what kind, ought to be adjudicated in an anomalously pragmatic context.

## Theories of Everything

Currently, physics' often stated goal is to be a theory of everything (TOE), but what does that mean, really? I believe that in its common usage, the term refers to a "theory of the normal type" (Thomas Kuhn's familiar term), to a theory that is much like the current theories in physics (i.e., mathematical, tied to quantifying measurement), only better, more encompassing. We have seen, however, that some advocate a physics whose subject matter includes the heretofore excluded realm of subjective phenomena.

In that case, if one intends the term to be taken literally, if one means a "theory of everything" to be just that, to cover consciousness, perception, beliefs, language, and so on, then I doubt very much that a physics predicated on the world of primary qualities and conceptualized as retaining the usual formal, logical-mathematical structure will be able to take us out of the circumscribed domain of primary qualities.[54] That view is supported by much of what has been presented in the previous chapters. Adequate treatment of language, perception, observation, the presence of the observer, self-reference, and the like seems quite beyond the capacity of a physics whose field of study is specified to be limited to the dehumanized, mathematized, reduced world of primary, objectively observable and measurable qualities. I cannot imagine how a field predicated on a conceptual and experimental arsenal that screens out (or, as Husserl put it, "brackets out")[55] an entire domain of experience *at the front end*, so to speak, could then ever recapture that discarded domain by using physics' usual conceptual and methodological resources: "a

---

[54] See Berger, 1978.
[55] Harvey, 1989, p. 47.

direct mathematization... in respect to the specifically sensible qualities of bodies is impossible in principle."[56] To make a crude analogy, it is as though one were to screen out color from a picture, and then expect that one somehow could capture and reconstruct or recapture the lost dimension from that constricted black-and-white residue.[57] Once a dimension has been removed, it is gone. This point was the essence of my early critiques of formalization.[58]

In either case, that is whether or not one envisions a TOE as encompassing subjective phenomena, what is seldom recognized or discussed are the intimate and tight linkages between any mathematization and the practice of remaining within the domain of *res extensa,* and therefore, how central the question of retaining mathematizing is to any proposal for a new physics. One of the few who did explore deeply this connection between mathematization and reductionism was Edmund Husserl, the important phenomenologically-oriented philosopher who came to philosophy after having been thoroughly trained as a mathematician.[59] He traced these links between mathematization and world view from their early stages in the work of Copernicus, Kepler, and Galileo (with Pythagorean precursors who "having discovered the mathematical relations intrinsic to the tuning of the lyre,... extended this intrinsic mathematical structure to the universe at large")[60] through Descartes' formalization of substance dualism and of its parallel, the dualism of primary and secondary qualities, and through the twists

---

[56] Husserl, quoted in Harvey, 1989, p. 17.
[57] Harris makes a similar point about the kind of "black-and-white" object of study that segregationism creates in and for linguistics (1998, p. 41).
[58] See Berger, 1974, 1978, 1985.
[59] His connection with the important logician Gottlob Frege was mentioned in chapter 12. His teachers were the prominent mathematicians Kronecker and Weierstrass, and his dissertation in Vienna was in mathematics. His first published book was *The Philosophy of Arithmetic* (1891).
[60] Harvey, 1989, p.14.

and turns in later philosophical thought (Hobbes, Locke, Berkeley, Hume, Kant). One of the main themes in his explorations was this equivalence of mathematizing and remaining in the domain of primary qualities; these are two sides of the same coin.[61]

As I say, this equivalence between mathematization and physical reductionism (retaining only the domain of primary qualities) is seldom explicitly stated or appreciated. We see that lack demonstrated in the examples cited above. Bohm and Chew believe that physics can deal with holisms via improved mathematics; de Quincey's ideas about "a radically different physics" (see above) are predicated on introducing new kinds of forces, strongly suggesting that quantification can be retained in a physics that is to take into account also the "qualitative-character-of-experience."[62] Pylkkö is something of an exception, although he vacillates; sometimes he seems to appreciate that link and consequently the incompatibility of mathematizing and having an adogmatic, *a*-onto-theo-logical, etc., science, but at other times he seems to retreat and say that one can approximate the kind of ametaphysical discipline he is seeking yet retain a mathematical approach.

I have been arguing for more than thirty years now in my own field of psychotherapy that mathematization or any basically similar kind of formalization must lead to frameworks that *cannot* encompass subjectivity; it necessarily leads to disciplines that are restricted to dealing with the domain of primary qualities and having Cheshire Cat residues as its objects of study.[63] Can physics still

---

[61] See Harvey, 1989, especially chapters 2 and 3.
[62] Griffin, 1998, p. 88.
[63] See Berger, 1974, 1978, 1985, 1991, 2002a, and most of the papers reprinted in Berger 2002b. I did not realize that these critiques largely reinvented the wheel, restating Heidegger's critique of enframing and its consequences. The difference is that my critiques draw on a formal structure, the state process formalism, as the principal tool for analyzing the situation and supporting my

remain physics if it does not basically remain a discipline of empirically and instrumentally derived quantified or quantifiable data interpreted via theories grounded in mathematics? *Should* it remain a mathematized discipline? And, most especially: What might a non-mathematized physics look like? What could its ingredients be? I believe that these basic questions deserve serious attention.

## EPILOGUE: CAN DISCIPLINES BE CHANGED?

Are physicists likely to begin to take seriously radical philosophical critiques and the alternative approaches they adumbrate? Are they likely to address the questions sketched above that follow from recognizing the close coupling between mathematization and restricting one's domain of inquiry to the world of *res extensa*? All the evidence suggests that this is highly improbable. In a paper to which I have already referred, Evelyn Fox Keller speaks of "cognitive repression in contemporary physics."[64] She attributes the unwillingness of most physicists to take seriously and address the fundamentally "logically conflictual"[65] basic premises of their enterprise not only to "the familiarity and success of older, established structures"[66] but also to deep psychodynamic affective needs (specifically the need to maintain an often hard-won and therefore shaky autonomy and differentiation from the first caregivers).[67] My own view as a clinician is that Ms. Keller's calling attention to the psychodynamic-defensive aspects is admirable, but that these are a good deal more complicated and obscure than she intimates.[68] In any case, such

---

arguments.
[64] Keller, 1979.
[65] Ibid., p. 719.
[66] Ibid., p. 720.
[67] See the discussions of ontogenesis, especially in chapters 9 and 12; also Winnicott, 1958, 1965; Balint, 1969; Loewald, 1980.
[68] See Berger, 1991, chapters 4 and 5; 2002a, chapter 6.

psychodynamics seem to manifest symptomatically in academic disciplines as an almost desperate need for highly structured, apparently consistent, reliable, veridical, almost sacred problem-free frameworks, and that means one may expect violent defensive maneuvers to arise as reactions when any such apparently security-giving "rigorous" foundations are challenged. (We may recall Tallis's lamenting the failure of his solidly-based critiques of physical reductionism to have any visible impact on his peers, the neuroscientists—see chapter 3.) It has been said that "nothing or no one can be as violent, dogmatic, or emotional" as a "fundamentalist" scientist.[69] We catch a glimpse of why that might be so.

I am convinced that covered-over residues of infancy-based affective needs leading to the zealous, rabidly defended maintenance of an apparently safe, true, secure, rationalizable conceptual structure are pervasive and at work not only in most or all professional fields, but also in socio-political movements, religious groups, sports, the arts, nationalisms, academia, and so on. An interesting sidelight is the phenomenon of strong polarization: each group seems to divide into two subpopulations on the basis of roughly the issues that Roy Harris labels "segregationalist" and "integrationist."[70] The former embrace firmly boundaried worlds and thus their "objects of study" are Cheshire Cat residues, while the latter are holistic and blur boundaries; the former cannot tolerate any elasticity or ambiguity or looseness in their structure. (These days, segregationalists seem to be the dominant majority everywhere.) According to Harris, because of their fundamental differences there cannot be a rapprochement between such polarized populations; neither can really hear the other, or see the

[69] Schaef, 1992, p. 92.
[70] Harris, 1998.

other's point. A look at the current scene certainly seems to bear out Harris's assessment.[71]

It may be taken for granted, then, that such conflicted polarizations within groups will not be budged by rational arguments or by appeals to empirical findings or human values A telling and representative example is the current conflict over environmental issues. Even the facts (e.g., about global warming, or about the effects of existing and future pollution) cannot be agreed on. That seems curious unless and until one recognizes that across the board, Western civilization's belief systems to a great extent are motivated and maintained by inaccessible, virtually invisible psychopathological forces (especially, by narcissistic needs, wishes, fears, destructive hostility).[72] Thus, in the case of physics specifically, the mainstream is quite unlikely to be open to hearing, taking seriously, and exploring the consequences of any truly unorthodox holistic criticisms that challenge the received view. As already noted, I see this situation in physics as a special case, a reflection, of a very general, pervasive phenomenon.

I began to discuss this matter of groups' resistance to change some time ago.[73] Later, in a monograph ostensibly about substance abuse but actually about pervasive societal psychopathology,[74] I emphasized its ubiquitous presence, and explained its manifestations in our society as a product of what I called the presence of pervasive "mid-range

---

[71]  I want to reemphasize that in my view, the difficulties and situations Harris describes are true not only in his own field, linguistics, but equally rampant in psychiatry, politics, psychology, and on and on.

[72]  I use the term "narcissism" in its clinical sense. Because it has been used in many and often vaguely specified ways, in my discussions of cultural psychopathology I tend to substitute the more general and less contentious diagnostic term "mid-range pathology," referring to those difficulties that diagnostically and symptomatologically lie between psychoses and neuroses and thus include, roughly, narcissistic and borderline characterological disorders—see Berger, 1991.

[73]  My first publication was a series of articles in a peace newsletter (Berger, 1986).

[74]  Berger, 1991. For an important consonant critique, see Berman, 2000b.

psychopathology" in our general population. Its manifestations are protean; that is one of the features that makes this pathology so difficult to see. The spectrum of surface symptoms ranges from substance abuse to violent crime, including such apparently diverse expressions as while collar crime, political crime in the highest places, destructive internal and international policies, highly unrealistic approaches to severe environmental issues and to the threats of living in a nuclear age (e.g., relying on antiquated and now in the long run ineffective political, military, economic, technological countermeasures), pseudo-religiosity and pseudomorality, rabid and occasionally violent fanaticism in sports, rampant obesity, a medical system dedicated to cure rather than to prevention, widespread disregard of traffic laws, and a highly inconsistent, sometimes corrupt legal system, to mention only a few of the manifestations. The common element is a defective, noxiously immature character structure spawned in an enframing Western civilization. It is interesting and utterly expectable that this common root remains unperceived. Among the general public as well as in the various professional disciplines, mystifying, misleading, collusive, fragmented, unsupportable "explanations" are offered for each separate manifestation of the symptoms (e.g.: What made those "good" kids do these terrible things? Why is our population so alarmingly obese? Why is there rampant corruption in politics?). Such fragmented and fragmenting pseudo-explanations are endlessly and heatedly debated. We again face a fracturing segregationalism, accompanied by the total failure to understand, let alone appreciate, the integrated, whole picture.

As far as the clinical implications of this pathology are concerned, I sought to show that, and how, psychotherapists of all stripes, neuroscientists and the medical profession in general, school systems, insurance companies, legal systems, patient advocate groups, families of patients, and of course patients themselves, all tend to develop and grimly hold on to views of psychological difficulties and of treatment approaches that actually are in the service of defensive needs; when one looks at the situation carefully and openly, one can see the the defended positions actually collude with the patient's (and society's) pathology, and serve to maintain it. More recently I elaborated on this perspective in the context of a therapeutic stance I labeled *praxial* psychotherapy which I contrasted to what I called "technotherapies."[75]

If, as I am claiming, groups resist any change "toward health"—i.e., a shift toward a position that might deprive them of the defensive strategies that currently support and maintain pathological needs and potentiate constructive movement—then what can be done by those who advocate such threatening changes? I recently began to ask whether what therapists have learned about facilitating change in individual patients, that hard-won knowledge accumulated over a century of clinical exploration, could somehow be transmuted and adapted so that it could be applied on a societal scale.[76] The principal focus and key common element of these clinical considerations is *defensiveness*, using that term in its specialized psychoanalytic sense,[77] and the concomitant kind of therapy loosely and ambiguously referred to "the analysis of defense."[78] On a larger scale, at the level of small and large groups, there does seem to be some sort of analogue to those manifestations and phenomena of irrational and rigid clinging to the status quo which in individuals we call pathologically defensive. Parallels between the two levels

---

[75] Berger, 2002a.
[76] Berger, 2002a, pp. 87-90, chapter 6; also 2002b, chapters 30 and 31; unpublished (2002); 1991, chapter 7.
[77] In psychoanalysis, defenses by definition are unconscious, and thus the term does not have its usual colloquial meaning (as in "you are being defensive").
[78] Gray, 1994; Berger, 2002a, chapter 5.

are not difficult to identify. At the level of groups and populations one can clearly recognize similarities between the various "defense mechanisms" (e.g., denial; projection) at work in the two levels. The question that I have specifically raised and begun to explore is: Given these parallels in defensive structures and *psychopathology*, is it possible to find or develop analogous societal parallels to the *psychotherapy* of individuals? Some of the difficulties inherent in such an enterprise are obvious; others are more subtle. At any rate, as one would expect there is little interest in or support for pursuing such a project. Indeed, were a proposal to do so ever to become visible, it would almost certainly generate strong and effective opposition. (It would stir up defensive reactions ranging from indifference to vilification.)

What, then, are the prospects for the unconventional holistic, ontogenetically-grounded approaches that I have sought to evolve in the present work? I have little confidence that disciplines actually do harbor the benign, healthy self-correcting, innate tendencies which Thomas Kuhn famously has identified in connection with his discussion paradigms and the dynamics of paradigm shifts.[79] I think that in a deeper sense these corrections have been and continue to be cosmetic. For example, in 300 years of physics there has been no visible interest in the field in exploring a move away from the constrictions that go hand in hand with the Cartesian bifurcations. Nevertheless, no one can be sure that this stasis is a permanent or an universal condition; there is always a chance that some felicitous combination of circumstances will make the kinds of approaches I have outlined and advocated less threatening, more interesting, more welcomed, timely, in some context. In any case, I must admit that even if these proposals never resonate in the

---

[79] See Berger, 2003.

various disciplines, gathering and organizing them into the present work has been an educational and gratifying (though often almost overwhelming) experience.

# REFERENCES

# INDEX

# REFERENCES

Abel, R. 1976. *Man Is the Measure: A Cordial Invitation to the Central Problems of Philosophy.* New York: Free Press.

Abram, D. 1996. *The Spell of the Sensuous.* New York: Random House.

Ackermann, R. J. 1988. *Wittgenstein's City.* Amherst, MA: University of Massachusetts Press.

Albert, D. Z. 1992. *Quantum Mechanics and Experience.* Cambridge, MA: Harvard University Press.

Anderson, A. R., ed. 1964. *Minds and Machines.* Englewood Cliffs, NJ: Prentice-Hall.

Armour, L., and Bartlett, E. T. 1980. *The Conceptualization of the Inner Life: A Philosophical Exploration.* Atlantic Highlands, NJ: Humanities Press.

Ashmore, M. 1989. *The Reflexive Thesis: Wrighting Sociology of Scientific Knowledge.* Chicago: University of Chicago Press.

Audi, R., ed., 1999. *The Cambridge Dictionary of Philosophy.* 2d ed. New York: Cambridge University Press.

Ayer, A. J. 1984. *Philosophy in the Twentieth Century.* New York: Vintage.

Balint, M. 1969. *The Basic Fault: Therapeutic Aspects of Regression.* London: Tavistock.

Bannister, D. 1966. Psychology as an exercise in paradox. *Bulletin of the British Psychological Society* 19:21-26.

Barratt, B. B. 1984. *Psychic Reality and Psychoanalytic Knowing.* Hillsdale, NJ: The Analytic Press.

Barrett, W. 1978. *The Illusion of Technique: A Search for Meaning in a Technological Civilization.* Garden City, NY: Anchor/Doubleday.

_____ 1986. *Death of the Soul: From Descartes to the Computer.* New York: Anchor Doubleday.

Berger, L. S. 1970. Barriers to communication between disciplines. *Journal of the Association of Advancement of Medical Instrumentation* 4:127-140.

_____ 1971. Thoughts on the semantics of information. *ETC.: A Review of General Semantics* 28:421-425.

_____ 1974. *The Logic of Observation in Psychotherapy Research.* Diss. University of Tennessee, Knoxville.

_____ 1978. Innate constraints of formal theories. *Psychoanalysis and Contemporary Thought, 1:* 89-117. (Chapter 1 in Berger, 2002b.)

_____ 1985. *Psychoanalytic Theory and Clinical Relevance: What Makes a Theory Consequential for Practice?* Hillsdale, NJ: Analytic Press.

_____ 1986. (June, August, September, October) Notes on depth psychology and peace. Louisville, KY: Council for Peacemaking and Religion Newsletter.

_____ 1991. *Substance Abuse as Symptom: A Psychoanalytic Critique of Treatment Approaches and the Cultural Beliefs That Sustain Them.* Hillsdale, NJ: Analytic Press.

_____ 1995a. Grünbaum's questionable interpretations of inanimate systems: "History" and "context" in physics. *Psychoanalytic Psychology* 12:439-449. (Chapter 5 in Berger, 2002b.)

_____ 1995b. The characteristics and limits of formal representation: Faulconer and Williams's "Temporality in human action" revisited. *Studies in*

*Psychoanalytic Theory* 4:48-57. (Chapter 2 in Berger, 2002b.)

_____ 1996a. Psychoanalytic neonate models and noncartesian frameworks. *Psychoanalytic Review* 33:49-65. (Chapter 6 in Berger, 2002b.)

_____ 1996b. Toward a non-Cartesian psychotherapeutic framework. *Philosophy, Psychiatry, & Psychology* 3:169-184. (Chapter 9 in Berger, 2002b.)

_____ 2000 *Praxis* as a radical alternative to scientific frameworks for psychotherapy. *American Journal of Psychotherapy* 54:43-54. (Chapter 11 in Berger, 2002b.)

_____ 2001. Psychotherapy, Biological Psychiatry, and the Nature of Matter: A View from Physics. *American Journal of Psychotherapy* 55:185-201. (Chapter 4 in Berger, 2002b.)

_____ 2002a. *Psychotherapy as* Praxis: *Abandoning Misapplied Science.* Victoria, BC: Trafford.

_____ 2002b. *Issues in Psychoanalysis and Psychology: Annotated Collected Papers.* Victoria, BC: Trafford.

_____ 2003. Review of S. Fuller, *A Philosophical History for our Times.* mentalhelp.net/books.

_____ (unpublished) "Group Self-Estrangement and Sociocultural Praxis." Proposal for a visiting fellowship submitted to School of Social Science, Institute for Advanced Study, Princeton, NJ, October 2002.

Bergman, G. 1959. *Meaning and Existence.* Madison: University of Wisconsin Press.

Berlin, I. 1994. *The Magus of the North: J. G. Hamann and the Origins of Modern Irrationalism.* London, UK: HarperCollins.

Berman, M. 1981. *The Reenchantment of the World*. Ithaca, NY: Cornell University Press.

———— 1989. *Coming to our Senses: Body and Spirit in the Hidden History of the West*. New York: Simon and Schuster.

———— 2000a. *Wandering God: A Study in Nomadic Spirituality*. Albany: State University of New York Press.

———— 2000b. *The Twilight of American Culture*. New York: Norton.

Bernstein, R. 1971. *Praxis and Action*. Philadelphia: University of Pennsylvania Press.

———— 1983. *Beyond Objectivism and Relativism: Science, Hermeneutics, and Praxis*. Philadelphia: University of Pennsylvania Press.

———— 1992. *The New Constellation*. Cambridge, MA: MIT Press.

Blakemore, C., and Greenfield, S., eds. 1987. *Mindwaves: Thoughts on Intelligence, Identity and Consciousness*. Cambridge, MA: Basil Blackwell.

Blattner, W.D. 2000. The primacy of practice and assertoric truth: Dewey and Heidegger. In M. Wrathall and J. Malpas, eds., *Heidegger, Authenticity, and Modernity: Essays in Honor of Hubert L. Dreyfus*, v.1. Cambridge, MA: MIT Press.

Blum, A., and McHugh, P. 1984. *Self-Reflection in the Arts and Sciences*. Atlantic Highlands, NJ: Humanities Press.

Bohm, D. 1976. *Fragmentation and Wholeness*. Jerusalem: Van Leer.

———— 1980. *Wholeness and the Implicate Order*. London: Routledge & Kegan Paul.

Bologh, R. W. 1979. *Dialectical Phenomenology: Marx's Method*. Boston: Routledge & Kegan Paul.

BonJour, L. 1985. *The Structure of Empirical Knowledge*. Cambridge, MA: Harvard University Press.

_____ 2002. *Epistemology: Classic Problems and Contemporary Responses*. Lanham, MD: Rowman & Littlefield.

Bowman, N. 1993. *Language, Culture, and Communication: the Meaning of Messages*. Englewood Cliffs, NJ: Prentice Hall.

Bruns, G. L. 1987. On the weakness of language in the human sciences. In A. Megill and D. N. McCloskey, eds., *The Rhetoric of the Human Sciences: Language and Argument in Scholarship and Public Affairs*. Madison: University of Wisconsin Press.

_____ 1989. *Heidegger's Estrangements: Language, Truth, and Poetry in the Later Writings*. New Haven: Yale University Press.

Bunt, L. N. H., Jones, P. S., and Bedient, J. D. 1976. *The Historical Roots of Elementary Mathematics*. Englewood Cliffs, NJ: Prentice-Hall.

Burtt, E. A. 1954. *The Metaphysical Foundations of Modern Physical Science*, rev. ed. Garden City, NY: Doubleday.

Cahoone, L. E. 1988. *The Dilemma of Modernity: Philosophy, Culture, and Anti-Culture*. Albany: State University of New York Press.

Capra, F. 1988. *Uncommon Wisdom: Conversations with Remarkable People*. New York: Simon & Schuster.

Caputo, J.D. 1978. *The Mystical Element in Heidegger's Thought*. New York: Fordham University Press.

Carnap, R. 1966. *Philosophical Foundations of Physics: An Introduction to the Philosophy of Science.* New York: Basic Books.

Chalmers, D. J. 1996. *The Conscious Mind: In Search of a Fundamental Theory.* New York: Oxford University Press.

Chomsky, N. 2000. *New Horizons in the Study of Language and Mind.* Cambridge, MA: MIT Press.

Cohen, D. 1996. *The Secret Language of the Mind: A Visual Inquiry into the Mysteries of Consciousness.* San Francisco: Chronicle Books.

Collingwood, R. G. 1945. *The Idea of Nature.* Oxford, UK: Clarendon Press.

Collins, A. W. 1987. *The Nature of Mental Things.* Notre Dame, IN: University of Notre Dame Press.

Collins, J., and Selina, H. 1999. *Introducing Heidegger.* Cambridge, England: Totem Books.

Cook, J. 1965. Wittgenstein on privacy. *Philosophical Review* 74:281-314.

Coulter, J. 1983. *Rethinking Cognitive Psychology.* New York: St. Martin's Press.

Crain, W. C. 2000. *Theories of Development: Concepts and Applications.* 4th ed. Upper Saddle River, NJ: Prentice Hall.

Crane, T. 2001. *The Elements of Mind: An Introduction to the Philosophy of Mind.* New York: Oxford University Press.

Critchley, S. 2001. *Continental Philosophy: A Very Short Introduction.* New York: Oxford University Press.

Cryan, D., Shatil, S., and Mayblin, B. 2002. *Introducing Logic.* Lantham, MD: Totem Books.

Dancy, J. 1985. *Introduction to Contemporary Epistemology.* New York: Basil Blackwell.

Dancy, J., and Sosa, E., eds. 1992. *A Companion to Epistemology.* Cambridge, MA: Blackwell.

Danto, A. C. 1989. *Connections to the World: The Basic Concepts of Philosophy.* New York: Harper & Row.

Dantzig, T. 1954. *Number: The Language of Science.* 4th ed., revised and augmented. New York: Free Press.

Davies, P. C. W., and Brown, J. R., eds. 1986. *The Ghost in the Atom: A Discussion of the Mysteries of Quantum Physics.* New York: Cambridge University Press.

Davis, D. R. 2002. The language myth and mathematical notation as a language of nature. In R. Harris, ed., *The Language Myth in Western Culture.* Richmond, UK: Curzon.

Davis, P. J., and Hersh, R. 1981. *The Mathematical Experience.* Boston: Houghton Mifflin.

de Boysson-Bardies, B. 1999. *How Language Comes to Children: from Birth to Two Years.* trans. M. B. DeBevoise. Cambridge, MA: MIT Press.

d'Espagnat, B. 1989. *Reality and the Physicist: Knowledge, Duration and the Quantum World,* trans. J. C. Whitehouse. New York: Cambridge University Press.

de Quincey, C. 2002. *Radical Nature: Rediscovering the Soul of Matter.* Montpelier, VT: Invisible Cities Press.

Detlefsen, M. 1986. *Hilbert's Program: An Essay on Mathematical Instrumentalism.* Hingham, MA: Kluwer.

Dossey, L. 1999. *Reinventing Medicine: Beyond Mind-Body to a New Era of Healing.* San Francisco: HarperCollins.

Eagleton, T. 1991. *Ideology: An Introduction.* New York: Verso.

Ellis, J. M. 1993. *Language, Thought, and Logic.* Evanston, IL: Northwestern University Press.

Engel, G. L. 1977. The need for a new medical model: A challenge for biomedicine. *Science* 196:129-136.

Feher, L. 1981. *The Psychology of Birth: Roots of Human Personality.* New York: Continuum.

Freud, S. 1965. *The Interpretation of Dreams,* trans. J. Strachey. New York: Avon Books.

Gabbard, G. O. 1994. Mind and brain in psychiatric treatment. *Bulletin of the Menninger Clinic* 58:427-446.

Gardener, H. 1985. *The Mind's New Science: A History of the Cognitive Revolution.* New York: Basic Books.

Gardner, S. 1999. *Kant and the Critique of Pure Reason.* New York: Routledge.

Gensler, H. J. 1984. *Godel's Theorem Simplified.* Lantham, MD: University Press of America.

_____ 2002. *Introduction to Logic.* New York: Routledge.

Gertler, B. ed. 2003. *Philosophical Accounts of Self-Knowledge.* Aldershot, U.K.: Ashgate.

Gill, J. H. 1989. *Mediated Transcendence: A Postmodern Reflection.* Macon, GA: Mercer University Press.

Golinkoff, R. M., and Hirsh-Pasek, K. 1999. *How Babies Talk: the Magic and Mystery of Language in the First Two Years of Life.* New York: Dutton.

Goodman, A. 1991. Organic unity theory: The mind-body problem revisited. *American Journal of Psychiatry* 148: 553-563.

Goodman, R. B., ed. 1995. *Pragmatism: A Contemporary Reader.* New York: Routledge.

Grant, M., ed. 2000. *The Raymond Tallis Reader.* New York: Palgrave.

Gray, P. 1994. *The Ego and Analysis of Defense.* Northvale, NJ: Jason Aronson.

Griffin, D. R. 1988. Of minds and molecules: Postmodern medicine in a psychosomatic universe. In D. R. Griffin, ed., *the Reenchantment of Science: Postmodern Proposals.* Albany: State University of New York Press.

———— 1998. *Unsnarling the World Knot: Consciousness, Freedom, and the Mind-Body Problem.* Berkeley: University of California Press.

Grof, S. 1985. *Beyond the Brain: Birth, Death and Transcendence in Psychotherapy.* Albany: State University of New York Press.

Grossman, R. 1992. *The Existence of the World: An Introduction to Ontology.* New York: Routledge.

Guignon, C. B. 1983. *Heidegger and the Problem of Knowledge.* Indianapolis, IN: Hackett.

Harding, D. E. 2002. *On Having No Head: Zen and the Rediscovery of the Obvious.* Carlsbad, CA: Inner Directions.

Harrington, A. 1996. *Reenchanted Science: Holism in German Culture from Wilhelm II to Hitler.* Princeton: Princeton University Press.

Harris, R. 1981. *The Language Myth.* London: Duckworth.

———— 1986. *The Origin of Writing.* LaSalle, IL: Open Court.

———— 1987. *The Language Machine.* Ithaca: Cornell University Press.

———— 1990. Scriptism. In N. Love, ed., *The Foundations of Linguistic Theory: Selected Writings of Roy Harris.* New York: Routledge.

———— 1995. *Signs of Writing.* New York: Routledge.

———— 1996. *The Language Connection: Philosophy and Linguistics.* Dulles, VA: Thoemmes Press.

———— 1998. *Introduction to Integrational Linguistics.* Oxford: Pergamon.

———— 2002. The role of the Language Myth in the Western cultural tradition. In R. Harris, ed., *The Language Myth in Western Culture.* Richmond, England: Curzon.

Harvey, C. W. 1989. *Husserl's Phenomenology and the Foundations of Natural Science.* Athens: Ohio University Press.

Heidegger, M. 1971. *Poetry, Language, Thought.* trans. A. Hofstadter. New York: Harper & Row.

———— 2002. *The Essence of Truth: On Plato's Parable of the Cave Allegory and Theaetetus.* trans. T. Sadler. NY: Continuum.

Heisenberg, W. 1958. *Physics and Philosophy: The Revolution in Modern Science.* Amherst, NY: Harper & Row.

Hempel, C. G. 1945. On the nature of mathematical truth. *The American Mathematical Monthly* 52:543-556.

Herbert, N. 1987. *Quantum Reality: Beyond the New Physics; An Excursion into Metaphysics and the Meaning of Reality.* New York: Doubleday.

Hersh, R. 1997. *What is Mathematics, Really?* London, UK: Jonathan Cape.

Heyting, A. 1971. *Intuitionism: An Introduction.* 3d ed. Amsterdam: North-Holland.

Hodges, W. 1977. *Logic: An Introduction to Elementary Logic.* New York: Viking Penguin.

Hodgson, D. 1991. *The Mind Matters: Consciousness and Choice in a Quantum World.* New York: Oxford University Press.

Holbrook, B. 1981. *The Stone Monkey: An Alternative, Chinese-Scientific, Reality.* New York: Morrow.

Hubbard, R., and Wald, E. 1993. *Exploding the Gene Myth: How Genetic Information Is Produced and Manipulated by Scientists, Physicians, Employers, Insurance Companies, Educators, and Law Enforcers.* Boston: Beacon Press.

Hunter, J. F. M. 1973. *Essays After Wittgenstein.* Toronto: University of Toronto Press.

_____ 1985. *Understanding Wittgenstein: Studies of Philosophical Investigations.* Edinburgh: Edinburgh University Press.

_____ 1990. *Wittgenstein on Words as Instruments: Lessons in Philosophical 'Psychology.'* Savage, MD: Barnes & Noble.

Ingleby, D. 1980. Understanding "mental illness." In D. Ingleby, ed., *Critical Psychiatry: the Politics of Mental Health.* New York: Pantheon Books.

Irvine, A. D., 2004. Russell's Paradox. In E. N. Zalta, ed., *The Stanford Internet Encyclopedia of Philosophy.*

Jackson, F. 1998. *From Metaphysics to Ethics: A Defense of Conceptual Analysis.* New York: Oxford UP.

Janik, A., and Toulmin, S. 1973. *Wittgenstein's Vienna.* New York: Simon and Schuster.

Johnston, P. 1993. *Wittgenstein: Rethinking the Inner.* New York: Routledge.

Jones, R. S. 1982. *Physics as Metaphor*. Minneapolis: University of Minnesota Press.

Jones, W. B. 1986. Physics and metaphysics: Harry Stapp on time. In D. R. Griffin, ed., *Physics and the Ultimate Significance of Time*. Albany, NY: State University of New York Press.

Kafatos, M., and Nadeau, R. 1990. *The Conscious Universe: Part and Whole in Modern Physical Theory*. New York: Springer-Varlag.

Kaplan, A. 1961. *The New World of Philosophy*. New York: Random House.

Katz, J. J. 1998. *Realistic Rationalism*. Cambridge, MA: MIT Press.

Kearney, C. 1994. *Modern Movements in European Philosophy: Phenomenology, Critical Theory, Structuralism*. 2d ed. Manchester, UK: Manchester University Press.

Keller, H. F. 1979. Cognitive repression in contemporary physics. *American Journal of Physics* 47:718-721.

Kim, J. 1998. *Philosophy of Mind*. Boulder, CO: Westview Press.

Kirk, S. A., and Kutchins, H. 1992. *The Selling of DSM: The Rhetoric of Science in Psychiatry*. Hawthorne, NY: Aldine de Gruyter.

Kleinman, A., and Good, B., eds. 1985. *Culture and Depression: Studies in the Anthropology of Cross-cultural Psychiatry of Affect and Disorder*. Berkeley: University of California Press.

Klenk, V. H. 1976. *Wittgenstein's Philosophy of Mathematics*. The Hague: Martinus Nijhoff.

Koch, S. 1961. Psychological science versus the science-humanism antinomy. *American Psychologist* 16:629-639.

_____ 1974. "Psychology as science." In C. S. Brown, ed., *Philosophy of Psychology*. New York: Barnes & Noble.

_____ 1985. "The nature and limits of psychological knowledge: Lessons of a century qua 'science.'" In S. Koch and D. E. Leary, eds., *A Century of Psychology as Science*. New York: McGraw-Hill.

Kohut, H. 1971. *The Analysis of the Self*. New York: International Universities Press.

_____ 1977. *The Restoration of the Self*. New York: International Universities Press.

Korab-Karpowicz, W. J. 2001. Martin Heidegger. *The Internet Encyclopedia of Philosophy*.

Kovel, J. 1978. Things and words: Metapsychology and the historical point of view. *Psychoanalysis and Contemporary Thought* 1:21-88.

Laplanche, J., and Pontalis, J.-B. 1973. *The Language of Psycho-Analysis*. trans. D. Nicholson-Smith. New York: Norton.

Laughlin, D. D. Jr., McManus, J., and d'Aquili, E. G. 1990. *Brain, Symbol and Experience: Toward a Neurophenomenology of Human Consciousness*. Boston: Shambhala.

Lawson, H. 1985. *Reflexivity: The Post-Modern Predicament*. La Salle, IL: Open Court.

Lawson, H., and Appignanesi, L. , eds. 1989. *Dismantling Truth: Reality in the Post-Modern World*. London, UK: Weidenfeld and Nicolson.

Lear, J. 1998. *Open Minded: Working out the Logic of the Soul*. Cambridge, MA: Harvard University Press.

Leavy, S. A. 1989. Time and world in the thought of Hans W. Loewald. *Psychoanalytic Study of the Child* 44: 231-240.

LeDoux, J. E., and Hirst, W. eds. 1986. *Mind and Brain: Dialogues in Cognitive Neuroscience.* New York: Cambridge University Press.

Levine, J. 2001. *Purple Haze: The Puzzle of Consciousness.* New York: Oxford University Press.

Lewontin, R. C., Rose, S., and Kamin, L. J. 1984. *Not in Our Genes: Biology, Ideology, and Human Nature.* New York: Pantheon.

Lindley, D. 1996. *Where Does the Weirdness Go? Why Quantum Mechanics is Strange but Not as Strange as You Think.* New York: Basic Books.

Lockwood, M. 1989. *Mind, Brain, and the Quantum: The Compound "I".* London, UK: Basil Blackwell.

Loewald, H. W. 1980. *Papers on Psychoanalysis.* New Haven: Yale University Press.

Lovitt, W., and Lovitt, H. B. 1995. *Modern Technology in the Heideggerian Perspective.* 2 vols. Lewiston, NY: Edwin Mellen Press.

Loy, D. 1988. *Nonduality: A Study in Comparative Philosophy.* New Haven: Yale University Press.

———— 1996. *Lack and Transcendence: The Problem of Death and Life in Psychotherapy, Existentialism, and Buddhism.* Atlantic Highlands, NJ: Humanities Press.

———— 2002. *A Buddhist History of the West: Studies in Lack.* Albany: State University of New York Press.

Lucas, J. R. 2000. *The Conceptual Roots of Mathematics: An Essay on the Philosophy of Mathematics.* New York: Routledge.

Luhrmann, T. M. 2000. *Of Two Minds: The Growing Disorder in American Psychiatry.* New York: Knopf.

Maher, J., and Groves, J. 1997. *Introducing Chomsky.* Cambridge, UK: Icon Books.

Mahler, M. S., Pine, F., and Bergman, A. 1975. *The Psychological Birth of the Human Infant: Symbiosis and Individuation.* New York: Basic Books.

Malin, S. 2001. *Nature Loves to Hide: Quantum Physics and the Nature of Reality, a Western Perspective.* New York: Oxford University Press.

Mansbach, A. 2002. *Beyond Subjectivism: Heidegger on Language and the Human Being.* Westport, CT: Greenwood.

Marías, J. 1067. *History of Philosophy.* New York: Dover.

Marsella, A. J., and White, G., eds. 1982. *Cultural Concepts of Mental Health and Therapy.* Boston: Reidel.

Mayes, G. R. 2000. Theories of Explanation. *The Internet Encyclopedia of Philosophy.*

McGinn, C. 1993. *Problems in Philosophy: The Limits of Inquiry.* Oxford, UK: Basil Blackwell.

_____ 1997. *The Character of Mind: An Introduction to the Philosophy of Mind.* New York: Oxford University Press.

McNeill, D., and Freiberger, P. 1993. *Fuzzy Logic: The Revolutionary Technology That Is Changing Our World.* New York: Simon & Schuster.

McTaggard, L. 2002. *The Field: The Quest for the Secret Force of the Universe.* New York: HarperCollins.

Melchert, N. 1995. *The Great Conversation* (Volume II): *Descartes Through Heidegger.* 2d ed. Mountain View, CA: Mayfield.

Miller, L. 1991. Brain and self: Toward a neuropsychodynamic model of ego autonomy and personality. *Journal of the American Academy of Psychoanalysis* 19:213-234.

Moore, T. 1992. *Care of the Soul: A Guide for Cultivating Depth and Sacredness in Everyday Life.* New York: HarperCollins.

Moravia, S. 1995. *The Enigma of the Mind: The Mind-Body Problem in Contemporary Thought.* trans. S. Stanton. New York: Cambridge University Press.

Nagel, E. 1961. *The Structure of Science: Problems in the Logic of Scientific Explanations.* New York: Harcourt, Brace & World.

Nagel, E., and Newman, J. R. 1958. *Gödel's Proof.* New York: New York University Press.

Nagel, T. 1974. What is it like to be a bat? *Philosophical Review* 83: 435-50.

_____ 1986. *The View from Nowhere.* New York: Oxford University Press.

Newman, F. 1991. *The Myth of Psychology.* New York: Castillo International.

Notturno, M. A. 1985. *Objectivity, Rationality and the Third Realm: Justification and the Grounds of Psychologism. A Study of Frege and Popper.* Boston, MA: Nijhoff.

Ogden, T. H. 2001. Reading Winnicott. *Psychoanalytic Quarterly* 70:299-323.

Olafson, F. 1987. *Heidegger and the Philosophy of Mind.* New Haven: Yale University Press.

_____ 1995. *What is a Human Being? A Heideggerian View.* New York: Cambridge University Press.

_____ 2001. *Naturalism and the Human Condition: Against Scientism .* New York: Routledge.

Parks, G. 1990. *Heidegger and Asian Thought*. Honolulu: University of Hawaii Press.

Pattison, G. 2000. *The Later Heidegger*. NY: Cambridge University Press.

Penrose, R. 1995. Must mathematical physics be reductionist? In J. Cornwall, ed., *Nature's Imagination: The Frontiers of Scientific Vision*. New York: Oxford University Press.

Percy, W. 1954. *The Message in the Bottle: How Queer Man Is, How Queer Language Is, and What One Has to Do with the Other*. New York: Noonday Press.

Piontelli, A. 1992. *From Fetus to Child: An Observational and Psychoanalytic Study*. New York: Routledge.

Pippin, R. B. 1991. *Modernism as a Philosophical Problem: On the Dissatisfactions of European High Culture*. Cambridge, MA: Blackwell.

Polt, R. 1999. *Heidegger: An Introduction*. Ithaca: Cornell University Press.

Potter, V. G. 1994. *On Understanding: A Philosophy of Knowledge*. New York: Fordham University Pres.

Prado, C. G. 1987. *The Limits of Pragmatism*. Atlantic Highlands, NJ: Humanities Press International.

———— 1992. *Descartes and Foucault: A Contrastive Introduction to Philosophy*. Ottawa: University of Ottawa press.

Priest, G. 2000. *Logic: A Very Short Introduction*. New York: Oxford University Press.

Protter, B. 1988. Ways of knowing in psychoanalysis: Some epistemic considerations for an autonomous theory of psychoanalytic praxis. *Contemporary Psychoanalysis* 24:498-523.

Richardson, J. 1986. *Existential Epistemology: A Heideggerian Critique of the Cartesian Project.* New York: Clarendon.

Pylkkö, P. 1998. *The Aconceptual Mind: Heideggerian Themes in Holistic Naturalism.* Philadelphia: Benjamins.

Quine, W. V. O. 1961 *From a Logical Point of View.* 2d ed., rev. Cambridge, MA: Harvard University Press.

———— 1968. Paradox. In *Mathematics in the Modern World.* Readings from *Scientific American.* San Francisco: Freeman.

———— 1986. *Philosophy of Logic.* 2d ed. Cambridge, MA: Harvard University Press.

Rangell, L. 1990. *The Human Core.* Madison, CT: International Universities Press.

Roberts, J. 1992. *The Logic of Reflection: German Philosophy in the Twentieth Century.* New Haven: Yale University Press.

Robinson, I. 1975. *The New Grammarians' Funeral: A Critique of Noam Chomsky's Linguistics.* New York: Cambridge University Press.

Rorty, R., ed. 1967. *The Linguistic Turn: Recent Essays in Philosophical Method.* Chicago: University of Chicago Press.

———— 1982. *Consequences of Pragmatism (Essays: 1972-1980).* Minneapolis: University of Minnesota Press.

———— 1991. *Essays on Heidegger and Others.* Philosophical Papers, vol. 2. New York: Cambridge University Press.

———— 1999. *Philosophy and Social Hope.* New York: Penguin.

Rosen, S. 1980. *The Limits of Analysis.* New York: Basic Books.

Rota, G-C. 1997. *Indiscrete Thoughts.* (F. Palombi, editor) Boston: Birkhäuser.

Russell, B. 1916. *Mysticism and Logic.* London: Longmans, Green and Co.

_____ 1919. *Introduction to Mathematical Philosophy.* NY: Macmillan.

_____. 1967. *The Autobiography of Bertrand Russell.* Boston: Allen & Unwin.

Ryder, J. ed. 1994. *American Philosophic Naturalism in the Twentieth Century.* Amherst, NY: Prometheus Books.

Sacks, O. 1995. Scotoma: Forgetting and neglect in science. In R. B. Silvers, ed., *Hidden Histories of Science.* New York Review of Books.

Sass, L. 1992. The Self and Its Vicissitudes in the Psychoanalytic Avant-Garde. In G. Levine, ed., *Constructions of the Self.* New Brunswick, NJ: Rutgers University Press.

Schaef, A. W. 1992. *Beyond Therapy, Beyond Science: A New Model for Healing the Whole Person.* New York: HarperCollins.

Schafer, R. 1976. *A New Language for Psychoanalysis.* New Haven: Yale University Press.

Scharfstein, B-A. 1980. *The Philosophers: Their Lives and the Nature of Their Thought.* New York: Oxford University Press.

_____ 1989. *The Dilemma of Context.* New York: New York University Press.

Schulte, J. 1993. *Experience and Expression: Wittgenstein's Philosophy of Psychology.* New York: Oxford University Press.

Schumacher, E. F. 1977. *A Guide for the Perplexed.* New York: Harper & Row.

Seager, W. 2001. Panpsychism. In E. N. Zalta, ed., *The Stanford Internet Encyclopedia of Philosophy.*

Senechal, M. 1990. Shape. In *On the Shoulders of Giants.* ed. L. A. Steen. Washington, DC: National Academy Press.

Shalom, A. 1985. *The Mind/body Conceptual Framework and the Problem of Personal Identity: Some Theories in Philosophy, Psychoanalysis and Neurology.* Atlantic Highlands, NJ: Humanities Press International.

Sheehan, J. J., and Sosna, M., eds. 1991. *The Boundaries of Humanity: Humans, Animals, Machines.* Berkeley: University of California Press.

Sheldrake, R. 2003. *The Sense of Being Stared At: And Other Unexplained Powers of the Human Mind.* New York: Crown.

Silver, R. B. 1995. *Hidden Histories of Science.* New York Review of Books.

Smith, B., and Smith, D. W. 1995. Introduction. In B. Smith and D. W. Smith, eds., *The Cambridge Companion to Husserl.* New York: Cambridge University Press.

Smith, G. B. 1996. *Nietzsche, Heidegger, and the Transition to Postmodernity.* Chicago: University of Chicago Press.

Smith, W. 1984. *Cosmos and Transcendence: Breaking Through the Barrier of Scientistic Belief.* Peru, IL: Sherwood Sugden.

_____ 1995. *The Quantum Enigma: Finding the Hidden Key*. Peru, IL: Sherwood Sugden.

Solnit, A. J. 1987. Review of Stem, 1985. *American Journal of Psychiatry* 144:1508-1509.

Solomon, R. C. 1972. *From Rationalism to Existentialism: The Existentialists and Their Nineteenth-century Backgrounds*. Lanham, MD: University Press of America.

Squires, E. 1990. *Conscious Mind in the Physical World*. New York: Adam Hilger.

Stapp, H. P. 1993. *Mind, Matter, and Quantum Mechanics*. New York: Springer-Verlag.

Stern, D. N. 1977. *The First Relationship: Infant and Mother*. Cambridge, MA: Harvard University Press.

_____ 1985. *The Interpersonal World of the Infant: A View from Psychoanalysis and Developmental Psychology*. New York: Basic Books.

_____ 1992. Commentary on constructivism in clinical psychoanalysis. *Psychoanalytic Dialogues* 2:331-363.

Sternberg, R. J. 2001. *Psychology: In Search of the Human Mind*. 3d ed. Orlando, FL: Harcourt College Press.

Stroll, A. 2000. *Twentieth-Century Analytic Philosophy*. New York: Columbia University Press.

_____ 2002. *Wittgenstein*. Oxford: Oneworld.

Swetz, F. J. 1987. *Capitalism & Arithmetic: The New Math of the 15th Century*. La Salle, IL: Open Court.

Szasz, T. 1996. *The Meaning of Mind: Language, Morality, and Neuroscience*. Westport, CT: Praeger.

Tallis, R. 1999a. *The Explicit Animal: A Defence of Human Consciousness*. reprint of the 1991 ed., with a new preface. New York: St. Martin's Press.

_____ 1999b. *On the Edge of Certainty: Philosophical Explorations.* New York: St. Martin's Press.

_____ 2002. *A Conversation with Martin Heidegger.* New York: Palgrave Macmillan.

Tarnas, R. 1991. *The Passion of the Western Mind: Understanding the Ideas that Have Shaped our World View.* New York: Ballantine.

Taylor, C. 1985. *Human Agency and Language.* Philosophical Papers vol. I. New York: Cambridge University Press.

Terrace, H. 1987. Thoughts without words. In C. Blakemore and S. Greenfield, eds., *Mindwaves: Thoughts on Intelligence, Identity and Consciousness.* Cambridge, MA: Basil Blackwell.

Tolman, C. 1987. Dialectical materialism as psychological metatheory. In H. J. Stam, T. B. Rogers, & K. J. Gergen, eds., *The Analysis of Psychological Theory: Metapsychological Perspectives.* Washington, DC: Hemisphere.

Toulmin, S. 1990. *Cosmopolis: The Hidden Agenda of Modernity.* New York: Free Press.

Ulmer, G. L. 1987. *Applied Grammatology: Post(e)-Pedagogy from Jacques Derrida to Joseph Beuys.* Baltimore, MD: Johns Hopkins University Press.

Valenstein, E. S. 1998. *Blaming the Brain: The Truth about Drugs and Mental Health.* New York: Free Press.

Wallace, E. IV, Radden, J., and Sadler, J. Z. 1997. The philosophy of psychiatry: Who needs it? *Journal of Nervous and Mental Disease* 185:67-73.

Walsh, W. H. 1963. *Metaphysics: An Exposition and Defense of a Controversial Branch of Philosophy.* New York: Harcourt, Brace & World.

Weinberg, S. *Dreams of a Final Theory: the Scientist's Search for the Ultimate Laws.* New York: Vintage.

Welton, D. 2000. *The Other Husserl: The Horizons of Transcendental Phenomenology.* Bloomington: Indiana University Press.

Wigner, E. P. 1967. *Symmetries and Reflections.* Bloomington: Indiana University Press.

Winnicott, D. W. 1958. *Through Paediatrics to Psycho-Analysis.* New York: Basic Books.

———— 1965. *The Maturational Processes and the Facilitating Environment.* New York: Basic Books.

Wittgenstein, L. 1978. *Remarks on the Foundations of Mathematics.* trans. G. E. M. Anscombe; ed. G. H. Von Wright, R. Rhees, and G. E. M. Anscombe. Cambridge, MA: MIT Press.

———— 1958a *Philosophical Grammar*, ed. R. Rhees, trans. A. Kenny. New York: Oxford University Press.

———— 1958b. *Philosophical Investigations.* 2d ed., trans. G. E. M. Anscombe. New York: Macmillan.

Woolfolk, R. L. 1998. *The Cure of Souls: Science, Values, and Psychotherapy.* San Francisco, CA: Jossey-Bass.

Young, J. 2002. *Heidegger's Later Philosophy.* New York: Cambridge University Press.

Zimmerman, M. E. 1993. Heidegger, Buddhism, and deep ecology. In C. Guignon, ed., *The Cambridge Companion to Heidegger.* New York: Cambridge University Press.

Zukav, G. 1979. *The Dancing Wu Li Masters: An Overview of the New Physics.* New York: Bantam.

Zuriff, G. E. 1992. Theoretical inference and the new psychoanalytic theories of infancy. *Psychoanalytic Quarterly* 59:18-36.

# INDEX

ISBN 1-41206072-9

9 781412 060721